Database Dreaming

Volume I

Relational Writings Revised

and Revived

C. J. Date

Published by:

115 Linda Vista, Sedona, AZ 86336 USA
https://www.TechnicsPub.com

Cover design by Lorena Molinari

First Printing 2022

Printed in the United States of America.

ISBN, print ed.   9781634629843
ISBN, Kindle ed.   9781634629850
ISBN, ePub ed.   9781634629867
ISBN, PDF ed.   9781634629874

Library of Congress Control Number: 2021953505

I take the opportunity here to include a few quotes from writings by Bertrand Russell that I happen to like. Some of them are relevant to the overall message of this book and some aren't. I'll leave it to you to decide which are which!

Most people would sooner die than think.
In fact they do.

Work is of two kinds:
first, altering the position of matter at or near the earth's surface
relative to other matter;
second, telling other people to do so.

Everything is vague to a degree you do not realize
till you have tried to make it precise.

I once received a letter from an eminent logician,
Mrs Christine Ladd Franklin,
saying that she was a solipsist,
and was surprised that there were no others.

———— ♦ ♦ ♦ ♦ ————

To all my old friends and colleagues at LEO—
stars and pioneers

About the Author

C. J. Date is an independent author, lecturer, researcher, and consultant, specializing in relational database technology. He is best known for his book *An Introduction to Database Systems* (8th edition, Addison-Wesley, 2004), which has sold some 900,000 copies at the time of writing and is used by several hundred colleges and universities worldwide. He is also the author of numerous other books on database management, including most recently:

- From Trafford: *Database Explorations: Essays on The Third Manifesto and Related Topics* (with Hugh Darwen, 2010)

- From Morgan Kaufmann: *Time and Relational Theory: Temporal Databases in the Relational Model and SQL* (with Hugh Darwen and Nikos A. Lorentzos, 2014)

- From O'Reilly: *Relational Theory for Computer Professionals: What Relational Databases Are Really All About* (2013); *View Updating and Relational Theory: Solving the View Update Problem* (2013); *SQL and Relational Theory: How to Write Accurate SQL Code* (3rd edition, 2015); *The **New** Relational Database Dictionary* (2016); *Type Inheritance and Relational Theory: Subtypes, Supertypes, and Substitutability* (2016)

- From Apress: *Database Design and Relational Theory: Normal Forms and All That Jazz* (2nd edition, 2019)

- From Technics: *Logic and Relational Theory: Thoughts and Essays on Database Matters* (2020); *Fifty Years of Relational, and Other Database Writings: More Thoughts and Essays on Database Matters* (2020); *Stating the Obvious, and Other Database Writings: Still More Thoughts and Essays on Database Matters* (2020); *E. F. Codd and Relational Theory, Revised Edition: A Detailed Review and Analysis of Codd's Major Database Writings* (2021)

Mr Date was inducted into the Computing Industry Hall of Fame in 2004. He enjoys a reputation that is second to none for his ability to explain complex technical subjects in a clear and understandable fashion.

Contents

Preface

A little while back I gave an online presentation based on the first chapter of this book, "My Life as a Writer." During the discussion that followed, one of the attendees raised the point that many of the shorter pieces I'd written over the years, ones I'd touched on in my presentation, were now quite hard to find. And it's true: Despite the fact that most of the pieces in question have been collected and published in various "Relational Writings" books over the years, most of those books now seem to be out of print. The attendee went on to suggest that I might want to do something about this state of affairs. He was right, and I did, and this book is the result (or part of the result, at any rate, as I'll explain in just a moment). To be specific, what I did was the following: I went back and reviewed all of those "Writings" books, looking for pieces that seemed to be worth reviving (or, rather, revising and reviving) at this time. Of course, some of them definitely weren't! However, out of a total of around 130 original papers, I did find some 20 or so that (a) seemed to me worth preserving and (b) hadn't already been incorporated in, or superseded by, more recent books of mine. So I tracked down the original versions of those 20 plus papers and set to work. When I was done, though, I found I had somewhere in excess of 600 pages on my hands—too much, in my view, for just one book, and so I split the pieces across two separate volumes. This is Volume I, of course; Volume II will appear in a few months time.

Let me say a word about my title, *Database Dreaming*. It's meant primarily as a respectful nod to the culture and belief system of the Aboriginal peoples of Australia (though it does also reflect my own personal dreams in this connection). One of the simplest and best introductions I know to Aboriginal Dreamings and the Dreamtime is in Bruce Chatwin's beautiful book *The Songlines*. Here are a few quotes:

> In Genesis, God first created the "living things" and then fashioned Father Adam from clay ... [In the Dreamtime] the Ancestors created themselves from clay, hundreds and thousands of them, one for each totemic species.

> Any species ... can be a Dreaming. A virus can be a Dreaming. You can have a chickenpox Dreaming, a rain Dreaming, a desert-orange Dreaming, a lice dreaming. In the Kimberleys they've now got a money dreaming.

Aboriginals [believe] that all the living things had been made in secret beneath the earth's crust, as well as all the white man's gear – his aeroplanes, his guns, his Toyota Land Cruisers – and every invention that will ever be invented; slumbering below the surface, waiting their turn to be called.

Structure of the Book

Actually there isn't much (structure, that is)—most of the chapters were originally written to stand alone and are thus, for the most part, independent of all the others. However, I've tried to arrange them in such a way that if you do want to read them in sequence, then there is a kind of flow to them. I've also done my best to edit out the worst of the overlaps and inconsistencies among them, though to what extent I've succeeded in that effort I'll let you be the judge.

Technical Background

My target audience is database professionals; thus, I assume you're reasonably familiar with both the relational model and the SQL language. However, there are a few technical terms that (a) are appealed to repeatedly and (b) might not be as familiar to you as all that, so I thought it would be a good idea to define and explain them here, in the preface. The terms in question are *relvar*, **Tutorial D**, and *commalist*.

Relvar: "Relvar" is short for *relation variable*. What all too many people still call just "relations" (meaning constructs in the database, that is) are indeed really variables; after all, their value does change over time as INSERT, DELETE, and UPDATE operations are performed, and "changing over time" is exactly what makes them variable. In fact, *not* distinguishing clearly between relation values and relation variables—or table values and table variables, in SQL—has led to an immense amount of confusion in the past, and indeed continues to do so to this day. In our work on *The Third Manifesto*, therefore, Hugh Darwen and I decided to face up to this problem right from the outset. To be specific, in that *Manifesto* we framed all of our remarks in terms of relation values when it really was relation values that we meant, and in terms of relation variables when it really was relation variables that we meant, and we abided by this discipline rigorously (indeed, one hundred percent). However, we also introduced two abbreviations: We allowed "relation value" to be abbreviated to just *relation* (exactly as we allow, e.g., "integer value" to be abbreviated to just *integer*), and we allowed "relation variable" to be abbreviated to *relvar*.

Tutorial D: I mentioned *The Third Manifesto* in the previous paragraph. Now, *The Third Manifesto* (the *Manifesto* for short) isn't a language definition; rather, it's a prescription for the functionality that its authors, Hugh Darwen and myself, claim a language must provide in order to be considered truly relational. But we did need a way of referring generically to any such language within our *Manifesto*, and we used the name **D** for that purpose. Note carefully, therefore, that **D** isn't a language as such, it's a family of languages; there could be any number of individual languages all qualifying as a valid member of that family. **Tutorial D** is one such.[1] **Tutorial D** is based on the relational algebra; it's defined more or less formally in the *Manifesto* book,[2] and it's used throughout that book and elsewhere—the present book included—as a basis for examples. In fact, I and others have been using that language for such purposes in books and presentations for many years now, and I think our experience in that regard has shown that it's both well designed and fairly self-explanatory.

Note that the names **D** and **Tutorial D** are always set in boldface as shown.

Commalist: This term is used heavily in syntax definitions and the like. It's short for "comma separated list." It can be defined as follows: Let *xyz* be some syntactic construct (for example, "attribute name"); then the term *xyz commalist* denotes a sequence of zero or more *xyz*'s in which each pair of adjacent *xyz*'s is separated by a comma. Within a given commalist, spaces appearing immediately before the first item or any comma, or immediately after the last item or any comma, are ignored. For example, if *A*, *B*, and *C* are attribute names, then the following are all attribute name commalists:

```
A , B , C

C , A , B

B

A , C
```

So too is the empty sequence of attribute names.

---

[1] By contrast, SQL isn't.

[2] *Databases, Types, and the Relational Model: The Third Manifesto*, by Hugh Darwen and myself (3rd edition, Addison-Wesley, 2007). *Note:* We've made a number of improvements to the language since that book was published, however. Those changes, along with much other relevant material, can be found on the website *www.thethirdmanifesto.com*.

Suppliers and parts: Many of the examples in this book makes use of the familiar suppliers-and-parts database. Here's the usual sample value:

S

SNO	SNAME	STATUS	CITY
S1	Smith	20	London
S2	Jones	10	Paris
S3	Blake	30	Paris
S4	Clark	20	London
S5	Adams	30	Athens

P

PNO	PNAME	COLOR	WEIGHT	CITY
P1	Nut	Red	12.0	London
P2	Bolt	Green	17.0	Paris
P3	Screw	Blue	17.0	Oslo
P4	Screw	Red	14.0	London
P5	Cam	Blue	12.0	Paris
P6	Cog	Red	19.0	London

SP

SNO	PNO	QTY
S1	P1	300
S1	P2	200
S1	P3	400
S1	P4	200
S1	P5	100
S1	P6	100
S2	P1	300
S2	P2	400
S3	P2	200
S4	P2	200
S4	P4	300
S4	P5	400

And here are definitions, expressed in **Tutorial D**, of the three relvars in this database:

```
VAR S BASE RELATION    /* suppliers */
  { SNO     CHAR ,
    SNAME   CHAR ,
    STATUS  INTEGER ,
    CITY    CHAR }
  KEY { SNO } ;

VAR P BASE RELATION    /* parts */
  { PNO     CHAR ,
    PNAME   CHAR ,
    COLOR   CHAR ,
    WEIGHT  RATIONAL ,
    CITY    CHAR }
  KEY { PNO } ;
```

```
VAR SP BASE RELATION    /* shipments */
   { SNO     CHAR ,
     PNO     CHAR  ,
     QTY     INTEGER }
   KEY { SNO , PNO }
   FOREIGN KEY { SNO }
         REFERENCES S
   FOREIGN KEY { PNO }
         REFERENCES P ;
```

Now read on ...

C. J. Date
Morristown, Vermont
2022

Chapter 1

My Life as a Writer

The only thing I was fit for was to be a writer, and this notion rested solely on my suspicion that I would never be fit for real work, and that writing didn't require any.

—Russell Baker:
Growing Up (1982)

This chapter was originally written as an essay to accompany a live presentation of the same name. Like that presentation, it consists of a series of miscellaneous thoughts, lessons, and anecdotes deriving from over half a century of life as a (mostly technical) writer. Of course, it goes without saying that any essay of such a nature is likely to be more than a little self-indulgent—well, this one certainly is, at any rate—so let me just apologize for that state of affairs right up front, and ask for your forbearance, and then let me get on with what I really want to say.

Publishing history: Portions of what follows have appeared in various forms in various other writings of mine over the years. However, the chapter as a whole is new. Copyright © C. J. Date 2022.

I've always loved good writing—both reading it, of course, and also trying to produce it, regardless of whether the writing in question has to do with technical or nontechnical matters. Even when I was at primary school in England, when I was only nine or ten years old,[1] when what I was producing was what in those days we called compositions ... My teacher at that time was called Mr Loveday. He bore a striking resemblance to Hardy, of Laurel & Hardy, so naturally we

---

[1] I know for a fact that I wasn't more than ten years old at the time because I started attending my secondary school, High Wycombe Royal Grammar School, in September 1951, and my eleventh birthday wasn't until January 1952.

called him Ollie; but he was an inspiring teacher, and I really liked him. Anyway, writing compositions: I enjoyed this activity, and I was good at it, even though I do say it myself. However—this is going to sound dreadfully like bragging, but it's true—I got tired (or at least, so I claimed to myself) of always getting full marks, ten out of ten, for my compositions, which I did without fail, week after week; so I decided one week to write one that was deliberately bad. I wrote a description of the sunset as I'd seen it once in the hills above our house. It was awful—I pulled out all the stops and wrote dreadful purple prose ("The mighty Sun in offended majesty yields to the threatening blackness of the oncoming night," etc.). I handed the essay in, wondering what would happen. It came back marked eleven out of ten.

Since then I've often wondered if Ollie was being too smart for me and was teasing me back, just as I'd been trying to tease him with my deliberately bad writing. But at the time I just took the incident at face value and assumed that *I* had been too smart for *him*.

But talking of good writing, here are a few pieces of advice that I've followed—or tried to follow, or at any rate been aware of so that when I ignored them I could at least claim it was a conscious decision on my part to do so—in all of my writing endeavors. The first is this:

- Delete all the adverbs.

  I don't know who came up with this one—it might have been Evelyn Waugh—and in any case it needs to be taken with a huge pinch of salt, of course; but I'm all too well aware that I tend to use too many adverbs myself, so I do try to prune them as much as I can. In other words: Examine every adverb in what you've written, and see if your text wouldn't be better off without it.

- Always consider deleting the first paragraph.

  Now this is a good one. I don't know who came up with it, but I do remember when I first encountered it I instantly took a look at my own writings to see whether I should indeed have deleted that first paragraph ... As I recall I didn't find any cases of where I should have done—well, of *course* I didn't—but I think that's because I had the advice in mind anyway, even though I'd never heard it spelled out in so many words before. The truth is, it's always quite difficult to start *any* piece of writing, and that's why opening paragraphs, or opening sentences, are so often bad, and often unnecessary anyway. More on this topic in a moment.

■ Read over your compositions, and wherever you meet with a passage which you think is particularly fine, *strike it out* [my italics].

And this is a *really* good one—I like it a lot. It's due to Dr Johnson.

SOME GREAT OPENERS

"Always consider deleting the first paragraph": Yes, that first paragraph is so hard to write, and people often make a hash of it. *Good* opening paragraphs, and/or sentences, tend to be memorable ones. For example, do you recognize these? (I love this kind of stuff.)

■ This is the most beautiful place on earth.

This one is close to perfect ... You simply have to read on, to find out what place it is that the author's talking about, and why he makes such a claim (yes, it's a he), and whether you think he's justified in making it. It's from *Desert Solitaire*, by Edward Abbey—one of my all-time favorite writers, and indeed a great personal hero. PS: The place in question is Arches National Monument (now Park), in Utah.

■ Call me Ishmael.

Moby Dick, of course (Herman Melville). Another wonderful book.

■ It was a bright cold day in April, and the clocks were striking thirteen.

1984 (George Orwell—another personal hero).

■ It is a truth universally acknowledged, that a single man in possession of a good fortune must be in want of a wife.

Pride and Prejudice, as I'm sure you knew (Jane Austen). This has to be one of the most famous (and possibly most parodied) opening lines in the whole of English literature.

■ It was love at first sight.

Catch-22 (Joseph Heller)—the best antiwar book ever, in my opinion.[2] *Note:* In case you find the answer here surprising, it might help if I add that the next sentence is as follows: "The first time Yossarian saw the chaplain he fell madly in love with him."

■ I have walked by stalls in the marketplace where books, dog eared and faded from their purple, have burst with a white hosanna.

Not so catchy, this one, but I like it. It has a great rhythm. It's from *Free Fall*, by William Golding.

■ There were 117 psychoanalysts on the Pan Am flight to Vienna and I'd been treated by at least six of them. And married a seventh.

I wouldn't put this book in anything like the same league as the others I'm quoting from here, but no one could argue this isn't a great opener. It's from *Fear of Flying*, by Erica Jong.

■ All this happened, more or less.

Slaughterhouse-Five, by Kurt Vonnegut (another great antiwar novel, incidentally).

DATABASE AND ME

How did I get into this business, anyway?

Well, to begin at the beginning: After three years at university (Cambridge University, in England), where I read mathematics, I went to work as a

---

[2] I have several marvelous stories (well, at least two) about Joseph Heller and *Catch-22* which this ~~margin~~ footnote is unfortunately too small to contain.

programmer for a British computer company called LEO.[3] That was in 1962. Then in 1967, after five years of working in London, I joined IBM at the IBM Development Lab at Hursley in Hampshire—out in the British countryside, in other words—as a programming instructor, where I got to teach among other things computing fundamentals, and System/360 Assembler Language, and PL/I, and OS/360 externals and internals.

Now, IBM had a very enlightened policy in those days, according to which, even if you were the best instructor in the world, you shouldn't just do instructing—you should rotate out of the Education Department every once in a while and get your hands dirty working down in the trenches, as it were. So in 1970, when it was my turn, I joined a small research department at IBM Hursley called "Ad Tech" (Advanced Technology), where, along with a colleague, Paul Hopewell, I was given the job of figuring out what the PL/I language should be doing about this comparatively new thing called *database*. That was the start of my database career.

I had no idea what a database was, of course. So I read a lot of technical papers and reference manuals and the like; in particular, I spent quite a lot of time playing around with IBM's own database product, a nightmare of a thing called IMS. I also studied, in depth, the proposals of another nightmarish thing called DBTG, which was being pushed by certain parties outside IBM as a potential standard in the database arena. *And* I read a research paper just published by one E. F. (Ted) Codd, from IBM Research, called "A Relational Model of Data for Large Shared Data Banks."

Now, Ted's paper wasn't exactly easy to read—almost everyone thought it was far too mathematical and abstract—but to me, it was basically just set theory, and set theory was perhaps the part of math that I'd enjoyed the most when I was a mathematician (sort of). In fact, here for the first time since I left university was something where my mathematical training looked like it might come in handy, and might even have some real practical application! So Paul Hopewell and I set about designing some PL/I extensions based on Ted's relational ideas, and Paul even implemented a kind of rough and ready prototype to show how those extensions might work out in practice. (I mustn't mislead you here, though. Despite the fact that our proposals were well received at the time, they never actually made it into the official PL/I language as such.)

---

[3] LEO was a true computing pioneer. The original LEO I machine was the first computer in the world designed and used for purely business, as opposed to scientific or military, purposes (the first application on LEO I ran successfully in November 1951). By the time I joined, however, the company was building and selling LEO III, a truly advanced machine that—as I didn't fully realize until several years later—was in numerous respects way ahead of its time.

Anyway, as a consequence of these activities, I found myself in some demand, both inside and outside IBM, as someone who seemed to be able to explain Ted's ideas to ordinary mortals, both in live lectures and in writing. Indeed, I found I had a knack for this kind of work; I mean, I found I really was able to explain Ted's ideas simply and clearly (probably because I'm a fairly slow learner myself, and was thus able to appreciate where other people might have difficulty). And after a while, I thought it would be a good idea to write a book on this stuff: the book, in fact, that I kind of wished had been available to me when I was learning this stuff myself. And so I did—I wrote what became the first edition of *An Introduction to Database Systems*. (I wrote it in 1972, but it wasn't published until 1975. I'll have more to say about that three-year gap in a few moments.)

What happened next? Well, in 1974, still working on database issues for IBM, I moved to the U.S. (actually to the IBM lab in Palo Alto, California, which was part of what's now known as Silicon Valley). For a while I continued to work on database extensions to PL/I, also to COBOL and Fortran (the three major "high level languages," as they were jointly and somewhat quaintly known at the time). Then, when the decision was made (finally!) to build what eventually became IBM's flagship product DB2, I moved into the technical planning area for that product.

Now, again I mustn't mislead you—my influence on that product was absolutely minuscule. (If you want to buy me a beer some time, you might persuade me to elaborate on that remark. Maybe.) Throughout those years of DB2 planning, though, my teaching activities continued, and indeed hugely expanded, and I slowly began to realize a few things:

- First, I was good at that teaching work, and enjoyed doing it.

- Second, I could be doing it for myself instead of for IBM.

- Third, IBM was increasingly not a good place for a software person to be anyway, especially a relational database person (several blood on the floor stories here, sadly beyond the scope of this chapter).

- Fourth, I was in great demand at the time, but I was probably riding a wave ... The market for lectures on relational database theory wouldn't last forever,[4] and I wouldn't be one of the leading players in that market forever, either.

So in 1983 I left IBM[5] and started working for myself (as a "database author, lecturer, researcher, and consultant," as I liked to say at the time). Then Ted himself left IBM a little bit later to do much the same kind of thing, and for a year or so we were effectively competing with each other. In 1985, therefore, our mutual friend Sharon Weinberg suggested that we get together and form a joint company, and we did.[6] And I continued in that partnership with Ted and Sharon until 1990 or so, and then I went back to working for myself again. And that's what I've done ever since, right up to the present day.

AN INTRODUCTION TO DATABASE SYSTEMS

As I've more or less said already, it was my database lecturing activities that gave me the idea of writing a book on databases. Indeed, there weren't any database books at that time, and I thought I could produce a pretty good one, given the chance. So I got the necessary permission from my IBM management, as well as encouragement from Ted Codd ("Such a book is very much needed"), to embark on such a project, and then I got down to work and completed the draft sometime in the middle of 1972. Then all hell broke loose ... Let me elaborate.

My draft contained extensive coverage of three different approaches to the database problem: the so called hierarchic approach, exemplified by IBM's IMS (first nightmare); the so called network approach, exemplified by DBTG (second nightmare); and Ted's new relational approach. Now, since I was employed by IBM, I had to get clearance from IBM before my book could be published (or indeed even submitted to a publisher for consideration), and so the draft had to

---

[4] Actually it should have done, but it didn't. The situation today is this: Some people think they already know that theory, but they don't; others think they don't need to know it, but they do. Unfortunately it's difficult to use this sorry state of affairs as the basis for any kind of positive marketing!—marketing what I have to sell, that is, by which I mean my lectures and my books.

[5] I actually left at 2:30 pm on Friday, May 13th, 1983, just before DB2 became generally available. By that time I'd become fairly disenchanted with the mess that IBM was making with its "relational"—or would-be relational—product line, and I didn't want to have anything more to do with it. Indeed, it seemed to me that by the time IBM was done with it, DB2 would be just as messy and complicated as IMS ever was. I believe events have proved me right here, too.

[6] Ted and Sharon later married.

be reviewed by various parties in IBM. I learned some things. First, none of those IBM reviewers felt they'd done their job until (a) they'd found at least one thing that had to be changed (usually many more things than just one, and usually things requiring major surgery on my text), and (b) they'd nominated at least two further people who ought also to do a review. Well, you can see how that was going to work out ... Not only that, but some reviewers were upset because I hadn't come out and stated categorically that IBM's own product IMS (Nightmare No. 1) was the best on the market, and in fact the greatest thing since sliced bread. Others were very concerned that I was so critical of DBTG (Nightmare No. 2), precisely because DBTG *wasn't* an IBM product, and hence that I, and by extension IBM, might be accused of disparaging the competition—we might even be sued. Still others were upset that I so obviously favored the relational approach, despite the fact that there weren't any relational products at the time—they claimed that I was therefore comparing apples and oranges (or real products vs. a hypothetical ideal), and in fact they made me change references to "the relational approach" throughout the book to say things like "relational theory" instead.[7]

That wasn't all. IBM had recently lost some major IMS accounts—especially in the U.K., as it happened, where of course I was still located—and certain parties in IBM were looking for someone to blame (a scapegoat, in other words) ... and Ted's research, and my book, were obvious targets. Indeed, it began to look as if my book was never going to be published at all. But then something else happened. IBM isn't as monolithic on the inside as it might appear on the outside, and another part of IBM was busy at the time with a joint project with the publishing company Addison-Wesley to produce a series of books on various aspects of systems programming ("The IBM Systems Programming Series"). Now, I'd deliberately not tried to get my book into that series because I didn't want it to be labeled as, and/or seen as, "an IBM book"—I'd written it myself, on my own time, and it was mine, and the opinions were mine. But Ted Codd sent them a copy of my draft,[8] and their reaction was "Well, this is exactly the kind of book we're looking for!" So now I had some senior IBM folks on my side, as it were—which was probably just as well,

---

[7] I had great fun changing all of those references back again in the second edition, because to have left them unchanged could have been seen as disparaging the competition again (some of those competitors looked as if they might be about to produce a relational product).

[8] By "them" here I mean the various IBM employees who constituted the IBM Systems Programming Series Editorial Board.

because I'd begun to realize that, being at the bottom of IBM as I was, I was never going to win this fight on my own.

Now, I don't know exactly what happened next, but I heard there were some pretty nasty senior level meetings inside IBM (more blood on the floor), and further that most if not all of the IBM Editorial Board were prepared to resign if they weren't allowed to publish my book. And so it did finally get published, albeit in that IBM series that I hadn't wanted it to be in. But that didn't happen until 1975, when it could have been published in 1972, and could thereby have had three years of having the field all to itself. Oh well.

Anyway, here are a few more things I learned:

- I discovered some interesting differences between U.S. and U.K. English! And I don't mean just differences in spelling, but actual differences in meaning. For example, the transitive verb "to table" means *to put on the agenda* in U.K. English but the exact opposite—*to take off the agenda*—in U.S. English. Likewise, the transitive verb "to sanction" means *to allow* in the U.K. but *to disallow* in the U.S. I could go on.

- I confirmed something that I'd known instinctively already: viz., that writing books is no way to make money—at least, not unless you're extremely fortunate and find yourself with a bestseller on your hands. (Actually that first book of mine did turn out to be a bestseller, of a kind— but only in technical book terms. Certainly I could never have survived on what it paid me. In terms of dollars earned vs. hours worked, in fact, the dollars I earned from that book worked out as way below the U.S. minimum wage at the time.)

- I learned, albeit not right away, not to trust publishers. *An Introduction to Database Systems* wasn't just my first published book, it was actually the first book on database technology published by anyone at all. But only just! One of the other publishers I approached at the time did offer me a contract (in fact I still had the draft contract in my possession, until I lost it—with so much else—in one of the California wildfires). Not being familiar with such matters, I showed that draft to a lawyer friend of mine ... who pointed out that it didn't actually guarantee that the publisher in question would ever publish my book at all; it merely said, in effect, that *if* they published my book, *then* they'd pay me such and such. In other words, they'd be perfectly within their rights not to publish the book at all, if they so decided. And I've always been a little suspicious of the fact that they did publish a book on the subject just two weeks after mine—quite literally!—by an author, James Martin, who was much better known in the computing world than I was. An unworthy thought, perhaps (and if so then I apologize to all concerned) ... but could it have been that they wanted to suppress my book so that Martin's book could have the field all to itself?

Anyway, I decided not to sign that contract, and signed the one with Addison-Wesley instead. And I continued to publish new books with Addison-Wesley exclusively for many years—basically up until the time when they were taken over by Pearson Education and became far less friendly and pleasant to deal with than they used to be, whereupon I switched my allegiance elsewhere.[9]

■   I found that (for me, at any rate) the right way to write a book is what later came to be known as WYSIWIG (pronounced whizzy wig, and standing for What You See Is What You Get). In other words, write as you speak (or speak as you write, perhaps?). That's why my books and presentations are all very obviously cut from the same cloth, as it were.

■   I had my consciousness raised!—regarding my use of personal pronouns, I mean. In the chapter on security, my original draft (which believe it or not was written entirely in longhand, by the way) contained the following text:

> When the user signs on to the system, he should provide a user ID, to say who he is. Ideally, he should then provide a password, to prove he is who he says he is.

Now, I'm not very proud of this (though I did at least think it was nice and punchy and made its point clearly and succinctly)—but I certainly didn't like what it got changed to by the copyeditor:

---

[9] What actually made me switch (the last straw, you might say) was the following:. Some years later I was working along with two coauthors (Hugh Darwen and Nikos Lorentzos) on a book on temporal data. We had an agreement with Addison-Wesley (or Pearson, I should say, because Addison-Wesley had been taken over by Pearson by that time) to publish it when it was done. Then they reneged!—they decided they didn't want to publish the book after all. I was pretty annoyed about it at the time, I can tell you; I don't think we actually had a formal contract in place, but what I'm quite sure of is that we had at least secured an oral agreement (which in California is supposed to be binding). However, the upshot was that we wound up placing the book elsewhere, and as I've said I stopped doing new books with Pearson from that point forward.

> When the user signs on to the system, **he or she** should provide a user ID, to say who **he or she** is. Ideally, **he or she** should then provide a password, to prove **he or she** is who **he or she** says **he or she** is [boldface added].

Well, I was able to change it to:

> When users sign on to the system, **they** should provide a user ID, to say who **they** are. Ideally, **they** should then provide a password, to prove **they** are who **they** say **they** are [boldface added].

That's better, though it's still not very good: But at least I got my consciousness raised, and that's a good thing, and I learned my lesson, and I've tried very hard not to offend in this regard ever since.

You Can't Please All of the People All of the Time

Well, that book of mine quickly went through several editions, of which the first few at least were pretty well accepted; I mean, they got largely positive reviews. Later editions, not so much ... Here are some reader comments (taken from the Amazon website) on the seventh edition: [10]

1. Next to unreadable.

2. I personally got nothing out of this book.

3. This is an absolutely horrible book.

4. Impossible to read.

5. The book pretty much consists of the author trying to make everything sound technical when, honestly, there isn't all that much substance to back him up.

6. The worst book I have ever [*sic*].

7. Written in a style that's unreadable.

---

[10] The book is currently in its eighth edition and has sold some 900,000 copies in total (all editions) at the time of writing.

8. Quite frankly there isn't anything here that you probably haven't figured out on your own.

9. Would be a nice reference guide for some middle manager who needs to know "the lingo," but that's it.

10. Date is a "genius" who simply cannot construct a simple intelligible sentence! ... People who can't write simply shouldn't be published!

11. This book is the worst piece of swill I have come across in awhile [*sic*]. There is absolutely no editing by anyone whom [*sic!*] has any knowledge of the english [*sic*] language.

12.[11] A Devil Awful Book! ... only able to communicate in language understandable to Einstein.

Gosh. I guess it's nice to be described as a genius (and even compared to Einstein, no less); but how to respond? Well ... there were some good reviews too, of course, but I'm not going to quote those. What I do want to say is this. The fat is, it's my belief that there's a serious issue underlying all of these negative remarks. Let me elaborate:

- First of all, I haven't changed the way I write, and earlier editions got much better reviews. So if anything has changed, it's the audience, not me.

- Second, I still get good reviews from overseas (as far as I recall the negative remarks just quoted were all from the U.S.).

- Third, the same goes for my live presentations, mutatis mutandis.

- Fourth, I could bolster my argument—if I had the time and you had the patience—with some truly appalling quotes on database matters taken off the Internet.

---

[11] Of course, There Must Always Be Twelve, as all relational aficionados know.

■ Fifth, I could bolster my argument still further by citing comments from various actual U.S. computer science professors (!) and other similar "experts."

In a nutshell, it seems to me that what we've been seeing is a general dumbing down of the computing community in the U.S. And speaking as a (naturalized) U.S. citizen, that dumbing down bothers me considerably ... So the net of what I'm saying is that I want to enter **a plea for better education** in the good old US of A. We used not to be satisfied with being second best, and we shouldn't be so now.

OTHER WRITINGS

Counting different editions as different books (which as far as I'm concerned they most certainly are), at the time of writing I've published well over 50 database books.[12] I've also had many of those books translated into foreign languages, made videos based on a number of them, written well over 200 additional technical papers, and also written four or five unpublished[13] and mostly nontechnical books.

So why am I still writing about databases after all these years? In fact there are several answers to this question:

■ I still find the subject fun and interesting; in fact, it seems to have infinite depth, and I'm still learning new things myself. (Perhaps that's the key; perhaps if I weren't still learning, I'd have dropped the whole thing a long time ago and become a park ranger or something.)

■ Explaining things on paper helps me understand them. As I've already said, I'm a slow learner, and working things out on paper helps me think.
     Note: Actually I have a story here. I've claimed for years that one of the virtues of the relational model is that it helps you *think precisely*; in particular, it helps you state or articulate problems in a precise manner.

---

[12] About a third of them with coauthors—though even in those cases it's true if immodest to say that (with just one partial exception) I was always the principal author, and the text as finally published was always written by me.

[13] That's *unpublished*, not unpublishable. And at least one of them never will be published because it existed only as a hard copy manuscript and was lost in that same wildfire I mentioned earlier.

Now, I've been teaching this relational stuff for many years; but it doesn't matter how many times you teach a given seminar, you can always get questions you've never heard before ... And on one occasion, I was making just that claim (that the relational model helps you think precisely), whereupon one student asked "Why is it important to think precisely?" Now that was right out of left field so far as I was concerned—certainly it was a question I'd never heard before. So I replied "Well, I don't know exactly." Which I thought was a pretty good response, off the top of my head.

■ As I've also already said, I like writing; but I found I really got a kick out of *technical* writing, by which I mean explaining complex technical issues in written prose, without sacrificing precision, accuracy, clarity, or comprehensibility. In fact I regard such writing (the activity of producing such writing, I mean) as a truly creative endeavor, and I guess we all need to do something creative with our life. Well, I do, anyway.

■ I believe (or at any rate I'd like to believe) that I have a useful contribution to make. Indeed, I continue to derive some quiet satisfaction from the fact that almost everything we do in our western civilization, on a daily basis, relies on technology that Ted invented and I helped pioneer, or at least popularize. Of course, like all people in such a position, I also worry about some of the uses—or abuses, rather—to which that technology might be put ... and with that ever in mind I support a variety of causes and organizations that do their best to fight such abuses. But that's another story.

Let me elaborate briefly on this notion of making a useful contribution. I see my work in this connection as falling into two broad categories:

■ Reporting on and explaining research by myself and colleagues

■ Counteracting and debunking some of the nonsense that's out there

And I'd like to devote the remainder of this chapter to discussing each of these two categories—or, more particularly, my activities in connection with them—in turn.

REPORTING ON RESEARCH

The context for most of the research I want to talk about here is *The Third Manifesto*, a detailed proposal by Hugh Darwen and myself for the future direction of data and database management systems. Here's the reference:

■ C. J. Date and Hugh Darwen: *Databases, Types, and the Relational Model: The Third Manifesto* (3rd edition, Addison-Wesley, 2007). See also the *Manifesto* website *www.thethirdmanifesto.com*.

Note: The reason we called our *Manifesto* "the third" was because we wanted it to be seen, at least in part, as a response to two previous ones: "The Object Oriented Database System Manifesto" by Malcolm Atkinson et al. (1989), and the "Third Generation Database System Manifesto" by Michael Stonebraker et al. (1990). Now, I don't want to get into detail on what it was we objected to in those previous manifestos (you can find the specifics if you're interested in the book mentioned above); however, I should at least note for the record that we didn't publish our own *Manifesto* until several years later (in early 1995, to be precise). The main reason for the delay was simply that we spent a great deal of thought and time in pinning our ideas down as carefully as we could. As a consequence, I think it's fair to say that, although we've added a few bits and pieces since 1995, the *Manifesto* remains in all essential respects just as it was when we originally formulated it.

Be all that as it may, one thing that's important to understand about *The Third Manifesto* is that it's not a language definition. Rather, it's a prescription for the functionality that Hugh Darwen and I claim a language must provide in order to be considered truly relational. But we did need a way of referring to such a language generically in our *Manifesto*, and we chose the name **D** for that purpose. Note carefully, therefore, that **D** isn't a language as such, it's a family of languages; there could be any number of individual languages all qualifying as a valid member of that family. **Tutorial D** is one such; it's defined more or less formally in the *Manifesto* book, and it's used throughout that book and elsewhere as a basis for examples. (As a matter of fact, I and others have been using that language for such purposes in books and presentations—we've even used it for a few small but genuine applications[14]—for many years now, and I think our

---

[14] So yes, there are implementations.

experience in that connection has shown that it's both well designed and fairly self-explanatory.)

Here then is a list of some of the things we've done in connection with our work on the *Manifesto*. *Note:* These items are (a) all things that we regard as research contributions, (b) all of them of considerable practical as well as theoretical interest, and (c) all very much interrelated.

- We've clarified the logical difference between relation values and variables. (More on this one in a few moments.)

- We've added explicit relational comparisons.

- We've developed a better understanding of the nature of relational algebra, including the relative significance of various operators and an appreciation of the importance of relations of degree zero.[15]

- We've added certain useful new operators, such as EXTEND and MATCHING.

- We've added image relations.

- We've clarified the concept of first normal form; as a consequence, we've embraced the concept of relation valued attributes in particular (see later for an example).

- We have a better understanding of updating in general—including the need for and importance of *multiple assignment* (see Chapter 13)—and view updating in particular.

- We have a better understanding of the fundamental significance of integrity constraints in general, and we have some good theoretical results regarding certain important special cases.

---

[15] I don't want to get into detail about those relations of degree zero here; let me just note that such relations play a role with respect to the relational algebra that's precisely analogous to the role played by the number 0 with respect to ordinary arithmetic. In other words, such relations are exactly as important in the relational context as the number 0 is in the ordinary arithmetical context, and a relational algebra without them is (or should be!) just as unthinkable as an arithmetic without 0. PS: Of course, SQL doesn't support such relations. So what does that tell you about SQL?

■ We've clarified the nature of the relationship between the relational model and logic (more specifically, predicate logic).

■ Finally, we have a clearer understanding of the relationship between the relational model and type theory (more specifically, we've clarified the nature of domains).

Let me elaborate briefly on this last item. The basic point can be summed up as follows: (a) Relations have attributes; (b) attributes have types (*aka* domains); hence, (c) relations are defined in terms of types, and so the theory of relations requires a supporting theory of types. Now, Ted Codd never provided any such thing ... so we did! In fact, the subtitle of our *Manifesto* book reads in its entirety as follows:

a detailed study of **the impact of type theory**
on the relational model of data,
including a comprehensive model of **type inheritance**

(boldface added). In some ways, in fact, we regard that theory of types as the most significant aspect of what our *Manifesto* has to offer.

Relation Values and Variables

Let me now come back as promised to that business of relation values and variables. The basic point is this: Historically, there's been a lot of confusion over the difference between relations as such, on the one hand, and relation *variables*, on the other. Forget about databases for a moment; consider instead the following simple programming language example. Suppose I say in some programming language:

```
VAR N INTEGER ... ;
```

Then N here isn't an integer; rather, it's a *variable*, whose *values* are integers as such (different integers at different times). We all understand that. Well, in exactly the same way, if I say in SQL—

```
CREATE TABLE T ... ;
```

—then T *isn't a table*; rather, it's a variable, a table variable or (as I'd prefer to call it, ignoring various SQL quirks such as duplicate rows and left to right column ordering) a relation variable, whose values are relations as such (different relations at different times).

Consider the famous suppliers-and-parts database. Now, I'm sure you're familiar with this example—you've probably seen it before many times, and it's in the preface anyway. But just to remind you, S is suppliers; P is parts; and SP is shipments of parts by suppliers. Here's a picture (the various attributes— SNO, PNO, CITY, and so on—I take to be all pretty much self-explanatory):

S

SNO	SNAME	STATUS	CITY
S1	Smith	20	London
S2	Jones	10	Paris
S3	Blake	30	Paris
S4	Clark	20	London
S5	Adams	30	Athens

P

PNO	PNAME	COLOR	WEIGHT	CITY
P1	Nut	Red	12.0	London
P2	Bolt	Green	17.0	Paris
P3	Screw	Blue	17.0	Oslo
P4	Screw	Red	14.0	London
P5	Cam	Blue	12.0	Paris
P6	Cog	Red	19.0	London

SP

SNO	PNO	QTY
S1	P1	300
S1	P2	200
S1	P3	400
S1	P4	200
S1	P5	100
S1	P6	100
S2	P1	300
S2	P2	400
S3	P2	200
S4	P2	200
S4	P4	300
S4	P5	400

Now, what this picture shows is one possible value for the database, made up of three relations. Well, more precisely, what it shows is three relation *values*: namely, the relation values that happen to exist in the database at some particular time. But if we were to look at the database at some different time, we'd probably see three different relation values appearing in their place. In other words, S, P, and SP here are really *variables*: relation variables, to be precise. For example, suppose the relation variable S currently has the value shown in the picture, and suppose we delete the tuples for suppliers in London:[16]

```
DELETE S WHERE CITY = 'London' ;
```

---

[16] As I hope you know, "tuple" is the formal relational term for the relational counterpart to what SQL calls a row (and in the relational context, at least, there are good reasons for preferring it).

Here's the result:

SNO	SNAME	STATUS	CITY
S2	Jones	10	Paris
S3	Blake	30	Paris
S5	Adams	30	Athens

Conceptually, what's happened here is that the old value of S has been replaced in its entirety by a new value. Of course, the old value (with five tuples) and the new one (with three) are somewhat similar, in a sense, but they certainly are different values. In fact, the DELETE just shown is logically equivalent to, and indeed shorthand for, the following *relational assignment*:

```
S := S WHERE NOT ( CITY = 'London' ) ;
```

As with all assignments, the effect here is as follows: The source expression on the right side is evaluated, and then the result of that evaluation—a relation value in the case at hand, since the source expression is a relational expression—is assigned to the target variable on the left side (a relation variable, of course), with the overall result already explained.

So DELETE is shorthand for a certain relational assignment. And an analogous remark applies to INSERT and UPDATE also, of course: They too are basically just shorthand for certain relational assignments. Thus, relational assignment is the only update operator we really need, logically speaking, and it's the only one that's included in the relational model.

We see, therefore, that there's a logical difference between relation values and relation variables. The trouble is, the relational community has historically used the same term, *relation*, to stand for both. (Of course, SQL makes an exactly analogous mistake—it uses *table* to mean sometimes a table value and sometimes a table variable.) And that practice has certainly led to confusion. In our *Manifesto*, therefore, we distinguish very carefully between the two: We talk about relation values when we mean relation values, and relation variables when we mean relation variables. However, we also abbreviate *relation value*, most of the time, to just *relation*—exactly as we abbreviate *integer value* most of the time to just *integer*. And we abbreviate *relation variable*, most of the time, to **relvar**; for example, we say the suppliers-and-parts database contains three *relvars*.

All right, so that's relations vs. relvars. That's a big item. But now I'd like to say just a little about a few further topics that we've investigated using the *Manifesto* as a framework. The ones I'd like to discuss briefly are (a) language design, (b) view updating, (c) type inheritance, and (d) temporal data—though there are many others I could talk about if I wanted to, including implementation; business rules, predicates, and constraints; multiple assignment; database design; and missing information. Anyway, here goes.

Language Design

Our own language design efforts have been focused on **Tutorial D**, of course, though other researchers have independently designed a variety of "**D**"s of their own. And it's our claim that **Tutorial D** in particlar is well designed, powerful, and easy to use—much more so than SQL, in fact, in each of these three respects. I'll give just one example here (deliberately a slightly nontrivial one) to illustrate the point. For simplicity, let's suppose the shipments relvar SP has just the attributes SNO and PNO (i.e., let's ignore quantities). Then the expression

```
SP GROUP { PNO } AS PNO_REL
```

evaluates to a relation with one tuple for each supplier currently mentioned in SP, containing (a) that supplier's supplier number and (b) a unary "nested" relation containing part numbers for all parts supplied by that supplier (i.e., it maps a relation without a relation valued attribute into one with one). For example, if the following is the current value of SP—

SNO	PNO
S2	P1
S2	P2
S3	P2

—then the result of the GROUP operation looks like this:

Attribute PNO_REL in this result is a relation valued attribute or RVA. As already noted in passing, yes, we do allow such things, even if they're usually not a very good idea (that's another topic I could elaborate on if necessary, but I don't really want to get into further detail here).

Here for interest is what I *think*—but I wouldn't bet good money on it—is an SQL analog of the foregoing **Tutorial D** expression:

```
SELECT DISTINCT X.SNO ,
                CAST ( TABLE ( SELECT Y.PNO
                               FROM    SP AS Y
                               WHERE   Y.SNO = X.SNO )
                       AS ROW ( PNO VARCHAR(6) ) MULTISET )
                AS PNO_REL
FROM      SP AS X
```

By the way, a **Tutorial D** expression for "going the other way," as it were (i.e., mapping the relation with the RVA—let's call it SPP—to the one without one) is also straightforward:

```
SPP UNGROUP PNO_REL
```

This time I'll leave the SQL analog to you!

The bottom line here is as follows: We require every specific **D** to abide by various well established principles of good language design, such as parsimony, orthogonality, generality, completeness, extensibility, and so on, and **Tutorial D** does so. (By contrast, SQL most certainly doesn't. SQL isn't a valid **D**.)

View Updating

View updating has been a thorny problem ever since the relational model first saw the light of day. Many, many papers and articles have been written on the subject over the years, and most of them have been quite depressing and/or negative in tone. Now, I don't claim the problem is 100% solved, either; however, I do believe the ideas of *The Third Manifesto* have allowed us to get much closer to a solution than anyone has managed before, as far as I'm aware. In fact, I'm going to make a somewhat contentious claim—to wit:

There's no such thing as a nonupdatable view.

Actually this claim is trivially true, in a sense. For consider: First, views are relvars (virtual relvars, agreed, but still relvars). Second, relvars are variables. Third, variables are updatable by definition!—to be a variable is to be updatable, and to be updatable is to be a variable.

Now, it's true that some updates on some variables will fail—but if they do, it's *because they violate some constraint*. This remark is true of base relvars in particular, and it's true of virtual relvars (views) as well. So yes, certain updates do fail on certain views, but they do so not because the views in question are inherently nonupdatable—rather, they do so because the updates in question violate some constraint. Indeed, a productive way to think about the issue is as follows:

- Let $B1, ..., Bn$ be base relvars and let V be a view defined in terms of $B1, ..., Bn$.

- Think of $B1, ..., Bn$, and V as all living alongside one another, with the view definition for V as an integrity constraint interrelating them.

Also, remember that multiple assignment is sometimes a logical necessity, [17] implying among other things that (e.g.) an update on V might sometimes require updates to two or more of $B1, ..., Bn$.

---

[17] A trivial illustration of that logical necessity is this: Sometimes, a delete on relvar S will require a corresponding delete on relvar SP—in which case the deletes in question will logically both be part of the same multiple assignment. For further discussion, see Chapter 13.

That's all I want to say on this topic here; if you want to know more, please see my book *View Updating and Relational Theory: Solving the View Update Problem* (O'Reilly, 2013).

Type Inheritance

On this subject, by contrast, I do want to get into a certain amount of technical detail. But it's a tricky area, and all I can do here is just touch on a few of the basic ideas.

To begin at the beginning: As I've already said, our *Manifesto* includes a theory of types; indeed, we regard the provision of that theory as one of the *Manifesto*'s main contributions. But thinking about types in general quickly leads to thinking about type inheritance in particular ... and we did that, and what we came up with was basically a whole new inheritance model, or theory, that's separate from the *Manifesto* as such but grafted on top of it, as it were. Which I'll now very briefly describe.

First of all, I should explain what we[18] mean by the term *type inheritance*, or just *inheritance* for short. Basically, we use that term to refer to that phenomenon according to which we can sensibly say, for example, that every circle is an ellipse, and hence that all properties that apply to ellipses in general apply to—i.e., *are inherited by*—circles in particular. Equivalently (albeit loosely): All circles are ellipses, but "most" ellipses aren't circles.

Now, I need to explain immediately that there's no consensus in this field, and some people would dispute even the foregoing apparent truism (i.e., that circles are ellipses). By way of illustration, here's a verbatim quote from the book *The C++ Programming Language*, by Bjarne Stroustrup (3rd edition, Addison-Wesley, 1997):

> In mathematics a circle is a kind of an ellipse, but in most programs a circle should not be derived from an ellipse or an ellipse derived from a circle. The often heard arguments "because that's the way it is in mathematics" and "because the representation of a circle is a subset of that of an ellipse" are not conclusive and most often wrong. This is because for most programs, the key property of a circle is that it has a center and a fixed distance to its perimeter. All behavior of a circle (all operations) must maintain this property ... On the other hand, an ellipse is characterized by two focal points that can be changed independently of each

---

[18] By "we" here I mean Hugh Darwen and myself, together with supporters of *The Third Manifesto* in general.

other. If those focal points coincide, the ellipse looks like a circle, but it is not a circle because its operations do not preserve the circle invariant. In most systems, this difference will be reflected by having a circle and an ellipse provide sets of operations that are not subsets of each other.

Well, we disagree (politely, of course) with Stroustrup here. In our approach, in very striking contrast, (a) a circle most certainly is an ellipse—just as it is "in mathematics," in fact, as Stroustrup rightly says, and also (and more to the point) just as it is in the real world—and (b) ellipse properties most certainly are inherited by circles. By which we mean that, for example, every ellipse has an area, and therefore every circle has an area also. More precisely:

a. Types ELLIPSE and CIRCLE are such that type ELLIPSE is a *supertype* of type CIRCLE and type CIRCLE is a *subtype* of type ELLIPSE.

b. There's an operator—AREA_OF, say—that, given an argument of type ELLIPSE returns the area of that ellipse, and that operator can be invoked with an argument of type CIRCLE, because circles *are* ellipses.

Of course, the converse is false—the subtype will have properties of its own that don't apply to the supertype. For example, circles have a radius, but ellipses in general don't; in other words, there's an operator—RADIUS_OF, say—that returns the radius of a given circle, but that operator can't be invoked with an argument that's "just an ellipse," because such ellipses aren't circles.

So operators are inherited. But constraints are properties too, of a kind, and therefore they're inherited too. For example, any constraint that applies to ellipses in general also applies to circles in particular (for otherwise some circles wouldn't be ellipses). By way of example, suppose ellipses are subject to the constraint that the length a of their major semiaxis is greater than or equal to the length b of their minor semiaxis; then that same constraint must be satisfied by circles also. (For circles the semiaxes coincide in the radius, and this particular constraint is satisfied trivially.)

Again, of course, the converse is false—there'll be constraints that apply to circles specifically but not to ellipses in general. In fact, the constraint $a = b$ is a case in point—it's a constraint that applies to circles specifically but not to ellipses in general.

Well, from simple ideas such as the foregoing (all of which, let me stress, are really nothing more than logical consequences of the even more fundamental notion that *types are sets*) we've constructed a complete and rigorous model of inheritance, one that supports:

a. Both single and multiple inheritance

That is, a given subtype can have any number of supertypes (loosely speaking). For example, type CIRCLE has just one, ELLIPSE—that's single inheritance—but type SQUARE might have two, RECTANGLE and RHOMBUS—that's multiple inheritance. Of course, the former is just a special case of the latter. But you need to understand that support for the latter is quite unusual! Many inheritance schemes described in the literature deal with single inheritance only. That's the way SQL is, for example.

b. Scalar, tuple, and relation inheritance

That is, the subtypes and supertypes we're talking about can be tuple or relation types as well as scalar types. For example, the relation type

```
RELATION { E CIRCLE , R SQUARE }
```

is a subtype of the relation type

```
RELATION { E ELLIPSE , R RECTANGLE }
```

And again such support is quite unusual—most inheritance schemes deal with scalar inheritance only. Again, that's the way SQL is, for example.

And, very importantly (but uniquely, and very controversially!), our model also supports what we call:

c. "Specialization by constraint" (S by C for short)

That is, if an ellipse has $a = b$ then it's a circle, and if it's a circle then it has $a = b$, and *the system is aware of both of these facts*. In particular, therefore, the fact that a given value of type ELLIPSE happens to have $a = b$ means that the value in question is "specialized"—in effect, by the system—to type CIRCLE.

Now, the idea that an ellipse is a circle if and only if it has $a = b$ is in strict accordance with the way the world works, of course, but—rather incredibly—*nobody* except us (as far as we know) has an inheritance scheme that supports it. Certainly SQL doesn't. Here's another quote to illustrate the point (actually this quote talks about classes instead of types, and squares and rectangles instead of circles and ellipses, but I'm sure you won't need me to translate for you):

> Is SQUARE a subclass of RECTANGLE? ... Stretching the x dimension of a rectangle is a perfectly reasonable thing to do. But if you do it to a square, then the object is no longer a square. This is not necessarily a bad thing conceptually. When you stretch a square you *do* get a rectangle ... But ... most object languages do not want objects to change class ... This suggests a design principle for classification systems: *A subclass should not be defined by constraining a superclass.*
> —James Rumbaugh: "A Matter of Intent: How to Define Subclasses"
> *Journal of Object Oriented Programming* (September 1996)

Notice the rationale—"most object languages don't want objects to change class." By contrast, we say: "Let's get the model right first, then worry about designing a language to support it afterward." And in our model, stretching a square does produce a rectangle (if you see what I mean). That's S by C. (Or G by C, to be more precise—G for generalization. S by C and G by C are two sides of the same coin, and we use "S by C" as a shorthand label for both considered together. Stretching a square produces a rectangle—OK, that's G by C. By the same token, squashing a rectangle produces a square—OK, that's S by C! Speaking pretty loosely, of course, in both cases.)

By the way, you might be wondering *why* object languages don't want objects to change class and therefore don't support S by C, since it seems so obviously the right thing to do. The answer, believe it or not, is because they support *pointers* ... The issue is far too arcane to get into details on here, but the fact is that pointers and S by C turn out to be simply, but fundamentally, incompatible. If we're right on this (and we think we are), then we say tough—it's just too bad for pointers, and they'll have to go.[19]

Be that as it may, our inheritance model, and as a matter of fact SQL's too, are both described in detail in my book *Type Inheritance and Relational Theory:*

---

[19] And if they do, then—since support for objects seems to *require* support for pointers—it follows that objects (as that term is usually understood) will have to go too. Interesting conclusion!

Subtypes, Supertypes, and Substitutability (O'Reilly, 2016). And I'd like to call your attention here to something I say in that book:

> There's no consensus on a formal, rigorous, and abstract type inheritance model. In our work on *The Third Manifesto*, therefore, we were more or less forced to develop an inheritance model of our own ... We're very serious about that model. We'd like it *not* to be seen as just an academic exercise. Rather, we'd like it to be considered by the community at large as a serious contender for filling the gap (i.e., as a candidate for the role that *is* "formal, rigorous, and abstract" and can be generally agreed upon by that "community at large"). We offer it here in that spirit.

Now, you might have noticed that I haven't said anything so far as to why inheritance is worth supporting in the first place! However, there seem to be at least two answers to this question:

■ First, the ideas of subtyping and inheritance do seem to arise naturally in the real world (as with ellipses and circles, or rectangles and squares). Thus, subtyping and inheritance look as if they might be useful tools for "modeling reality."

■ Second, if we can recognize such general patterns—patterns of subtyping and inheritance, that is—and build intelligence regarding them into our application and system software, we might be able to achieve certain practical economies. For example, a program that works for ellipses might work for circles too, even if it was originally written with no thought for circles at all (perhaps type CIRCLE hadn't even been defined at the time the program in question was written).

That said, I should say too that most of the existing literature seems more concerned—I'm tempted to say, *much* more concerned—with the second of these goals than it is with the first; in other words, it seems to be principally interested in inheritance as a mechanism for designing, building, and (re)using *programs*. Our own focus, by contrast, is more on the first than the second; that is, we're interested in inheritance as a conceptual tool for designing, building, and (re)using *data structures*. (After all, we're database people, and data structures are important to us.) In other words, what we're looking for is an inheritance model that can be used to "model reality"—certain aspects of reality, at any rate—much as the relational model itself can also be used to model certain aspects of reality.

Temporal Data

Here's another really big issue that I'd like to say a little more about. This time I'll start with the pertinent reference:

- C. J. Date, Hugh Darwen, and Nikos A. Lorentzos: *Time and Relational Theory: Temporal Databases in the Relational Model and SQL* (Morgan Kaufmann, 2014)

Nikos is the prime mover in this work (he began working in this area in the late 1980s).

Now, much of the research in the temporal database field seems to assume that the relational model is incapable of dealing with temporal data, and hence that it needs extension of some kind. Consider by way of example the following (genuine) research paper titles:

- A Temporally Oriented Data Model

- The Time Relational Model

- The Historical Relational Data Model (HRDM) Revisited

- Temporal Extensions to the Relational Model and SQL

And so on. What these titles (and many others like them) have in common is that they all tend to suggest is that something radical is needed: major surgery to the relational model, at the very least, or possibly even something entirely new. Our position, by contrast, is: No, don't do *anything* to the relational model! We believe, and we believe our book shows clearly, that the relational model needs no extension, and no correction, and no subsumption—and above all no perversion—in order for it to be able to support temporal data.

Now, I don't want to mislead you here—we do define a bunch of new "temporal" operators, for example—but everything we "add" to the relational model is, in the final analysis, just shorthand for something the relational model

can already do. But let me get a little more specific. Consider the following
relation:

```
┌─────┬───────────┐
│ SNO │ DURING    │
╞═════╪═══════════╡
│ S1  │ [d04:d07] │
│ S1  │ [d05:d10] │
│ S1  │ [d09:d09] │
│ S2  │ [d05:d06] │
│ S2  │ [d03:d03] │
│ S2  │ [d07:d08] │
└─────┴───────────┘
```

The intended interpretation of this relation is: *Supplier SNO was under
contract throughout interval DURING.* For example, we see among other things
that supplier S1 was under contract throughout the interval from day 4 (*d04*) to
day 7 (*d07*), inclusive. Now, in our book, we define all kinds of "new"
constructs for dealing with relations like the one just shown, including:

■ Two new operators, PACK and UNPACK

■ Generalized versions of regular projection, join, etc. ("U_ operators")

■ Generalized join dependencies ("U_JDs")

■ New constraints, PACKED ON and WHEN / THEN

And on and on. Now, I can't possibly get into details of all of these matters here;
I'll just say one thing, to give a slight hint. Let SD be the relation in the picture
on the previous page. Then I can think you can see some problems with that
relation:

■ *Redundancy:* For example, the relation tells us twice that supplier S1 was
under contract on day 6.

■ *Circumlocution:* For example, the relation takes three tuples to tell us what
it could have told us with just one, viz., that supplier S1 was under contract
throughout the interval [*d04:d10*].

Well, we can get rid of these problems by "packing" relation SD "on attribute DURING," thus:

```
PACK SD ON ( DURING )
```

Here's the result:

SNO	DURING
S1	[*d04:d10*]
S2	[*d03:d03*]
S2	[*d05:d08*]

As you can see, this relation doesn't suffer from either the redundancy problem or the circumlocution problem that SD suffers from. But let me stress again that all of these "new" things (PACK and all the rest) are, in the last analysis, just shorthand for combinations of things that can already be done—albeit not very easily, in some cases—by means of features already present in the relational model.

DEBUNKING SOME OF THE NONSENSE

OK, that's all I want to say here regarding the first "useful contribution" I claim my writing provides: reporting on, and explaining, research by myself and colleagues. Now I turn to the second: counteracting and debunking some of the nonsense that's out there. Actually, all I want to do here is cite a few horrible examples of the nonsense in question, suppressing the sources in order to protect the guilty. For the debunkings as such, you can go and read my books (if you really want to!).

By the way, you might be thinking it's not very gentlemanly of me to attack other writers in this fashion (not cricket, I might have said, if I still lived in the U.K.). But I disagree—even when the writer in question is someone for whom I generally have a lot of respect, which is indeed sometimes the case. I've devoted my entire professional career to advocating for, and doing my best to advance, a certain technology, a technology that for all kinds of reasons I regard as truly important. So if someone attacks that technology, I'm going to defend it! Of course, if the attack in question turns out to be merited, then I'll modify my position; I'm a scientist, and that's one way progress is made in science. By the way, I have a great quote in this connection:

> In science it often happens that scientists say, "You know, that's a really good argument, my position is mistaken," and then they actually change their minds, and you never hear that old view from them again. They really do it. It doesn't happen as often as it should, because scientists are human and change is sometimes painful. But it happens every day. I cannot recall the last time something like that happened in politics or religion.
>
> —Carl Sagan:
> *The Burden of Skepticism* (1987)

And another quote, also pertinent (I'm not sure of the source for this one, though I've seen it attributed to Neil deGrasse Tyson, but I like it a lot):

> The great thing about science is that it works even if you don't believe in it.

Anyway, here's the first horrible example (it's from a document purporting to give advice on how to use a relational DBMS):

> Don't use joins ... Oracle and SQL Server have fundamentally different approaches to the concept ... You can end up with unexpected result sets ... You should understand the basic types of join clauses ...
> Equijoins are formed by retrieving all the data from two separate sources and combining it into one large table.
> Inner joins are joined on the inner columns of two tables.
> Outer joins are joined on the outer columns of two tables.
> Left joins are joined on the left columns of two tables.
> Right joins are joined on the right columns of two tables.

What *is* this guy smoking? (Yes, it's a guy.)

Next horrible example (from a database consultant in the U.K.):

> [Your] instructor probably told you that the relational view was not only mathematically correct, provably correct, or something similar, but also far more flexible than anything that preceded it. That explanation is fairly simple and perhaps a little embarrassing for the computer world, because **the relational theory of data is wrong**. Data cannot always be represented in terms of entities, attributes, and relationships.

So set theory and predicate logic are wrong?

Here's one from a database consultant in the U.S.:

> These rules get more and more complex as you add domains to the database. When you multiply feet by pounds, you get work expressed in foot-pounds. But not always—a man's height multiplied by his weight is nonsense, not foot-pounds. The relation or entity where the attributes reside matters quite a bit.

The writer is suggesting that there might be such a thing as "a domain of feet" or "a domain of pounds." Really? What exactly would such domains contain?

My next example is from a well known database textbook:

> [It] is important to make a distinction between stored relations, which are *tables,* and virtual relations, which are *views* ... [We] shall use *relation* only where a table or a view could be used. When we want to emphasize that a relation is stored, rather than a view, we shall sometimes use the term *base relation* or *base table.*

There are so many things wrong with this one, I hardly know where to begin.

This next is also from a textbook, though thankfully one that's not so well known:

> Fifth normal form concerns dependencies that are rather obscure. It has to do with relations that can be divided into subrelations ... but then cannot be reconstructed. The condition under which this situation arises has no clear, intuitive meaning. We do not know what the consequences of such dependencies are or even if they have any practical consequences.

Frankly, I find this one rather amazing ... Can you imagine saying, in a what's supposed to be a *textbook*, "I have no idea what I'm talking about"? Because that's basically what the writer is doing here.

One last horrible example (this one is from a book on object orientation):

> A newer form of database manager, the *relational model,* ... [removes] information about complex relationships from the database ... Although the relational model is much more flexible than its predecessors, it pays a price for this flexibility. The information about complex relationships that was removed from the database must be expressed as procedures in every program that accesses the database, a clear violation of the independence required for modularity.

Trees should not be destroyed to make books as bad as this one.

Let me close on a positive note ... Here's a quote I like a lot and indeed thoroughly approve of:

> I would like to see computer science teaching set deliberately in a historical framework ... Students need to understand how the present situation has come about, what was tried, what worked and what did not, and how improvements in hardware made progress possible. The absence of this element in their training causes people to approach every problem from first principles. They are apt to propose solutions that have been found wanting in the past. Instead of standing on the shoulders of their precursors, they try to go it alone.

This one is from Maurice Wilkes. What he's saying is: *Education is important!* And education is what I've tried to provide, and it's a major reason why I write. And that's a great note to end on, and so I will. Thank you for your attention.

Chapter 2

The Principle

of Cautious Design

This short chapter describes and illustrates The Principle of Cautious Design (POCD), a simple guiding principle that I propose should be adhered to in the design of formal systems in general. Examples of such systems include programming languages, "query languages," databases, application programs, and many others— including, of course, the relational model.

> *Publishing history: This is a revised version of a paper that first appeared in The Relational Journal For DB2 Users 2, No. 3 (June/July 1990) and was later republished in my book Relational Database Writings 1989-1991 (Addison-Wesley, 1992). This version copyright © C. J. Date 2022.*

I introduced and first described *The Principle of Cautious Design* ("the POCD" for short) in an early paper on referential integrity and foreign keys [6]. Among other things, that paper proposed a set of guidelines to be followed in the way foreign keys should be deployed in the design of a relational database, and the POCD played a significant role in that proposal. It seemed to me, however, that cautious design was a principle that could and should apply in all kinds of situations in addition to that particular and comparatively narrow one, and I wrote the present chapter to expound on it further.

THE POCD AND THE RELATIONAL MODEL

By definition, designing a relational database involves a process of mapping from informal constructs in the real world to formal constructs in the relational model. Reference [6] includes a brief discussion of that process, and it's convenient to begin by repeating the essentials of that discussion here.

First of all, of course, the relational model is a formal system. But the intent of that formal system is to be used, and to be useful, in representing certain aspects of the real world—and the real world, I take it, isn't a formal system. It follows that the process of mapping to the formal relational model from the informal real world is necessarily not formal either, but only intuitive. (A mapping between two systems can be defined formally only if both of those systems are themselves formal in turn.) And it thereby follows further that there must be a certain element of subjectiveness in defining the rules of the formal relational model—basically, those rules have to be defined in such a way as to seem, intuitively, to be a good fit with the way the real world behaves. But of course it's always possible to argue about matters of intuition; hence, the design of the relational model itself depends, necessarily, on certain judgment calls on the part of those responsible for doing that design.

THE POCD AND PRIMARY KEYS

Now for an illustration. The two bullet items immediately following are repeated pretty much verbatim from the original version of this chapter, except that I've had to edit them in certain minor ways for present purposes:

■   The relational model [*i.e., as originally defined*] insists that a foreign key must always reference a primary key, not an alternate key.[1] Now, it's certainly possible to think of situations in which it might seem desirable to relax this rule. However, it's my opinion that the minor additional functionality provided by relaxing the rule is significantly outweighed by the additional complexity it causes—complexity, be it noted, not just for the user who wants to take advantage of the relaxed version of the rule, but rather for everybody. Personally, I've never seen a situation in which there was a genuine need to have a foreign key reference an alternate key; it has always turned out, in the examples I've seen, that the design of the database wasn't very good and could be improved to avoid that apparent need.

---

[1] An alternate key is a "candidate key" (i.e., a unique identifier) that's not the primary key. For example, if every employee has both a unique employee number and a unique social security number—in other words, if "employee number" and "social security number" are both candidate keys—then "employee number" might be chosen as the primary key, and "social security number" would then be an alternate key. The original idea was that every table must have exactly one primary key, plus N alternate keys for some $N \geq 0$.

■　However, given that—as in effect I've already said—such matters are always somewhat subjective, I would also argue that a good general principle is to stay with the simple version of the rule for as long as possible, waiting until such time as a genuine need to relax it comes along (if it ever does). If and when that happens, then that'll be the time to relax the rule. Such an approach will guarantee the maximum simplicity for the maximum time, and (more important) will guarantee that extensions to the model are made in an evolutionary, not revolutionary, manner.

Well, I don't think you could find a better example than the foregoing to illustrate the thesis of the present chapter! I wrote the original version of that text in 1988 or so, and of course I believed what I was saying (about keys in particular) at the time. But I subsequently came to realize that in fact there *are* situations in which (a) insisting that one candidate key be made primary (i.e., be "more equal than the others"), and (b) insisting moreover that foreign keys always reference primary keys specifically, didn't make very good sense. So I changed my position—in fact, I wrote an essay to that effect, called "Primary Keys Are Nice but Not Essential" [10].[2] But the fact that I was able to do so—change my position, I mean—is precisely because I'd followed *The Principle of Cautious Design* in the first place. *Now read on ...*

THE POCD DEFINED

The general principle articulated in the second bullet item in the previous section is *The Principle of Cautious Design*, and as I've said I believe it's applicable to formal systems in general, not just the relational model in particular. Here's a definition:

> **Definition (*The Principle of Cautious Design*):** A guiding principle in the design of formal systems, including databases, DBMSs, database

---

[2] In other ways, I still believe that every table has to have at least one candidate key. Moreover, I have no serious objection to the idea of labeling exactly one of those candidate keys "primary" if desired. I even have no objection to such a key enjoying some syntactic advantage over other candidate keys—though personally I'd prefer to drop the qualifiers *primary* and *candidate* and *alternate* and refer to them all as just keys, in which case there wouldn't be such a thing as a primary key any longer, and so it couldn't enjoy any syntactic advantage a fortiori. But what I definitely do (now!) have a serious objection to is the idea that a "primary" key might have some special *semantic* role to play, such as being the only permissible target for a foreign key reference.

languages, and many other such systems. It can be stated thus: Given a design choice between options *A* and *B*, where *A* is upward compatible with *B* and the full consequences of going with *B* aren't yet known, the cautious decision is to go with *A*.

Going with *A* permits subsequent "opening up" of the design to *B* if such opening up becomes desirable—indeed, that's exactly what happened with keys in the example described in the previous section. By contrast, going with *B* prohibits subsequent "closing down" of the design to *A*, even if such closing down later turns out to be desirable (i.e., if it becomes clear that *B* was a bad choice in the first place).

The language SQL provides an illustration.[3] The designers of SQL had a choice between prohibiting duplicate rows (*Option A*) and permitting them (*Option B*). The cautious decision would have been to prohibit them (*Option A*); they could then have been supported in the future, if a clear need for such support were ever demonstrated. Unfortunately, the designers chose to permit them (*Option B*). Of course, this decision turned out for all kinds of reasons to be an extremely bad one, but now there's no compatible way for SQL to go back to *Option A*.

Note: As the foregoing example might suggest, *The Principle of Cautious Design* can help avoid situations in which the language (or the DBMS, or the database, or whatever else it is that's being designed) provides certain options that users have to be explicitly told not to exercise or "take advantage of." As I've written elsewhere, in fact, such options are basically just rope to hang yourself with.

THE POCD AND FOREIGN KEYS

Note: This section is an extended version of a discussion that originally appeared in reference [6].

In reference [2], Codd implicitly opened the door to the possibility of having a single foreign key referring two or more distinct target tables.[4] I elaborated on

---

[3] Actually it provides numerous illustrations.

[4] Once he'd explicitly articulated that position, in fact (which as far as I know he first did in reference [3]), he never backed down from it.

this idea in reference [5], suggesting a possible syntax somewhat along the following lines:

```
FOREIGN KEY { <column name commalist> }
   REFERENCES [ <quantifier> ] { <table name commalist> }
```

Explanation:

- The *<column name commalist>* identifies the columns constituting the foreign key being defined.

- The *<table name commalist>* identifies the pertinent target tables. *Note:* I assume here for simplicity that (a) all target tables must be base tables specifically, and (b) every target key must have unqualified column names that are identical to those of the referencing foreign key. Both of these points deserve more discussion (actually a lot more discussion!), but such discussion would be out of place here.

- The *<quantifier>* is EXACTLY ONE OF, AT LEAST ONE OF, or EACH OF,[5] and it and the braces surrounding the *<table name commalist>* can be omitted if that list in fact names only one table. *Note:* For the purposes of this discussion I take the semantics of the various possible *<quantifier>*s to be intuitively obvious.

By way of example, consider the suppliers table (table S) from the usual suppliers-and-parts database. Here's the usual sample value for this table:

S

SNO	SNAME	STATUS	CITY
S1	Smith	20	London
S2	Jones	10	Paris
S3	Blake	30	Paris
S4	Clark	20	London
S5	Adams	30	Athens

As you can see, this table has four columns, viz., SNO (supplier number), SNAME, STATUS, and CITY. Its sole key—which you can take to be the

---

[5] The quantifier EACH OF was spelled ALL OF in the original paper [5].

primary key if you like—is column SNO (note the double underlining in the picture). [6]

The supplies-and-parts database also contains a shipments table (table SP), with columns SNO, PNO, and QTY, in which SNO is a foreign key referencing the sole key of table S:

```
FOREIGN KEY { SNO } REFERENCES S
```

Now suppose we decide for some reason to split this table "horizontally" into three restrictions, viz., LS, PS, and AS, representing London suppliers, Paris suppliers, and Athens suppliers, respectively:[7]

```
LS { SNO , SNAME , STATUS }
PS { SNO , SNAME , STATUS }
AS { SNO , SNAME , STATUS }
```

(The CITY column can obviously be dropped with this design.) Then the SNO foreign key definition in connection with table SP would look like this:

```
FOREIGN KEY { SNO }
   REFERENCES EXACTLY ONE OF { LS , PS , AS }
```

Alternatively, suppose we decide for some reason to split the original table S "vertically" into three projections, viz., SN, ST, and SC, like this:

```
SN { SNO , SNAME }
ST { SNO , STATUS }
SC { SNO , CITY }
```

Then the SNO foreign key definition in connection with table SP would look like this:

```
FOREIGN KEY { SNO }
   REFERENCES EACH OF { LS , PS , AS }
```

---

[6] Although I no longer believe in the primacy (as it were) of primary keys, I do still usually mark them in tabular pictures, as here, by doubly underlining the pertinent column names. PS: Yes, I know, supplier names are also unique in the example. But that's just a fluke—it's just a matter of the sample table value I chose for the example. It doesn't mean SNAME is a candidate key. (In a different sample value, it could be that two distinct suppliers both have the same name.)

[7] Of course, AS is a reserved word in SQL. Never mind, reserved words are a bad idea anyway.

However, I quickly came to feel the foregoing scheme was much *too* general, and I publicly stepped back from it in reference [6]. Let me explain why I now feel this way.

The Horizontal Split

Consider the "horizontal split" design once again. First of all, that design clearly requires an integrity constraint to be declared, and of course enforced, to the effect that no supplier number appears in more than one of the tables LS, PS, and AS:[8]

```
CONSTRAINT ... IS_EMPTY ( LS JOIN PS ) AND
               IS_EMPTY ( PS JOIN AS ) AND
               IS_EMPTY ( AS JOIN LS ) ;
```

Much easier just to declare SNO as a key for S! (It's likely to be easier to implement, too—but that's just a bonus, and I shouldn't really even be mentioning it in a discussion of this nature.)

Second, why would anyone want such a "horizontal split" design, anyway?[9] It certainly makes certain queries more difficult to formulate (as well as certain constraints, as we've already seen). For example, consider the query "What's the city for supplier S1?" An SQL formulation of this query with the original design is straightforward, even trivial:

```
SELECT CITY
FROM   S
WHERE  SNO = 'S1'
```

But with the horizontal split it has to look something like this:

```
SELECT 'London' AS CITY
FROM   LS
WHERE  SNO = 'S1'
UNION
SELECT 'Paris' AS CITY
FROM   PS
WHERE  SNO = 'S1'
UNION
```

---

[8] I deliberately show this constraint in **Tutorial D** [15], not SQL, because an SQL analog would be excessively cumbersome (exercise for the reader).

[9] I hope it goes without saying that performance is *not* an acceptable answer to this question.

```
SELECT 'Athens' AS CITY
FROM   AS
WHERE  SNO = 'S1'
```

Consider too what happens to both the foregoing constraint and the foregoing query—not to mention the foreign key constraint from table SP—if new supplier cities (Rome, Oslo, Madrid, and so on) become legal.

Well, the only reason I can see for going for the horizontal split design in the first place is that we might want to say different things about suppliers depending on what city they're in—for example, London suppliers might have a favorite beer; Paris suppliers a favorite wine; and Athens suppliers a favorite philosopher. But if that's the case, then surely there should be a single "master" or "anchor" suppliers table S, containing just the common properties such as STATUS, and then tables LS, PS, and AS can contain the special properties that apply to London, Paris, and Athens suppliers, respectively. The foreign key from table SP would then reference that master table:

```
FOREIGN KEY { SNO } REFERENCES S
```

(An identical foreign key specification would also have to appear as part of the definition of each of tables LS, PS, and AS.) This seems to me to be a much cleaner design—assuming, that is, that we want to go with a horizontal split design at all. And note in particular that there's now no need for that EXACTLY ONE OF quantifier in any of those foreign key specifications.

The Vertical Split

I turn now to the "vertical split" example. First of all, note that we now need a constraint to the effect that each of tables SN, ST, and SC contains the same set of supplier numbers (in other words, the projections of all three tables on column SNO should all be equal):

```
CONSTRAINT ... SN {SNO } = ST { SNO } AND
               ST {SNO } = SC { SNO } AND
               SC {SNO } = SN { SNO } ;
```

(Note the slight arbitrariness involved here, too: It would be sufficient to specify just two of the three equality tests—but which one should we drop? And why? And what are the implications?)

In fact, it could be argued in connection with this constraint that we're dealing with foreign keys again. For example, for table SN we might specify:

```
FOREIGN KEY { SNO } REFERENCES EACH OF { ST , SC }
```

But then we'd presumably also need (for table ST):

```
FOREIGN KEY { SNO } REFERENCES EACH OF { SC , SN }
```

And for table SC:

```
FOREIGN KEY { SNO } REFERENCES EACH OF { SN , ST }
```

Well, this hardly seems right ... After all, exactly what foreign key delete rules would make sense in such a situation, do you think? Which table should be in charge, as it were? Surely it would be better, as in the horizontal split example, to introduce some kind of master or anchor table—though here that master table (which again we might as well call just S) would probably contain nothing except the pertinent supplier numbers.[10] If we did introduce such a table, then the foreign key constraints from SN, ST, and SC would each reduce to just

```
FOREIGN KEY { SNO } REFERENCES S
```

What's more, the corresponding foreign key specification for the shipments table SP would also be just

```
FOREIGN KEY { SNO } REFERENCES S
```

(Without that master table, in fact, it's not at all clear what should be done about the SNO foreign key in the shipments table.)

Once again, a much cleaner design!—and note that there's now no need for that EACH OF quantifier in any of those foreign key specifications.

Cautious Design

The foregoing subsections cast serious doubt on the question as to whether the quantifiers EXACTLY ONE OF and EACH OF would ever be needed in

---

[10] As a matter of fact such a design does have quite a lot to recommend it, albeit for reasons that are beyond the scope of the present discussion. See reference [9].

practice. As for AT LEAST ONE OF, it's hard to find a sensible example of its use—not to mention the fact that it would probably be hard to implement efficiently. So let's apply *The Principle of Cautious Design* and prohibit all three quantifiers until a genuine requirement for them arises (if it ever does).[11]

FURTHER EXAMPLES

Here for interest are a few more instances of *The Principle of Cautious Design* in action:

- *PENDANT:* In the same paper [5] in which I discussed the quantifiers EXACTLY ONE OF, etc., I also introduced three foreign key delete rules, viz., CASCADES, RESTRICTED, and NULLIFIES.[12] However, a question I'm often asked—or was often asked at the time, at any rate—was: "Why just these three possibilities? Why not, e.g., a rule that deletes a target row when the last row referencing it is deleted?" Such a rule could be used, e.g., to trigger the automatic deletion of a department when the last employee is removed from that department. (It's sometimes characterized as "Last one out switch off the lights," or—a version I prefer—"Last one to leave the country, please switch off the politicians.")

  As a matter of fact, such a rule was actually proposed at one time for inclusion in the SQL standard, under the name PENDANT (?), though I don't think it ever actually became part of the standard as such. Anyway, regardless of whether it did or not, it seems to me that *The Principle of Cautious Design* would be a strong argument against it.

- *Relation valued attributes:* During the early years of the relational model it was widely believed—indeed, I believed it myself, and stated as much in my own early books and papers—that the values at row and column

---

[11] Which I don't believe it ever has. As indicated in footnote 4, however, Codd didn't agree with this position; rather, he insisted that it was necessary "right now" (as it were) to allow two or more target tables for the same foreign key [3,4]—despite the fact that he explicitly required the single target table discipline to be followed in what he called the extended relational model, RM/T [2].

[12] NULLIFIES was included because at the time I believed in nulls. That was a mistake on my part, for which I hereby apologize; inded, it might be seen as an example of a situation where I should have abided by the POCD but didn't. (Just to be clear, I no longer support *anything* to do with nulls, other than to eliminate them entirely.) As for CASCADES and RESTRICTED, I do continue to support them, but these days I prefer to spell them CASCADE and NO CASCADE, respectively.

intersections in table must always be "atomic." One particular consequence of this state of affairs was the rule that no relation could ever contain other relations nested inside itself; that is, relation valued attributes (RVAs for short) were prohibited.

The source of the "atomic values" idea was, of course, Codd himself, who stressed it repeatedly in most if not all of his database writings (with the sole and interesting exception of his very first paper on the relational model [1]). Subsequently, however, I came to understand that the position doesn't really make sense;[13] indeed, the very idea of "atomic values" doesn't really make sense. Certainly it was never precisely defined. When I finally understood the true situation, therefore, I realized that RVAs in particular were not only legitimate but sometimes, though perhaps not very often, actually desirable. And so I began to advocate for their acceptance (see, e.g., reference [12]). So the history here—first prohibiting RVAs and then later permitting them—can be seen as another example of following *The Principle of Cautious Design.*

■ *Coercions:* Coercions are implicit data type conversions. They're widely regarded as a very bad idea, because they're a rich source of errors (errors that, to make matters worse, probably won't be caught until run time). In the design of our language **Tutorial D**, therefore [15], Hugh Darwen and I have always prohibited them—but of course we would "open up" our design and allow them if a strong enough case in their favor were ever to be presented.

As a kind of aside, let me give some examples of the difficulties coercions can cause. The examples in question are repeated from reference [13]; they're all based on the language PL/I, which admittedly might be considered rather antiquated by now, but they do illustrate some of the pitfalls very well. *Note:* In any case (and regardless of what you might think about PL/I), it's unfortunately true, and relevant to mention, that SQL is rife with coercions, too. In particular, SQL sometimes (but not always) coerces a table of cardinality one to the single row it contains, and sometimes (but not always) coerces a row of degree one to the single value it contains—both of which are coercions that, in my view, are particularly inappropriate, and unfortunate in the extreme.

---

[13] Thanks largely to the efforts of my friend and colleague Hugh Darwen.

Example 1:

```
IF 1 < X < 5 THEN CALL Q ;
```

Surprise: Q is always called, even if X is outside the range one to five. Why? Because 1 < X yields either TRUE or FALSE, which are represented in PL/I by the bit strings '1'B and '0'B, respectively. These values are then coerced to numeric 1 and 0, respectively, both of which are less than 5.

Example 2:

```
DO J = 1 , J = 2 ; loop ; END ;
```

Surprise: The second iteration of *loop* is executed with J = 0, not 2. Why? Because J = 2 is a comparison which (thanks to the assignment of 1 to J, which holds during the first iteration of *loop*) returns FALSE ('0'B), which then gets coerced to 0.

Example 3:

```
A = B & C ; IF A = B & C THEN CALL Q ;
```

Surprise: Q isn't necessarily called. Why not? Well, assume A, B, and C are bit string variables, each just one bit in length. Then the first statement assigns the value of the expression B & C to A. But the IF statement *doesn't* then compare the value of A with the value of that expression B & C; instead, it evaluates the expression (A = B) & C, and goes on to call Q if and only if *that* expression evaluates to TRUE! E.g., suppose B and C are both '0'B; then A becomes '0'B as well, and the expression (A = B) & C thus becomes ('0'B = '0'B) & '0'B, or in other words effectively TRUE AND FALSE, which is FALSE.

Example 4:

```
DECLARE A FIXED DEC(3,1)  INIT (    9.1 ) ;
DECLARE B BIT(3)          INIT ( '101'B ) ;
DECLARE C CHAR(4)         INIT ( '+12.' ) ;
```

Surprise: A > B, B > C, and C > A are all TRUE. Why? Well, A > B is TRUE because the bit string '101'B is coerced to the value 5, and 9.1 is greater than 5; B > C is TRUE because the bit string '101'B is coerced to the character string '101' and that character string is greater than the character string '+12.';[14] and C > A is TRUE because the character string '+12.' is coerced to 12 and 12 is greater than 9.1.[15]

■ *Types and domains:* Types and domains are the same thing. Now, Codd never agreed that such was actually the case, but after several years of arguments from myself and others he did eventually and, I think, rather reluctantly come round to the idea that the constructs might perhaps have something in common. For example, in his book on RM/V2 [4] he says the following:

> In [various early papers I] introduced domains as declared data types ... It has become clear that domains as data types go beyond what is normally understood by data types in today's programming languages. Consequently ... when domains are viewed as data types, I now refer to them as *extended data types* ... [An extended data type] is conceptually similar to a ... data type [as] found in many programming languages.

Actually there's absolutely no respect in which domains do "go beyond what is normally understood by data types in today's programming languages"; to say it again, types and domains are the exact same thing. But even if we accept for the sake of the argument that domains might have something extra to offer, *The Principle of Cautious Design* would surely say: Let's stay with just types for now;[16] let's see how much mileage we can get out of doing that; and then, if it ever turns out that we need something extra, let's extend the type concept accordingly at that time. As it is, however, we have a situation where (a) a huge amount of time and energy (and paper) has been wasted on debating the issue—arguing, that is, both for and against the proposition that types and domains are one and the same—and (b) a huge number of people are still confused, even today, over

---

[14] At least this was true in the original IBM implementation of PL/I, where character strings were represented using EBCDIC. The EBCDIC codes for "1" and "+" are hexadecimal F1 and 4E, respectively.

[15] As a friend of mine once remarked to me—this must have been sometime in the late 1960s—whatever else you might say about it, there's one thing that PL/I is most definitely not, and that's "the language of least astonishment."

[16] I mean, it was obvious right from the outset that types did at least do the kinds of things that Codd was arguing at the time that he wanted domains to do—so it was obvious right from the outset that the concepts at least overlapped, even if they weren't identical.

this whole business. Not to mention (c) the various ad hoc notions that Codd found it necessary to introduce over the years, such as "domain check override," in order to shore up the already suspect position that domains and types were different things.

■ *Recursively defined types:* Any given DBMS will come equipped with certain built-in (system defined) types, such as BOOLEAN, INTEGER, RATIONAL, and so on. Suitably skilled and authorized can then define further (user defined) types in terms of those built-in ones; for example, the type POINT might be defined in terms of two values, the *x* and *y* coordinates, both of type RATIONAL. Of course, further types can then be defined in terms of those user defined types; for example, the type LINESEG might be defined in terms of two values, the begin and end points, of type POINT. And so on. So the question arises: Could it ever make sense for a type to be defined, either directly or indirectly, in terms of itself?

Well, Hugh Darwen and I were faced with exactly this question in our work on *The Third Manifesto* [15], where we wrote the following:

> [It's an] open question [as to] whether ... recursively defined [relation] types should be permitted. We don't feel obliged to legislate on this question so far as our model is concerned; for [present purposes], however, we follow *The Principle of Cautious Design* and assume, where it makes any difference, that such types aren't permitted.

However, I subsequently came to the conclusion—see reference [11]—that recursively defined *relation* types, at any rate, should be explicitly prohibited. But we wouldn't be able to impose such a rule now if we hadn't followed the POCD in the first place.

CONCLUDING REMARKS

This chapter has had a slightly "philosophical" flavor—unavoidably so, since we're dealing with an informal topic, and hence one that involves judgment calls. Even so, I believe *The Principle Of Cautious Design* can serve a variety of very practical purposes. One such is the refutation of the opposite point of view!—namely, the point of view that the formal system in question should provide a plethora of essentially equivalent options and alternatives ("bells and whistles") in the interests of "flexibility" and "generality." This latter point of view is founded on what I've referred to elsewhere as *The Principle Of Spurious Generality* [7]. Application of this latter "principle" leads to systems that are claimed to be more general but in fact aren't (at least, not to any significant degree); what's more, the tiny increase in generality, if any, they provide is more than offset by the accompanying increase in complexity. An obvious example of a formal system that suffers in this respect is provided by the SQL language, with its numerous and unfortunate redundancies (see, e.g., reference [14]). You can probably provide further examples of your own.

REFERENCES

1. E. F. Codd: "Derivability, Redundancy, and Consistency of Relations Stored in Large Data Banks," IBM Research Report RJ599 (August 19th, 1969).

2. E. F. Codd: "Extending the Database Relational Model to Capture More Meaning," *ACM Transactions on Database Systems 4*, No. 4 (December 1979).

3. E. F. Codd: "Domains, Keys, and Referential Integrity in Relational Databases," *InfoDB 3*, No. 1 (Spring 1988).

4. E. F. Codd: *The Relational Model for Database Management Version 2* (Addison-Wesley, 1990).

5. C. J. Date: "Referential Integrity," Proc. 7th International Conference on Very Large Data Bases, Cannes, France (September 1981). Republished in slightly revised form in C. J. Date, *Relational Database: Selected Writings* (Addison-Wesley, 1986). *Note:* This reference and reference [6] are both effectively superseded by reference [8].

6. C. J. Date: "Referential Integrity and Foreign Keys – Part II: Further Considerations," in C. J. Date, *Relational Database Writings 1985-1989* (Addison-Wesley, 1990). *Note:* This reference and reference [5] are both effectively superseded by reference [8].

7. C. J. Date: "Database Graffiti," in C. J. Date, *Relational Database Writings 1994-1997* (Addison-Wesley, 1998). *Note:* A revised version of this reference is included in the companion volume to the present book.

8. C. J. Date: "Inclusion Dependencies and Foreign Keys," in C. J. Date and Hugh Darwen, *Database Explorations: Essays on The Third Manifesto and Related Topics* (Trafford Publishing, 2010).

9. C. J. Date: *Database Design and Relational Theory: Normal Forms and All That Jazz*, 2nd edition (Apress, 2019).

10. C. J. Date: "Primary Keys Are Nice but Not Essential," in reference [9].

11. C. J. Date: "Gödel, Russell, Codd: A Recursive Golden Crowd," in *Fifty Years of Relational, and Other Database Writing: More Thoughts and Essays on Database Matters* (Technics Publications, 2020).

12. C. J. Date: "Relation Valued Attributes," in *Fifty Years of Relational, and Other Database Writing: More Thoughts and Essays on Database Matters* (Technics Publications, 2020).

13. C. J. Date: "Equality," in *Stating the Obvious, and Other Database Writing: Still More Thoughts and Essays on Database Matters* (Technics Publications, 2020).

14. C. J. Date: "Redundancy in SQL," in *Stating the Obvious, and Other Database Writing: Still More Thoughts and Essays on Database Matters* (Technics Publications, 2020).

15. C. J. Date and Hugh Darwen: *Databases, Types, and the Relational Model: The Third Manifesto*, 3rd edition (Addison-Wesley, 2007). See also the website *www.thethirdmanifesto.com*.

Chapter 3

SQL on IMS(?)

*When I wrote the paper that ultimately became this chapter, back in the 1980s, several commercial DBMSs (though not in fact IMS) were advertised as providing some kind of relational interface. Such an interface would, it was claimed, allow relational operations to be performed on data that had originally been created without any thought of users being able to operate on it in such a manner. So I wrote the paper to show that trying to provide such an interface involves certain inherent and possibly insuperable difficulties, using the hypothetical case of adding an SQL interface to IMS to illustrate some of the problems.[1] But I must stress that "SQL on IMS" is used only by way of example; more generally, it seems to me that similar kinds of problems are likely to arise in trying to provide **any** kind of relational interface to **any** nonrelational system—a state of affairs that makes the overall discussion still relevant, even though the original paper was written over 30 years ago.*

Let's consider the issue a little more carefully. Assume that users of some nonrelational DBMS wish to obtain the benefits of a relational system for their data. How might that goal be achieved? One way would be to migrate the data from the old nonrelational system to a relational system but to provide support in that new system for the old nonrelational operations, so that new relational applications could be developed while old nonrelational ones continue to operate unchanged. Another would be to support the new relational operations on the old unmigrated data, so that new relational applications could be developed to operate against existing data. In what follows I show that neither of these

---

[1] Despite the fact that SQL is a very long way from being a truly relational language! Given this state of affairs, in fact, I considered replacing all pertinent appearances of the word "relational" in the original paper by the phrase "relational (or would-be relational)." But of course it would be intolerably tedious—tedious for you the reader, I mean—if I'd actually carried out this threat. So I have to leave it to you just to imagine that such a replacement has indeed been made wherever applicable. Thank you for your understanding.

approaches is likely to work well in practice, advertising claims to the contrary notwithstanding.

One further point: Of course, there's another possible interpretation (not considered in detail in what follows) of the phrase "SQL on IMS," viz.: Would it be possible to implement an SQL system using IMS purely as an access method?—in which case the notion of using SQL to access existing IMS data wouldn't arise. The answer to this question is "Yes, of course it would be possible"—but I don't think anyone would ever dream of doing such a thing. Quite apart from anything else, IMS was never designed or built with such a use in mind, and it seems certain that most of its features (including, most likely, its hierarchic structuring features in particular!) would simply never be used in such an implementation. And in any case, such a system would of course be of no use at all in dealing with the real problem, viz., the problem of migrating from nonrelational to relational technology.

Publishing history: This is a heavily revised version of, and supersedes, a paper that first appeared under the title "Why Is It So Difficult to Provide a Relational Interface to IMS?" in InfoIMS 4, No. 4 (4th Quarter 1984) and was later republished in my book Relational Database: Selected Writings (Addison-Wesley, 1986). This version copyright © 2022 C. J. Date.

Support for the relational model is commonly regarded, with good reason, as a sine qua non for modern database systems. One indicator of the widespread acceptance of relational ideas is provided by the extensive list of nonrelational systems—IDMS, DATACOM/DB, ADABAS, Model 204, System 2000, TIS, and others—that now claim to be relational, or at least to support a relational interface. But among this list of what some call "born again" relational systems, IMS is conspicuous by its absence. Why?

Of course, a relational interface to IMS, if such a thing were possible, would be an attractive proposition. It would mean, among other things, that an installation that was currently committed to IMS could reap the benefits of the relational approach—or at least some of those benefits—without having to migrate any existing data and (more important) without having to rewrite any existing programs. Unfortunately, however, there's good evidence to suggest that a true relational interface to IMS will never be anything more than a pipedream. The purpose of this chapter is to explain why this is so—and, by extension, why a true relational interface to *any* nonrelational system is likely to be a difficult thing to achieve.

Of course, there's an obvious converse question too: Would it be possible to provide a DL/I interface to an SQL system such as DB2?[2] Such an interface would arguably be an even more attractive proposition: An IMS installation would be able to migrate to that system, and thereby obtain all of the advantages of SQL—at least for new applications—and still not have to rewrite any programs. I'll consider this converse question toward the end of the chapter.

Note: In order to focus the discussion, it's convenient to make a number of simplifying assumptions:

■ I'll assume, where it makes any difference, that the relational interface we'd like IMS to support is, specifically, the DB2 dialect of the language SQL. However, many of the points made in what follows apply with little change to any SQL dialect and indeed to any relational language, not just to SQL as such. As already indicated, they also apply (at least in some cases) to other nonrelational systems, not just to IMS.

■ I'll also assume that "IMS support for SQL" means, specifically, that SQL operations are to be implemented by translating them into DL/I calls. I discount the alternative possibility of bypassing DL/I entirely and translating SQL statements directly into I/O operations against the stored IMS data, for reasons I'll explain later.

■ For most of the chapter I choose to ignore IMS Main Storage databases. Main Storage databases are really a very special case in IMS; their behavior is significantly different from that of other kinds of IMS databases (for example, they support different data types). However, one pertinent aspect of their behavior is mentioned explicitly at the end of the section immediately following.

---

[2] DL/I is the native IMS language. It has nothing to do with the programming language PL/I, except for the fact that (deliberately, I presume) it has a similar name.

SOME FUNDAMENTAL INCOMPATIBILITIES

There are some very fundamental incompatibilities between SQL and IMS. The principal, though not the only, source of those incompatibilities is the comparative lack of discipline imposed in IMS; the user in IMS is given more freedom than is perhaps consistent with the general database objectives of control, stability, data independence, and so forth. As a result, there are many situations in IMS in which the meaning of the data is at least partly hidden in procedural code, instead of being made explicit in some IMS data definition. And, needless to say, it's often impossible to expose such hidden meanings through a disciplined relational interface, which requires all of the information in the database to be represented explicitly in the data as such.[3]

The following subsections go into more detail on some of the various incompatibilities.

Segments vs. Rows

The basic data aggregating mechanism is different in the two systems—in IMS it's the segment, in SQL it's the row. An IMS segment is basically just a byte string; an SQL row, by contrast, is an ordered collection of discrete, named, typed values. Thus, all of the following are possible in IMS and not in SQL:

a. *Anonymous or undefined fields:*[4] For example, a given segment[5] might be defined to be 100 bytes long, with bytes 1-10 defined as field A, bytes 91-100 defined as field Z, and bytes 11-90 undefined. Perhaps more realistically, anonymous fields can be used—and indeed are used—as a means of allowing two or more different segment types to occupy the same position in the hierarchy. For example, a given segment type might be

---

[3] These remarks are considerably oversimplified, but they're true enough for present purposes—true to a first approximation, I suppose we might say.

[4] Actually SQL too can have anonymous fields (or columns, rather)—and in fact that's a big problem in SQL!—but only if the table in question itself has no name. But base tables (and views) in particular are always named, and columns in such tables are therefore always named as well.

[5] I'd really prefer to say "a given segment type" here, but unfortunately (as my text immediately goes on to explain) the term "segment type" has, at best, only the fuzziest of meanings in the IMS world. At the same time it's virtually impossible to explain how IMS works without making frequent use of the term anyway. Please note, therefore, that all such uses in what follows should really—but won't—have a great deal of additional verbiage surrounding them in order to explain exactly what they denote in whatever the pertinent context happens to be. Please note also that (in a feeble attempt on my part to avoid the problem) I do often talk about "segments" when what I should really be saying is "segment types."

defined to be 100 bytes long, with just one named field SEGTYPE (bytes 1-4, say). The user program can then test that field (e.g., "if SEGTYPE = '0001' this is a type 1 segment, if SEGTYPE = '0002' it's a type 2 segment," and so on), and depending on the result of the test can then map the segment in question to an appropriate set of program variables internally.

b. *Arbitrarily overlapping fields:* For example, bytes 5-14 of some segment type might be defined as field A and bytes 5-12 as field B. This feature might very well be used in conjunction with the technique just mentioned under a. above for allowing different segment types to appear at the same position in the hierarchy, but of course it's not limited to such use. A more reasonable example might be in subdividing composite fields—for example, bytes 10-17 might be defined as a DATE field, with bytes 10-13, 14-15, and 16-17 redefined as YEAR, MONTH, and DAY fields, respectively. However, even if it's true that composite fields would be a desirable addition to SQL—they might be or they might not, depending on exactly what's meant by the term—allowing arbitrarily overlapping byte string fields is hardly the best approach to that problem.

c. *Different data types for the "same" field:* For example, bytes 5-14 of some segment type might be defined as type P (packed decimal) and bytes 5-12 as type X (hexadecimal). As the example might suggest, this feature could be used in conjunction with the technique mentioned under a. for allowing two or more different segment types to occupy the same position in the hierarchy, but again it's not restricted to such use.

Each of a., b., and c. above implies that an IMS segment can't simply be mapped or equated to an SQL row, in general.

Field Types

Even if the IMS segment in question is "well behaved," in the sense that none of a., b., and c. from the previous subsection applies, the basic field / column data types are different in the two systems. The IMS types are as follows:

```
C (character)      : corresponds to SQL CHAR

X (hexadecimal)    : no SQL equivalent

P (packed decimal) : no SQL equivalent
```

Note in particular that IMS type P does *not* correspond to SQL type DECIMAL—they differ in at least the following ways:

■ Data types are mostly not checked in IMS, so there's no guarantee that a type P field actually does contain a valid packed decimal number—though if it doesn't, then user programs could fail at run time.

■ Field comparisons in IMS are usually performed bit by bit from left to right, regardless of data type. In IMS, therefore, packed decimal "-1" might well be considered greater than packed decimal "+1"! It follows that if an IMS segment is to masquerade as an SQL row, a new SQL data type corresponding to IMS type P will have to be invented (e.g., "IMS DECIMAL"?), with its own (bizarre) comparison rules. Analogous remarks apply to type X also.

In addition, of course, SQL DECIMAL is capable of representing noninteger values, though that fact is irrelevant to the present discussion.

Note: It might appear from the foregoing that IMS types C, P, and X are in fact all the same—they're all just byte strings, and they could all map to SQL type CHAR. Such is not the case, however; there are some subtle differences among them, one of which is discussed in the subsection immediately following (others are beyond the scope of this chapter).

Variable Length Segments

IMS segments can be of variable length. So of course can SQL rows—but with the following critical difference:

a. Basically, an SQL row is of variable length if and only if it includes one or more variable length fields (columns)—i.e., fields that are explicitly defined to the system to be of variable length.

Note: Actually there are certain additional circumstances under which an SQL row can also be considered to be of variable length, at least in DB2, but those circumstances are of no concern to the ordinary SQL user.

b. In IMS, by contrast, there's no notion of a variable length field. Instead, a variable length segment is defined as a byte string of a fixed *maximum* length, made up of a set of fields also of fixed lengths. If a particular instance of such a segment is shorter than the maximum length, then fields at the right are simply considered to be missing, either in whole or in part. For example, suppose segment type S (maximum length 100 bytes) is defined to consist of fields A, B, C, and D, in that order, and each of A, B, C, and D is 25 bytes; and suppose a particular instance of S is only 65 bytes long. Then the last 10 bytes of field C and the whole of field D are simply considered as missing from that instance.

Assuming the IMS user is "sensitive" to a missing or partly missing field—in other words, assuming the field in question has been named in a SENFLD statement in the pertinent "Program Control Block" or PCB)—then on retrieval that field will be filled in the user's I/O area with blank characters (for type C) or binary zeros (for type X) or packed decimal zeros (for type P). Note that "missing" in IMS is thus not the same as "null" in SQL! However, an IMS search against a missing field will always return "not found," regardless of the specified search condition.

Each instance of a variable length segment of course includes a length field that specifies the actual length of that particular instance. Moreover, if field sensitivity isn't in effect—i.e., if the PCB doesn't include any SENFLD statements for the segment in question—then that length field is exposed to the user (on both retrieval and update operations). In particular, the user is responsible for specifying a value for that field when an instance of that segment is stored. As for retrieval, the length field can be (and has been) used as the basis for distinguishing between different segment types that have been allowed to occupy the same position in the hierarchy (see the remarks on this topic in the first subsection above); for example, "if length = 52 this is a type 1 segment, if length = 86 it's a type 2 segment." This trick might obviate the need for a separate SEGTYPE field.

Segment / Row Ordering

The collection of all segments of a given type in a particular hierarchy is ordered in IMS,[6] whereas the collection of all rows in a particular table is unordered in

---

[6] Actually IMS defines a total ordering over *all* segments (i.e., of all types) within a given database. It goes without saying that SQL has nothing analogous.

SQL; in fact, in SQL, a given set of rows is guaranteed to be returned to the user in a specific order only if the retrieval request includes an appropriate ORDER BY clause. These facts taken together suggest that if IMS segments are to be surfaced as rows through an SQL interface, then all SQL SELECTs against those rows will have to include an ORDER BY clause that specifies the ordering that IMS will in fact use (ignoring for the moment the point that not all IMS orderings can in fact be specified in SQL terms anyway—see below). For otherwise SQL programs that operate on IMS data (if such a thing is even possible) will very likely contain some unpleasant, and hidden, data dependencies.

Given the foregoing, incidentally, it seems particularly unfortunate that SQL doesn't allow a program that retrieves data via some cursor to update that data via the cursor in question, if the definition of that cursor does includes an ORDER BY clause.

However, to say it again, not all IMS orderings are expressible in SQL anyway. In fact, the only kind that does have an SQL analog is ordering via a unique "sequence field" (more precisely, ordering via a unique "fully concatenated key"; for brevity, however, I'll continue to use the more usual IMS term "sequence field"). Segments in IMS that don't have a sequence field are ordered in one of the following ways:

a.   If the segments have no sequence field at all, then the possibilities are FIRST, LAST, and HERE.

b.   If the segments do have a sequence field but it's not unique, then that sequence field serves as the major ordering item, but the set of duplicates with respect to a given sequence field value are ordered (again) FIRST, LAST, or HERE within that major sequence.

FIRST and LAST mean the ordering is controlled by time of arrival— FIRST means a new segment is stored in front of existing segments, LAST means it's stored after existing segments. HERE means the ordering is controlled by the user program: A new segment is stored at a position specified procedurally by user program code. And the fact that a particular segment is stored "here" and not "there" carries meaning, of course—but it's meaning that's embedded in the logic of the program and thus can't automatically be surfaced through a pure relational interface.

Note: FIRST, LAST, and HERE are all examples of what's called "essential ordering." An ordering is essential if and only if information would be lost if that ordering were destroyed. Note that ordering by a unique sequence field is *in*essential by this definition, because it would still be possible to find, e.g., the employee with the fourth highest employee number, even if employees weren't originally ordered by employee number in the database. By contrast, relational systems deliberately don't support any form of essential ordering. For a justification for this position, see Chapter 6 ("The Essentiality Paper") of my book *E. F. Codd and Relational Theory, Revised Edition* (Technics Publications, 2021).

Main Storage Databases

One final, albeit minor (?), incompatibility: In the case of Main Storage databases, IMS update operations have unconventional semantics. Specifically, if a transaction T updates a segment S and then retrieves that segment S again, it doesn't see the effect of its own update! The reason is that IMS doesn't actually apply the update to the database until successful "end of transaction" (COMMIT time), and this state of affairs is unfortunately exposed to the user.

DEFINING A "FLAT VIEW" OF IMS DATA

Despite everything I've said in this chapter so far, it would be technically possible, given some collection of IMS data, to construct a variety of what for brevity I'll call "flat views" over that data. Of course, such a flat view wouldn't be the same thing as an SQL table, for all of the reasons outlined in the previous section—though it might be close, if the IMS data is "well behaved" and doesn't involve any anonymous fields, essential orderings, or other such nonrelational constructs. (However, experience suggests that IMS databases are rarely—perhaps never—"well behaved" in this sense.)

The definition of such a flat view would involve a variety of IMS operations (both definitional and manipulative) that traverse various predefined paths through the IMS hierarchy. Consider the following example:

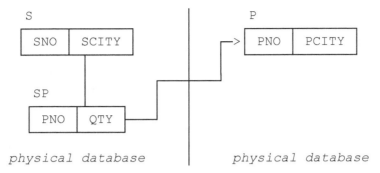

What the picture shows is an IMS version of the familiar suppliers-and-parts database (or a simplified version of that database, rather). Note that it involves two separate but interrelated "physical databases," one with two segment types, S ("suppliers") and SP ("shipments") and one with just one, P "parts"). Segment type S has two fields:

■ SNO (supplier number) : unique sequence field

■ SCITY (supplier city)

Likewise, segment type P also has two fields:

■ PNO (part number) : unique sequence field

■ PCITY (part city)

Finally, segment type SP also has two fields:

■ PNO (part number) : unique sequence field (see below)

■ QTY (quantity)

There's also a pointer from any given SP segment instance to the pertinent P segment instance in the other physical database. (Please note, however, that the pointer in question is hidden from the user.)

Now, at most one shipment can exist for a given supplier / part combination at any given time; thus, field SP.PNO is "unique within parent," "parent" here meaning "supplier." In fact, though, segment type SP has two parents: Segment type S is the *physical* parent and segment type P is the *logical* parent. (By the same token, SP is a physical child of S and a logical child of P.) The pointer from segment type SP to segment type P is a logical parent pointer. [7]

I remark in passing that, in general, IMS would permit field SP.PNO to be virtual—i.e., inherited from segment P—but we want to use it as the sequence field for segment type SP, and to be used for such a purpose it must be physical, not virtual. The SP segments for a given S segment are thus sequenced in PNO order.

Note carefully that both of these two databases are well behaved, in the sense in which I'm using that term in this chapter.

Now, given these two "physical" databases, we can define the following "logical" database (note the primed segment names S′ and SP′):

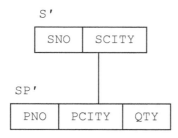

logical database

Note: For reasons that don't need to concern us here, the SP′ segment would actually consist of *four* fields, viz., PNO, QTY, PNO again, and PCITY, in that order. I choose to ignore this particular detail.

Finally, we can "flatten" this logical hierarchy by means of appropriate DL/I operations—probably making use of what are known as *path calls*—and present it to a "relational" user in a form that looks something like this (note the double primed name SP″):

```
SP''
┌──────┬───────┬──────┬───────┬──────┐
│ SNO  │ SCITY │ PNO  │ PCITY │ QTY  │
└──────┴───────┴──────┴───────┴──────┘
```

Points arising:

---

[7] Don't let yourself be confused by the nomenclature here—the pointer is a physical pointer all right, but it's called logical because what it points to is a logical parent.

1. Observe first that the definition of this flat view requires both (a) a lot of predefinition of physical access paths on the disk and (b) considerable IMS expertise in constructing the view given those access paths. "Relational" users would thus probably not be able to define such views for themselves dynamically as the need arose (contrast CREATE VIEW in SQL).

2. In fact, I've omitted one important definitional step—namely, that of defining a Program Communication Block (PCB) for the logical hierarchy. For simplicity I assume the missing PCB defines a hierarchy identical to the one shown as the "logical database" above.

3. Actually "logical database" is a considerable misnomer anyway, because IMS logical databases are just as physical, in a sense, as IMS physical databases are. Certainly they involve all kinds of physical access paths on the disk, just as physical databases do.

4. Be that as it may, what I'm suggesting is that some IMS expert (perhaps the IMS database administrator) would be responsible for writing flat view definitions—in particular, for writing the necessary DL/I calls to be invoked as part of the translation process from SQL to IMS. In the case at hand, it might be desirable to extend that definition process to remove fields SCITY and PCITY from the flat view[8] (since SP″ as shown above isn't in third normal form). For simplicity, however, I'll continue to assume those fields are indeed visible in the view.

Now let's consider the question of which SQL operations could be supported on the flat view SP″.[9] First retrieval (SELECT operations):

■ SELECT clause

The only "SELECT items"—i.e., the only things that can appear in the commalist of items in the SELECT clause—are the field names SNO, SCITY, PNO, PCITY, and QTY. Literals, aggregate operator invocations

---

[8] And to define two further flat views, of course, one for suppliers and one for parts.

[9] By *supported* here, I mean, of course, "supported via automatic translation to an appropriate set of DL/I calls." Obviously, almost anything can be supported if there's someone who's prepared to handcode a procedural program to do the job, but that's not the point. For similar reasons I discount the possibility that a flat view might be defined that doesn't depend on predefined hierarchic paths.

such as AVG (QTY), and other operational expressions such as QTY + 150 can't be supported. Also (most significant) DISTINCT can't be supported either—unless, just conceivably, the SELECT commalist includes both SNO and PNO, in which case DISTINCT would be a no op anyway.

■ FROM clause

Almost certainly, only a single table name—SP″ in the case at hand—will be allowed to appear in the FROM clause; in particular, therefore, it won't be possible to join that table with any other. (One problem with join is that it generates a new table that's completely different from any existing table, in general. If IMS needed to materialize such a new table, it would first need to create a data definition for it, and unfortunately IMS definitions can't be created dynamically.)

Note: The foregoing might be a little too extreme. I mean, it might be possible to support joins after all, so long as the joins in question correspond to predefined hierarchic paths (if such joins haven't already been factored into the flat view definition, that is). For example, suppose view SP″ is replaced by the following two views—

```
S'''   ( SNO , SCITY )
SP'''  ( SNO , PNO , PCITY , QTY )
```

—corresponding, approximately, to the segments S′ and SP′ in the logical hierarchy shown earlier Then the SQL join

```
SELECT ...
FROM    S''' , SP'''
WHERE   S'''.SNO = SP'''.SNO
```

can obviously be implemented by traversing the hierarchic path between S′ and SP′ in that hierarchy. In the flat view SP″, by contrast, that join has been built into the view definition itself.

■ WHERE clause

Basically, only restriction conditions can be supported in the WHERE clause. (A restriction condition is a boolean expression involving only literals and/or fields of the row in question; it can be evaluated as true or false for a given row by examining just that row in isolation.) Furthermore, not all restriction conditions will be legal:

a. At its most complex, the condition will have to take the form "($c1$) AND ($c2$)," where $c1$ is a restriction condition on S′ and $c2$ is a restriction condition on SP′. The reason for this limitation is that S′ and SP′ are at different levels of the (logical database) hierarchy, and IMS can't handle conditions that involve an OR between levels.

b. For reasons explained in the section "Some Fundamental Incompatibilities," comparison operators other than "equals" and "not equals" might have to be disallowed, at least in some cases.

c. Comparisons between fields won't be allowed.

d. Comparands can't be specified by means of operational expressions such as QTY + 150.

e. LIKE comparisons can't be supported (except for trivial cases).

f. IS NULL comparisons can't be supported.

Since only restriction conditions are supportable, the following SQL constructs will also not be allowed:

g. Scalar comparison operators (e.g., "=", ">") with a subquery

h. IN, =ANY, etc. with a subquery

i. EXISTS

■ GROUP BY clause

Can't be supported.

■ HAVING clause

Can't be supported.

■ ORDER BY clause

Can't be supported, other than as described earlier.

Finally, UNION also can't be supported.

Turning now to update operations: First of all, of course, limitations similar to those described above for the WHERE clause apply to these operations also, mutatis mutandis. Note too that as mentioned previously, view SP″ isn't in third normal form (in fact, it's not even in second); as a result, strange update behavior is only to be expected. But the situation is worse than it would be in a "pure" relational system in a number of ways, as described below.

Consider first the UPDATE operation itself:

■ QTY is updatable, with no hidden surprises.

■ SCITY is also updatable, but with side effects, owing to the fact that the information that a certain supplier is located in a certain city appears not once but many times in the view. Of course, that same information is represented only once on the disk; as a result, changing a supplier's city in one SP″ row causes the same change to occur instantaneously in all other SP″ rows for that supplier. Of course, it could be argued, and reasonably argued, that this side effect is desirable, and indeed a good thing; but it does have to be explained to the user, and it does mean that the user's view of the data is more complicated than the simple data structure

```
SP''( SNO , SCITY , PNO , PCITY , QTY )
```

would suggest if taken by itself.

■ PCITY might or might not be updatable, depending on the IMS "replace rule" for segment type P. If it is, then considerations analogous to those described above for field SCITY apply.

■ *SNO and PNO can't be updated at all.* In general, if V is a "relational" view of some IMS database D, and if F is a field in V, then it looks as if F won't be updatable in V if it's either (a) a component of the primary key of V or (b) a component of a foreign key in V that corresponds to a parent / child link in D.

Note: The second of these two limitations is particularly unfortunate, because updating foreign keys is not only legal but commonplace in a relational system. For example, given this table—

```
EMP ( EMPNO , ENAME , DEPTNO , SALARY )
```

—moving some employee from department D1 to department D2 is accomplished precisely by updating the foreign key field DEPTNO for that employee accordingly.

As for other update operations on SP'':

- DELETE is always legal; under certain circumstances, however, it could have the side effect of deleting the corresponding P segment also, depending on the IMS "delete rule" for that segment.

- INSERT will fail if no corresponding S segment exists. It might or might not fail if no corresponding P segment exists (depending on the IMS "insert rule" for that segment). If it succeeds, then (a) if no corresponding P segment exists, then one might automatically be created; (b) if a corresponding P segment does exist, then either PCITY in that segment will be replaced by PCITY from the new SP'' row, or the other way around. Of course, all of this is dependent (once again) on various IMS rules. What will happen if SCITY in the new SP'' row is different from SCITY in the existing S segment is unclear.

In general, the behavior of INSERT, DELETE, and UPDATE is very difficult to explain in an SQL framework, as the foregoing outline should be sufficient to illustrate. The situation is somewhat ironic, as a matter of fact:

a. Whatever the behavior of those operations actually is, the IMS rules will have to be exposed at the SQL interface in order to explain that behavior.

b. However, SQL currently has no framework in which to couch any such explanations, because SQL currently doesn't support foreign keys[10] (of course, this is a well known SQL deficiency).

---

[10] No longer true.

c. At the same time, the IMS rules are both less and more than the rules that I, at any rate, feel are desirable for a relational system.

In addition, of course, if the IMS databases aren't "well behaved"—in particular, if they involve any essential ordering—then the behavior of INSERT specifically will be hard to explain at the relational level (in fact, it might be unpredictable).

Finally, note that a "flat view" mechanism along the lines indicated in this section would require a new catalog to be built on top of the existing IMS catalog (or on top of the existing IMS data definitions, at any rate). The purpose of that new catalog would be to show the flat views that were available; to serve as a repository for the definitions of those views in terms of IMS data; to indicate what operations were legal against those views and (in the legal cases) what their semantics were; and so on. As a result, the system (or the DBA?) would be faced with all the usual problems of having to keep two separate catalogs in synch.

WHAT ABOUT BYPASSING DL/I?

I've been assuming so far that an SQL interface to IMS would be implemented by mapping SQL operations to DL/I code ("cascading through DL/I"). What about the possibility of bypassing DL/I entirely and translating SQL operations directly into I/O operations against the stored IMS data? In other words, would it be possible to provide a component (which I'll call *the SQL data manager*) whose function would be to provide SQL access to IMS data in much the same way that the DL/I data manager provides DL/I access to such data in IMS today?

If such an approach were possible, it would certainly overcome some of the objections raised earlier in this chapter. For example, such an SQL data manager could support the SQL ORDER BY clause by performing a dynamic sort if necessary, instead of having to be constrained by just those orderings that are statically predefined. However:

■ There'd still be difficulties: for example, data that doesn't conform to its declared data type, anonymous and overlapping fields, missing fields, essential ordering, and so on. At the very least it would seem that a separate set of SQL definitions would be required for the stored data, over and above the existing DL/I definitions; and so once again there'd be the problem of keeping two sets of definitions in synch (not to mention the fact that some of the data might not even be definable in SQL terms anyway).

■ It might be possible to deal with some of the difficulties mentioned in the previous bullet item by means of exit routines, whose function would be to "clean up" the IMS data before exposing it to SQL. But in order to be able to write such routines it would first of all be necessary to understand what the IMS data means—and as explained earlier, some of that meaning will in general be buried in procedural user code. Thus, the person writing those exit routines might have to study many user programs in order to discover that meaning. And can there be any guarantee that the process of discovering that meaning is ever complete?

■ Perhaps more to the point, consider what would be involved in constructing such an SQL data manager. It would obviously be at least as difficult as the original task of constructing the DL/I data manager of IMS in the first place. In fact, of course, it would be much harder, for at least the following reasons:

    a. SQL is a much richer language, functionally speaking, than DL/I.

    b. An optimizer would be required, for exactly the same reason that an optimizer is required in a "pure" SQL system—namely, because performance would almost certainly be intolerable without it.

■ To pursue the last point a little further: Such an optimizer would most likely require a considerable amount of original invention. In fact, it looks to me like a research problem, because almost all existing work on relational optimization assumes that the target storage structure is based on indexing or hashing or a combination of the two, and almost nothing has been published (so far as I'm aware) on optimizing against IMS-style pointer-based structures.

From all of the above, I conclude that building an "SQL data manager" that would operate directly against IMS stored data:

■ Would be a nontrivial undertaking;

■ Would probably require a certain amount of hand tailoring by the DBA (at the very least, in the way of additional data definition);

■ Might belong more in the realm of research than in that of commercial products;

■ Might not even be technically feasible;

■ Might not solve all of the problems even if it is; and

■ Might not be cost effective even if it does.

CONCLUDING REMARKS

In this chapter, I've sketched some of the difficulties I perceive in attempting to provide SQL access to existing IMS data. I've shown that, in general, a genuine relational interface is an impossibility; however, I've also shown that, in some cases at least, a "flat view" interface might be possible after all. But note clearly that such an interface would almost certainly support:

a. Predefined views only,

b. Using predefined hierarchic paths only, and possibly

c. Retrieval operations only (thanks to the complexity and apparently arbitrary behavior of update operations).

Note moreover that those retrieval operations would be limited in relational terms to just (a) "projection" (in quotes because there'd be no possibility of duplicate elimination), and (b) certain forms of restriction ("certain forms" because such restrictions would be subject to a number of complex and apparently arbitrary limitations). Join wouldn't be supported at all, except possibly for the case of a join that traverses a predefined hierarchic path. Furthermore, if the IMS data isn't "well behaved," then those flat views won't be "well behaved" either. Now, I don't say such an interface might not serve some useful practical purpose; but I do say it wouldn't be relational.

Of course, I've been limiting my attention to IMS specifically. Now, it might be that, considered as a target for a relational interface, IMS is more complex than other nonrelational systems; nevertheless, the reader should realize that (as noted near the beginning of this chapter) problems analogous to those discussed, though possibly less severe, are likely to arise with other systems also. If you're considering investing in a nonrelational system that claims to support a relational interface, therefore, you're advised to make sure you understand exactly what that interface really involves before you commit yourself. *Look before you leap* is the watchword.

I close as promised with a brief note on the converse question—namely, would it be possible to support a DL/I interface to an SQL system such as DB2? The short answer (as you'll probably have guessed) is no, it's not:

■ First, of course, all of the points raised in the section "Some Fundamental Incompatibilities" apply equally in the opposite direction. For example, it doesn't seem possible to simulate the behavior of HERE-style ordering or IMS-style variable length segments on top of SQL rows.

■ Second, support for the DL/I update operations would require SQL support for foreign keys (and a lot more besides). What's more, it's not even clear (as indicated earlier in this chapter) that equivalents of all of the IMS update rules are even desirable in a relational system, and I for one would argue that they're not.

■ Third, there are problems even with retrieval operations (even if the IMS data is completely "well behaved," though the problems are considerably worse if it isn't). For example, DL/I operations are crucially dependent on various notions of "current position" (current segment, current parent, etc.). The notion of "current parent" might break down because (again) SQL doesn't support foreign keys—a given "child" might in fact not have any "parent" in the SQL database. As for the notion of "current segment," it's not even all that well defined. For example, exactly which segment is "current" after a "not found" condition seems to depend on the underlying IMS access method (HISAM, HIDAM, etc.).

In addition to all the above, of course, there's the point that an implementation of DL/I on a relational system—if such a thing were possible at all—would almost certainly perform very poorly, because it would involve the simulation of a row level (or segment level) language on top of a set level interface. Note that it would indeed be on top of a set level interface; true relational systems deliberately don't provide any lower level interface to the data, in order to prevent the possibility of users bypassing the relational controls and thereby subverting the system in a variety of ways. In fact, this last point can be seen as yet another distinction between genuine relational systems, on the one hand, and "born again" relational systems on the other—in the latter case, there's always the possibility that a user can get in under the covers (i.e., using the previously existing interface) and perform some operation that undermines the system in some way. A true relational system doesn't permit such subversive behavior.

ACKNOWLEDGMENTS

I'm grateful to Ted Codd for encouraging me to write the original paper (the one that eventually became the present chapter) in the first place. I'm also grateful to Colin White for his numerous helpful comments on various drafts of that paper, and to Doug Hembry for assistance with technical questions regarding the behavior of variable length segments in IMS.

Chapter 4

Why Quantifier Order

Is Important

From experience in teaching specialist classes on relational databases and relational database theory, I've found that database professionals tend to be somewhat leery of both the relational calculus in general and the quantifiers EXISTS and FORALL in particular. This is a pity, since the concepts involved aren't really unfamiliar, nor are they as difficult to understand as you might think—and they're certainly very powerful, and indeed fundamental. At the same time there's one slightly tricky aspect involved in using them correctly, and that's what this short chapter is primarily concerned with.

Publishing history: What follows is a heavily revised version of, and supersedes, a paper that first appeared under the title "Quantifiers and Ambiguity: Order Makes a Difference" in The Relational Journal for DB2 Users 2, No. 2 (April/May 1990) and was later republished under the present title in my book Relational Database Writings 1989-1991 (Addison-Wesley, 1992). This version copyright © 2022 C. J. Date.

My subject in this chapter is the logic quantifiers EXISTS and FORALL(written in more formal contexts as a reversed uppercase *e*, "∃", and an inverted uppercase *a*, "∀", respectively). EXISTS ("there exists") is the *existential* quantifier, FORALL ("for all") is the *universal* quantifier. Both are part of the relational calculus, where they're used in the construction of boolean or truth valued expressions; hence, both can be used in a language that's based on that calculus to help in the formulation of database queries, constraints, view definitions, and the like.

Of course, it's true that most commercial DBMSs don't support FORALL (at least, not directly); however, they typically do support EXISTS, because EXISTS—or at least an approximation to it [2]—is included in the SQL standard. Thus, you probably have a basic familiarity with EXISTS already, but possibly not with FORALL. Be that as it may, I'll begin by briefly explaining them both.

BASIC SYNTAX AND SEMANTICS

To be a little more precise about the matter, *quantifiers* is the term used in logic to refer generically to constructs of the form EXISTS x or FORALL x (and I'll explain what that "x" is in just a moment). The term derives from the verb *to quantify*, which simply means *to express as a quantity*—that is, to say how much of something there is or how many somethings there are. Thus, the quantifiers can be explained as follows:

■ Let x be a variable that ranges over some set X. For example, X might be the set of people that work for IBM, and permitted values of x would then be IBM employees.[1]

■ Let $p(x)$ be a boolean or truth valued expression involving x—for example, the expression "x is Albanian."

Then:

■ The expression

```
EXISTS x ( p ( x ) )
```

is also a boolean expression, and it evaluates to TRUE if there exists at least one value of x such that $p(x)$ evaluates to TRUE and to FALSE otherwise. In the example, EXISTS x ($p(x)$) is TRUE if IBM has at least one Albanian employee and FALSE otherwise.

Note: Here and throughout this chapter I assume we're dealing with conventional two-valued logic (2VL) only, not three-valued logic (3VL).

---

[1] Perhaps I should explain that x here isn't a variable in the conventional programming language sense, it's a variable in the sense of logic. More specifically, it's an example of what's usually referred to—at least in the relational calculus context—as a *range* variable.

The picture becomes much more complex if we have to take *n*-valued logic into account for *n* = 3, or indeed for any *n* > 2.

■ The expression

```
FORALL x ( p ( x ) )
```

is also a boolean expression, and it evaluates to TRUE if *p*(*x*) evaluates to TRUE for all values of *x* and to FALSE otherwise. In the example, FORALL *x* (*p*(*x*)) is FALSE if IBM has at least one employee who's not Albanian and TRUE otherwise.

Of course, the foregoing explanations are recursive; that is, the expression *p*(*x*) might itself involve one or more quantifiers. As a result, expressions of the form (e.g.)

```
EXISTS x ( FORALL y ( EXISTS z ( ... ) ) )
```

(etc., etc.) are perfectly legal, in general; in other words, quantified expressions can contain further quantified expressions nested within themselves to arbitrary depth.

Now, you might have realized already that EXISTS and FORALL can be thought of—indeed, defined—as an *iterated OR* and an *iterated AND*, respectively. Again let *p*(*x*) be a boolean expression involving *x*, and let *x* range over the set $X = \{x1, x2, ..., xn\}$. Then

```
EXISTS x ( p ( x ) )
```

is a boolean expression, and it's equivalent to, and hence shorthand for, the expression

```
p ( x1 ) OR p ( x2 ) OR ... OR p ( xn ) OR FALSE
```

Likewise,

```
FORALL x ( p ( x ) )
```

is a boolean expression, and it's equivalent to, and hence shorthand for, the expression

```
p ( x1 ) AND p ( x2 ) AND ... AND p ( xn ) AND TRUE
```

Observe in particular, therefore, that EXISTS x ($p(x)$) and FORALL x ($p(x)$) evaluate to FALSE and TRUE, respectively, if the set X over which x ranges happens to be empty.

By the way, given that EXISTS and FORALL are basically just iterated OR and iterated AND, respectively, it's clear that every expression that involves quantification is equivalent to one that doesn't. Thus, you might be wondering, not without some justification, just what this quantification business is really all about ... Why all the fuss? The answer is as follows: We can define EXISTS and FORALL as iterated OR and AND *only because the sets we have to deal with are—thankfully—always finite* (because we're operating in the realm of computers, and computers are finite in turn). In pure logic, where there's no such restriction, those definitions aren't valid.[2]

Perhaps I should add that, even though we're always dealing with finite sets and EXISTS and FORALL are thus indeed merely shorthand, they're extremely *useful* shorthand. For my part, I certainly wouldn't want to have to formulate queries and the like purely in terms of OR and AND, without being able to use the quantifiers. Also (and much more to the point), the quantifiers allow us to formulate queries and the like without having to know the precise content of the database at the pertinent time—which wouldn't be the case if we always had to use the explicit iterated OR and AND equivalents.

FORALL IS STRICTLY UNNECESSARY

Having introduced the two quantifiers, I must now explain that we don't really need both—either can be defined in terms of the other, by virtue of the following equivalence, or *identity*:

```
FORALL x ( p ( x ) )  ≡  NOT EXISTS x ( NOT p ( x ) )
```

Note that this equivalence is intuitively reasonable. For example, let $p(x)$ be the expression "The person x is mortal." Then:

---

[2] To spell the point out: Again consider the expression EXISTS x ($p(x)$). If x ranges over an infinite set, then any attempt to use an "iterated OR" algorithm for evaluating that expression will inevitably be flawed, since the algorithm might never terminate (it might never find a value of x that makes $p(x)$ true). Likewise, any attempt to use an "iterated AND" algorithm for FORALL x ($p(x)$) will also inevitably be flawed, since again the algorithm might never terminate (it might never find a value of x that makes $p(x)$ false).

- FORALL x ($p(x)$) means "For all persons x, x is mortal," or more colloquially "Everyone is mortal"—which is true, of course.

- NOT EXISTS x (NOT (x ($p(x)$) means "There doesn't exist a person x such that it's not the case that x is mortal," or more colloquially "No one is immortal"—which is obviously equivalent to "Everyone is mortal," and is thereby also true.

It follows that any expression involving FORALL can always be replaced by an equivalent expression involving EXISTS instead, and vice versa. As the basis for another example, let x and y both range over the set of integers. Then the (true) statement[3]

```
FORALL x ( EXISTS y ( y > x ) )
```

("For all integers x, there exists some bigger integer y") is equivalent to the statement

```
NOT EXISTS x ( NOT EXISTS y ( y > x ) )
```

("There's no integer x such that there doesn't exist some bigger integer y"). But it's usually easier to think in terms of FORALL rather than in terms of EXISTS and a double negative; in other words, a language that's supposed to be user friendly should ideally support both quantifiers. Certainly it's a criticism of SQL—which supports only EXISTS[4]—that "FORALL type" queries aren't very easy to formulate, nor are they easy to understand. (What's more, extending SQL to provide direct support for FORALL wouldn't be an easy thing to do. But that's not the topic of the present chapter. See reference [2] for further discussion.)

---

[3] Of course, I'm using the term *statement* here in its ordinary natural language sense. I certainly don't want you to think that I think that an expression and a statement are the same thing in a programming language context—there's an important logical difference between them. (*Exercise:* Define that difference as carefully as you can.)

[4] That word *supports* should really be in quotation marks here [2].

QUANTIFIER ORDER

Now I come to my main point. Suppose we have an expression that involves a sequence of two or more quantifiers, all adjacent to one another. If the quantifiers are all of the same type (i.e., all existential or all universal), then the order in which they appear doesn't matter. For example, if $q(x,y)$ is a boolean expression involving range variables x and y, then the expressions

```
EXISTS x ( EXISTS y ( q ( x , y ) ) )
```

and

```
EXISTS y ( EXISTS x ( q ( x , y ) ) )
```

are clearly equivalent. (For example, if x and y again both range over the set of integers, and if $q(x,y)$ is the expression $y > x$, then both expressions mean "There exist two integers x and y such that y is bigger than x.")

If the quantifiers are of different types, though, the order definitely does matter. For instance, we already know that if x and y range over the integers, then the expression

```
FORALL x ( EXISTS y ( y > x ) )
```

("For all integers x, there exists a bigger integer y") is TRUE. By contrast, the expression

```
EXISTS y ( FORALL x ( y > x ) )
```

("There exists an integer y that's bigger than all integers x"), which is obtained from the first expression by simply inverting the order of the quantifiers, is FALSE. (Note in particular that this second expression says among other things that there exists an integer y that's bigger than itself!)

QUERY-BY-EXAMPLE

The discussion in the previous section probably seems straightforward enough. However, matters can be a little trickier in practice, especially if the language we have to deal with is one in which the quantification is only implicit. An example of such a language is Query-By-Example (QBE).[5] Here's an example of a query expressed in QBE. *Note:* The dialect of QBE I'm using here is essentially that proposed by Zloof in his original paper (reference [4]), not the dialect used in the IBM product QMF [1]. See the further remarks on this point at the end of this section.

SALES	DEPT	ITEM
	P.	_ink

SUPPLY	ITEM	SUPPLIER
	_ink	¬Smith

Explanation: The user here has asked the system to display two blank tables on the screen, one for SALES and one for SUPPLY, and has made entries in them as shown. To elaborate:

- "Smith" is a *constant element* (i.e., a literal).

- "_ink" is an *example element* (i.e., a range variable, identified as such by that leading underscore character).

- "¬" means negation.

- "P." stands for "Print" (meaning "Retrieve" or "Get").

Thus, the intuitive, and correct, interpretation of the overall formulation is as follows:

> Get departments that sell some item, such as ink, that's available from someone who's not Smith (i.e., from someone other than Smith).

Note in particular that the row in the SUPPLY table in the QBE formulation is *implicitly* existentially quantified. In fact, the formulation overall is equivalent to the following relational calculus expression:

```
SALES.DEPT WHERE EXISTS SUPPLY
               ( SUPPLY.ITEM = SALES.ITEM AND
                 SUPPLY.SUPPLIER ≠ 'Smith' )
```

---

[5] QUEL is another, though I don't think QUEL suffers from the kinds of problems I'll be describing in the rest of this section.

(I'm playing the usual punning trick here by which a table name can be used to refer to an implicitly declared range variable that ranges over the table with the same name. For example, references in the WHERE clause to the name SUPPLY denote a range variable that ranges over the table called SUPPLY. SQL plays this same trick, of course, as I'm sure you know.)

Here's another QBE example:

SALES	DEPT	ITEM
	P.	_ink

SUPPLY	ITEM	SUPPLIER
¬	_ink	Smith

The correct interpretation of this one is:

> Get departments that sell some item, such as ink, that isn't available from Smith.

This time, the implicitly quantified row in the SUPPLY table is explicitly negated. The query is thus equivalent to the following relational calculus expression:

```
SALES.DEPT WHERE NOT EXISTS SUPPLY
                    ( SUPPLY.ITEM = SALES.ITEM AND
                      SUPPLY.SUPPLIER = 'Smith' )
```

Or alternatively:

```
SALES.DEPT WHERE FORALL SUPPLY NOT
                    ( SUPPLY.ITEM = SALES.ITEM AND
                      SUPPLY.SUPPLIER = 'Smith' )
```

So far, so good; each of the foregoing examples has involved only a single quantifier. But what about this one?—

SALES	DEPT	ITEM
	P.	_ink

SUPPLY	ITEM	SUPPLIER
¬	_ink ¯ink	Smith

This one's ambiguous! Its interpretation depends on the order in which the rows in table SUPPLY are considered—and QBE unfortunately doesn't specify any such order. (As a matter of fact, it not only fails to specify an order for the rows within the tables, it also fails to specify an order in which the tables as such are to be considered.) In the example, therefore, if we take the negated row first, the formulation is equivalent to:

```
SALES.DEPT WHERE NOT EXISTS SUPPLY1
                ( EXISTS SUPPLY2
                        ( SUPPLY1.ITEM = SALES.ITEM AND
                        ( SUPPLY2.ITEM = SALES.ITEM AND
                        SUPPLY1.SUPPLIER = 'Smith' ) )
```

SUPPLY1 and SUPPLY2 here represent two distinct range variables, both ranging over the SUPPLY table, and the intuitive interpretation is :

Get departments that sell some item, such as ink, that isn't available from Smith (and possibly not from anyone at all).

On the other hand, if we take the nonnegated row first, the formulation is equivalent to:

```
SALES.DEPT WHERE EXISTS SUPPLY2 NOT
                ( EXISTS SUPPLY1
                        ( SUPPLY1.ITEM = SALES.ITEM AND
                        ( SUPPLY2.ITEM = SALES.ITEM AND
                        SUPPLY1.SUPPLIER = 'Smith' ) )
```

Intuitive interpretation:

Get departments that sell some item, such as ink, that *is* available from someone, but not from Smith.

So which interpretation is correct? And how do we know? And whichever it is, how can we formulate the other?

Note: An interesting sidelight on the foregoing is the following: In the document from which I took the example [3], the author was actually trying to formulate a different query entirely!—namely, "Get departments that don't sell anything available from Smith," for which a correct formulation would be as follows:

SALES	DEPT	ITEM
¬	P._d _d	_ink

SUPPLY	ITEM	SUPPLIER
	_ink	Smith

Relational calculus equivalent:

```
SALES1.DEPT WHERE NOT EXISTS SALES2
                 ( EXISTS SUPPLY
                         ( SALES2.DEPT = SALES1.DEPT AND
                         ( SALES2.ITEM = SUPPLY.ITEM AND
                           SUPPLY.SUPPLIER = 'Smith' ) )
```

The author was trying to show that negation is troublesome in QBE, and I think he succeeded.

Here's an example for you to try. Given the following simplified form of the usual suppliers-and-parts database, with definition as follows—

```
S    { SNO , CITY }
     KEY { SNO }

P    { PNO , CITY }
     KEY { PNO }

SP   { SNO , PNO }
     KEY { SNO , PNO }
     FOREIGN KEY { SNO } REFERENCES S
     FOREIGN KEY { PNO } REFERENCES P
```

—what possible interpretations are there for the following QBE formulation?

S	SNO	CITY
	P._x	_c

SP	SNO	PNO
¬	_x	_y

P	PNO	CITY
	_y	_c

Also show the output produced by each interpretation, given the following sample data (where for space reasons I've abbreviated London to LHR and Paris to CDG, respectively):

S	SNO	CITY
	S1	LHR
	S2	CDG

SP	SNO	PNO
	S1	P1

P	PNO	CITY
	P1	CDG
	P2	CDG

Answers are given in the appendix to this chapter.

Note: Precisely because of the ambiguities discussed above, the ability to negate a row was omitted from the dialect of QBE implemented in the IBM product QMF [1]. Thus, problems like those discussed don't occur in that product. However, the effect of the omission is to make it impossible to formulate certain "FORALL type" queries in the QBE dialect supported by QMF, and hence to make that dialect strictly less powerful (i.e., less expressive) than SQL. Here, for instance, is an example of a query—"Get cities for suppliers who don't supply any parts"—that can't be expressed in the QMF dialect of QBE but can easily be expressed in SQL as follows:

```
SELECT  S.CITY
FROM    S
WHERE   NOT EXISTS
      ( SELECT *
        FROM    SP
        WHERE   SP.SNO = S.SNO )
```

CONCLUDING REMARKS

I hope this chapter has made it clear why it's important for both users and designers of formal query languages to have a good understanding of EXISTS and FORALL. While I realize some people might regard this state of affairs as unfortunate, I don't think it's as unfortunate as the alternative, which is wrong answers from the database.

ACKNOWLEDGMENTS

I'm grateful to Charley Bontempo and Hugh Darwen for helpful discussions.

REFERENCES

1. IBM Corporation: *Query Management Facility General Information*, IBM Form No. GG26-4071.

2. C. J. Date: "EXISTS Is Not 'Exists'!", Chapter 14 of the present book.

3. John Owlett: "A Theory of Database Schemata: Studies in Conceptual and Relational Schemata," Doctoral Dissertation, Wolfson College, Oxford, England (October 1979).

4. M. M. Zloof: "Query By Example," Proc. NCC 44 (May 1975).

APPENDIX

Here are answers to the questions posed in the body of the chapter. First of all, there are two possible interpretations. The first is:

```
S.SNO WHERE NOT EXISTS SP
             ( EXISTS P ( SP.SNO = S.SNO AND
                          SP.PNO = P.PNO AND
                          P.CITY = S.CITY ) )
```

("Get supplier numbers for suppliers who don't supply any part that's stored in their own city"). The second interpretation is:

```
S.SNO WHERE EXISTS P
          ( NOT EXISTS SP ( SP.SNO = S.SNO AND
                            SP.PNO = P.PNO AND
                            P.CITY = S.CITY ) )
```

("Get supplier numbers for suppliers for whom there exists a part stored in their own city that they don't supply").

Given the specified sample data, the first interpretation gives as output a table containing both S1 and S2; the second gives a table containing just S2.

Chapter 5

An Optimization Problem

I wrote the first version of what follows soon after attending a presentation by Mike Stonebraker [2]. In that presentation, Mike sketched a sample database containing information concerning rectangles (Mike called them "boxes"), which might be seen as a simple abstraction of certain kinds of spatial data. He then discussed a simple query against that database—"Find all rectangles that overlap the unit square"—and demonstrated rather convincingly that (a) formulating such a query in a conventional SQL DBMS is highly nontrivial, and moreover that (b) such a DBMS would have great difficulty in handling that formulation with any kind of reasonable performance. Mike then used his analysis as the basis for an argument to show why and how relational DBMSs should be extended to allow users to define their own data types (a position with which I wholeheartedly agree).

Although it wasn't the major emphasis of his presentation, one point that struck me about Mike's example was that it raised a number of interesting questions regarding relational optimization, which I subsequently pursued. This chapter is the result.

Publishing history: This is a heavily revised version of, and supersedes, a paper that first appeared in my book Relational Database Writings 1989-1991 (Addison-Wesley, 1992). This version copyright © 2022 C. J. Date.

We're given a database concerning rectangles, in which we're allowed to assume that the rectangles in question are all "square on" to the X and Y axes (i.e., their sides are all either vertical or horizontal). Thus, each such rectangle can be uniquely identified by the coordinates $(x1,y1)$ and $(x2,y2)$ of its bottom left and top right corners, respectively (see Fig. 1):

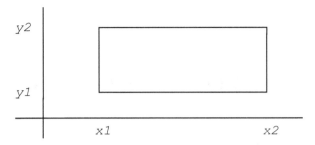

Fig. 1: The rectangle (*x1,y1,x2,y2*)

Fig. 2 is a repeat of Fig. 1, except that it shows how the given rectangle (*x1,y1,x2,y2*) overlaps "the unit square," i.e., the rectangle (0,0,1,1):

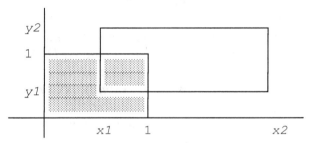

Fig. 2: The rectangle (*x1,y1,x2,y2*) and the unit square (0,0,1,1)

Here in outline is a possible CREATE TABLE statement for an SQL table in which each row represents one such rectangle:[1]

```
CREATE TABLE RECTANGLES ( RID , X1 , Y1 , X2 , Y2 , ... ,
       UNIQUE ( RID ) ,
       UNIQUE ( X1 , Y1 , X2 , Y2 ) ,
       CHECK ( X1 < X2 AND Y1 < Y2 ) ) ;
```

Note the CHECK clause in particular, which specifies an integrity constraint to the effect that for any given rectangle, *x1* is strictly less than *x2* and *y1* is strictly less than *y2*.

---

[1] The RID column ("rectangle ID") is included for completeness, but it has no part to play in the rest of the discussion—it's merely corroborative detail, intended to add an air of verisimilitude to an otherwise bald and unconvincing narrative.

Suppose now that we wish to find all of the rectangles that overlap the unit square. The "obvious" formulation of this query in SQL is:[2]

```
SELECT  *
FROM    RECTANGLES
WHERE   ( X1 ≥ 0 AND X1 ≤ 1 AND Y1 ≥ 0 AND Y1 ≤ 1 )
        /* bottom left corner inside unit square */
OR      ( X2 ≥ 0 AND X2 ≤ 1 AND Y2 ≥ 0 AND Y2 ≤ 1 )
        /* top right corner inside unit square */
OR      ( X1 ≥ 0 AND X1 ≤ 1 AND Y2 ≥ 0 AND Y2 ≤ 1 )
        /* top left corner inside unit square */
OR      ( X2 ≥ 0 AND X2 ≤ 1 AND Y1 ≥ 0 AND Y1 ≤ 1 )
        /* bottom right corner inside unit square */
OR      ( X1 ≤ 0 AND X2 ≥ 1 AND Y1 ≤ 0 AND Y2 ≥ 1 )
        /* rectangle totally includes unit square */
OR      ( X1 ≤ 0 AND X2 ≥ 1 AND Y1 ≥ 0 AND Y1 ≤ 1 )
        /* bottom edge crosses unit square */
OR      ( X1 ≥ 0 AND X1 ≤ 1 AND Y1 ≤ 0 AND Y2 ≥ 1 )
        /* left edge crosses unit square */
OR      ( X2 ≥ 0 AND X2 ≤ 1 AND Y1 ≤ 0 AND Y2 ≥ 1 )
        /* right edge crosses unit square */
OR      ( X1 ≤ 0 AND X2 ≥ 1 AND Y2 ≥ 0 AND Y2 ≤ 1 )
        /* top edge crosses unit square */
```

Note: I recommend strongly that you take the time to convince yourself that this formulation is correct before you continue reading.

With a little further thought, however,[3] it can be seen that the query can be expressed much more simply as follows:

```
SELECT  *
FROM    RECTANGLES
WHERE   ( X1 ≤ 1 AND Y1 ≤ 1
        /* bottom left corner is "downwind" of (1,1) */
AND       X2 ≥ 0 AND Y2 ≥ 0 )
        /* top right corner is "upwind" of (0,0) */
```

So the question is: Can we prove, formally, that these two formulations are equivalent?

The question isn't an idle one, of course; the real issue is whether the system optimizer could transform the original long formulation into the short version. I'll return to that "real" issue later. For now, however, I have another

---

[2] Just how obvious it really is can, I think, fairly be judged from the fact that reference [2] got it wrong (it omitted the last two of the nine ORed terms). *Note:* I use the conventional mathematical symbols "≤" and "≥" in place of the symbols that SQL would actually require, viz., "<=" and ">=", respectively.

[3] Actually the transformations needed require rather a lot of "further thought," as we'll see.

recommendation for you—viz., I recommend that you try to find a proof for yourself before reading any further. If you do manage to find one, or at least attempt to do so, then I believe you'll be in a much better position to appreciate the message of the rest of the chapter.

RESTATING THE PROBLEM

First of all let me define some shorthands, as follows:[4]

```
A  :  X1 ≥ 0       G  :  Y2 ≥ 0
B  :  X1 ≤ 1       H  :  Y2 ≤ 1
C  :  Y1 ≥ 0       I  :  X1 ≤ 0
D  :  Y1 ≤ 1       J  :  X2 ≥ 1
E  :  X2 ≥ 0       K  :  Y1 ≤ 0
F  :  X2 ≤ 1       L  :  Y2 ≥ 1
```

Then the boolean expression in the WHERE clause in the original "long" formulation of the query becomes:

```
     ( A AND B AND C AND D )       t1
OR ( E AND F AND G AND H )       t2
OR ( A AND B AND G AND H )       t3
OR ( E AND F AND C AND D )       t4
OR ( I AND J AND K AND L )       t5
OR ( I AND J AND C AND D )       t6
OR ( A AND B AND K AND L )       t7
OR ( E AND F AND K AND L )       t8
OR ( I AND J AND G AND H )       t9
```

And the corresponding expression in the short formulation becomes just:

```
B AND D AND E AND G
```

Let's agree to refer to the nine terms that are ORed together in the original long formulation as *t1*, *t2*, ..., *t9*, respectively (as suggested by the labels to the right above). Then the problem is to prove that the expression

```
t1 OR t2 OR t3 OR t4 OR t5 OR t6 OR t7 OR t8 OR t9
```

---

[4] Note that the expressions $X1 \geq 1$, $X2 \leq 0$, $Y1 \geq 1$, and $Y2 \leq 0$ are missing from the list. Are these omissions intuitively reasonable, do you think? Justify your answer!

is logically equivalent to the "target" expression

```
B AND D AND E AND G
```

LEMMAS

Before I embark on the proof per se, it's useful to state a number of lemmas, some of them well known results from logic, others easily proved from the arithmetic interpretations of the expressions *A, B, C,* etc. *Note:* The symbols *X, Y, Z,* etc., in those lemmas stand for boolean (or logical or truth valued) expressions.

The first few are well known identities from logic, and I state them here without proof:

```
X AND ( X OR  Y )  ≡  X
X OR  ( X AND Y )  ≡  X

X AND ( Y OR  Z )  ≡  ( X AND Y ) OR  ( X AND Z )
X OR  ( Y AND Z )  ≡  ( X OR  Y ) AND ( X OR  Z )

( X OR  Y ) AND ( Z OR  W )
              ≡  ( X AND Z ) OR  ( X AND W ) OR
                 ( Y AND Z ) OR  ( Y AND W )
( X AND Y ) OR  ( Z AND W )
              ≡  ( X OR  Z ) AND ( X OR  W ) AND
                 ( Y OR  Z ) AND ( Y OR  W )
```

Similar identities apply in the case of more complex expressions, of course, such as

```
( X AND Y ) OR ( Z AND W ) OR ( U AND V )
```

I'll skip the details here.

The proofs of the next four identities are trivial from the arithmetic meanings of the expressions *A, I, C,* etc.:

```
A OR I  ≡  TRUE
C OR K  ≡  TRUE
F OR J  ≡  TRUE
H OR L  ≡  TRUE
```

The proofs of the next four pairs of identities are again trivial from the arithmetic meanings of the expressions *B*, *I*, *D*, etc.:

```
B AND I  ≡  I          B OR I  ≡  B
D AND K  ≡  K          D OR K  ≡  D
E AND J  ≡  J          E OR J  ≡  E
G AND L  ≡  L          G OR L  ≡  G
```

The proofs of the next four pairs of identities are again trivial from the arithmetic meanings of the expressions *A*, *E*, *C*, etc., together with the fact that the integrity constraint X1 < X2 AND Y1 < Y2 holds:

```
A AND E  ≡  A          A OR E  ≡  E
C AND G  ≡  C          C OR G  ≡  G
F AND B  ≡  F          F OR B  ≡  B
H AND D  ≡  H          H OR D  ≡  D
```

SOLVING THE PROBLEM

I'm now in a position to show that the two formulations of the query are indeed equivalent. The proof begins by systematically grouping together terms of the original expression that share subexpressions. For example, terms *t1*, *t3*, and *t7* share the subexpression *A* AND *B*, which can be factored out, thus:

```
t1 OR t3 OR t7

≡   [ ( A AND B ) ] AND
    [ ( C AND D ) OR ( G AND H ) OR ( K OR L ) ]

≡   [ ( A AND B ) ] AND
    [ ( C OR G OR K ) AND ( C OR G OR L ) AND
      ( C OR H OR K ) AND ( C OR H OR L ) AND
      ( D OR G OR K ) AND ( D OR G OR L ) AND
      ( D OR H OR K ) AND ( D OR H OR L ) ]
```

Next, examining the eight parenthesized triplet terms here—i.e., (*C* OR *G* OR *K*), (*C* OR *G* OR *L*), and so on, which I'll refer to just for the moment as "term 1," "term2," and so on—we see that:

```
C OR K  ≡  TRUE, so terms 1 and 3 can be dropped;
H OR L  ≡  TRUE, so terms 4 and 8 can be dropped;
G OR L  ≡  G, so L can be dropped from terms 2 and 6;
C OR G  ≡  G, so C can be dropped from term 2;
D OR K  ≡  D, so K can be dropped from terms 5 and 7;
D OR H  ≡  D, so H can be dropped from term 7;
terms 5 and 6 are now identical, so one can be dropped.
```

The part of the expression involving those eight triplet terms thus reduces to the following:

```
G AND ( D OR G ) AND D
```

And this expression in turn reduces to just:

```
D AND G
```

It follows that

```
t1 OR t3 OR t7  ≡  A AND B AND D AND G
```

But we saw in the previous section that A ≡ A AND E, so we can rewrite the foregoing equivalence thus:

```
t1 OR t3 OR t7  ≡  ( B AND D AND E AND G ) AND A
```

Analogous arguments can be used to show that:

- *t1* OR *t4* or *t6* (common subexpression *C* AND *D*) is equivalent to:

  ```
  ( B AND D AND E AND G ) AND C
  ```

- *t2* OR *t4* or *t8* (common subexpression *E* AND *F*) is equivalent to:

  ```
  ( B AND D AND E AND G ) AND F
  ```

- *t2* OR *t3* or *t9* (common subexpression *G* AND *H*) is equivalent to:

  ```
  ( B AND D AND E AND G ) AND H
  ```

- *t5* OR *t6* or *t9* (common subexpression *I* AND *J*) is equivalent to:

  (B AND D AND E AND G) AND (I AND J)

- *t5* OR *t7* or *t8* (common subexpression *K* AND *L*) is equivalent to:

  (B AND D AND E AND G) AND (K AND L)

Note: Of course, it's legitimate to do as I've done (i.e., use individual terms of the original expression over and over again in the foregoing reductions), because $X \equiv (X$ OR $X)$ for all X.

It follows from all of the above that the complete original expression

t1 OR t2 OR t3 OR t4 OR t5 OR t6 OR t7 OR t8 OR t9

is equivalent to

(B AND D AND E AND G) AND term

where *term* is

(A OR C OR F OR H OR (I AND J) OR (K AND L))

Regrouping this latter gives:

(A OR F) OR (I AND J) OR (C OR H) OR (K AND L)

Now taking the first and second parenthesized terms together and the third and fourth likewise, this expression is seen to be equivalent to the following (call it *term'*):

[(A OR F OR I) AND (A OR F OR J)] OR
[(C OR H OR K) AND (C OR H OR L)]

But

(A OR I) ≡ (F OR J) ≡ (C OR K) ≡ (H OR L) ≡ TRUE

So each of the four triplet terms in *term'* reduces to TRUE; hence *term'* is identically true, and hence so is *term*, and thus the entire original expression

```
t1 OR t2 OR t3 OR t4 OR t5 OR t6 OR t7 OR t8 OR t9
```

reduces to just

```
B AND D AND E AND G
```

—i.e., to the desired target expression. QED.

DISCUSSION

I've now proved formally that the long and short formulations of the query are equivalent as claimed. As indicated earlier, however, the real issue is whether the system optimizer would be able to do the transformation—i.e., to transform the original long version into the equivalent short one. What do you think?

My own first thought is this: The proof I've given is certainly rather complex, but it is at least *constructive*, in the sense that it actually does what an optimizer would have to do (i.e., it actually constructs the short version by performing a series of transformations on the long one). By contrast, other proofs I've seen have been merely *existential*—by which I mean they've shown that each of the two formulations, long and short, implies the other (and hence that the two are equivalent, and hence that a transformation procedure must exist), but they haven't actually done the transformation. Such an approach wouldn't be of much use if the short version wasn't known ahead of time.

If we examine the transformations of that constructive proof a little more closely, however, then a number of facts, some of which might seem a little unfortunate, will become apparent:

1. The transformations rely on certain elementary properties of logic—for example, the *absorption law* X AND (X OR Y) $\equiv X$. Some optimizers might possess such knowledge, but others probably don't.

2. The transformations also rely on elementary properties of arithmetic—specifically, knowledge of the fact that zero is less than one (and one is greater than zero). Most optimizers probably don't possess such knowledge; some might not even know that $a < a$ is always false, or that ">" is the inverse of "<" (i.e., $a > b$ is true if and only if $b < a$ is true).

3. The transformations also rely on the fact that certain integrity constraints hold—specifically, the constraints that $x1 < x2$ and $y1 < y2$. Transformations that rely on certain constraints holding are referred to as *semantic* transformations, and an optimizer that performs such transformations is said to be doing semantic optimization [1]. So far as I know, no DBMS on the market today does anything very significant by way of semantic optimization; in fact, most current DBMSs don't even allow constraints to be declared, let alone enforce them.[5]

4. The transformations also rely on a somewhat tricky set of choices regarding exactly which transformation laws to use, and in which order. For example, my proof used certain terms of the original expression over and over again in the overall reduction process. This fact effectively implies that a certain term, X say, had to be transformed into the expression X OR X OR X OR ... OR X (as many X's as needed for the said repeated use). Such a transformation doesn't seem particularly obvious, to say the least. Considerations such as this one tend to suggest that the optimizer might run into combinatorial explosion problems.

From all of the above I conclude that it's unlikely, given the present state of the art, that a conventional relational optimizer (even a "good" one) would in fact be able to perform the desired transformation. I would be delighted to be proved wrong in this regard.

CONCLUDING REMARKS

There seem to be a number of conclusions that can be drawn from the discussions of this chapter.

1. We should of course continue to strive to make optimizers more and more "intelligent." However, there'll always be optimizations that are beyond the abilities of the optimizer at any given stage in its development. Thus, there needs to be a mechanism by which an appropriately skilled user can add specialized, user written optimization code to the vendor-provided

---

[5] Apart from a few pragmatically important special cases such as key and foreign key constraints. PS: Even if I'm wrong here, I don't think it materially affects the argument overall or the bigger picture.

optimizer. This mechanism will presumably be part of the "user defined type" facility (see the next point below).

2. I've argued elsewhere that a true relational system should allow users to define their own types.[6] Of course, the user defined type mechanism would also have to allow operators to be defined in connection with those types, because types without operators are useless. Thus we might define a RECTANGLE type, for example, together with an OVERLAPS operator that returns TRUE if and only if its two RECTANGLE operands overlap. The code that supports the OVERLAPS operator would be, precisely, an "efficient" (optimized) implementation of the query discussed in this chapter (or, rather, a generalized version thereof).

3. The discussions of this chapter show clearly that it's not enough for the optimizer to be be able to perform purely relational transformations—it also needs to be able to do logical transformations, arithmetic transformations, and so on. It also needs to be aware of any integrity constraints that might be in effect and to be able to take advantage of them.

4. Finally, as my late friend and colleague Adrian Larner once said to me, "Doing logic is hard and error prone for humans, and should be left to computers." If you tried to prove for yourself the equivalence of the two formulations of the "overlaps" query—or even if you just tried to follow the details of my own proof—then I'm quite sure you won't need any further convincing of the truth of this observation.

ACKNOWLEDGMENTS

I'm grateful to Mike Stonebraker for drawing my attention to the rectangles problem in the first place. I'm also grateful to Hugh Darwen and Adrian Larner for alternative proofs of the equivalence of the long and short formulations and for much enlightening correspondence on the larger matters discussed in this chapter.

---

[6] This is the point Stonebraker was making in reference [2].

REFERENCES

1. Jonathan J. King: "QUIST: A System For Semantic Query Optimization In Relational Databases," Proc. 7th International Conference on Very Large Data Bases, Cannes, France (September 1981).

2. Michael Stonebraker: "Three-Dimensional DBMSs" (presentation), DB Expo 90: The National Database Exposition and Conference, San Francisco, Calif. (May 27-29, 1990).

Chapter 6

Watch Out for Outer Join

The outer join operator is subtle—a lot subtler than many people realize. I wrote the original version of what follows after carrying out an investigation into the support provided for that operator by several different commercial DBMS products at that time. I was frankly amazed at the number of ways vendors could get it wrong![1] It was quite clear that the subtleties I have in mind here, though surely not unknown, were nevertheless not at all widely appreciated at the time (and very likely still aren't). So I felt it would be a service to identify and explain some of those subtleties in a paper—now a chapter—that could act as a "single source" reference for the material in the future.

Publishing history: This is a heavily revised version of, and supersedes, a paper that first appeared in InfoDB 5, No. 1 (Spring / Summer 1990) and was later republished in my book Relational Database Writings 1989-1991 (Addison-Wesley, 1992). This version copyright © C. J. Date 2022.

For the purposes of this chapter I assume you're at least broadly familiar with both:

a. The outer join operator per se—including the fact that it comes in a variety of different flavors (left, right, and full outer θ-join, and left, right, and full outer natural join);[2] and

---

[1] Whether the products in question still include the "support" I'll be describing I frankly have no idea, nor do I very much care. That's not the point. The point is, language design is hard, and it needs to be done by competent and knowledgeable professionals.

[2] A historical note here: The term *outer join* was invented by Ian Heath in 1971. Ian and I were both employees of IBM in the U.K. at the time, and I was working with him—in fact, we were sharing an office—when he came up with the concept, and the term.

b.   The kinds of problems the outer join operator is intended to solve.

A detailed discussion of such matters can be found in many places; see, e.g., reference [3]. Here I content myself with a single example, based on a very much reduced version of the usual suppliers-and-parts database. Refer to Fig. 1.

a.   S

SNO	SNAME	STATUS	SCITY
S2	Jones	10	Paris
S5	Adams	30	Athens

SP

SNO	PNO	QTY
S2	P1	300
S2	P2	400

b.   Regular (i.e., inner) natural join of S and SP

SNO	SNAME	STATUS	SCITY	PNO	QTY
S2	Jones	10	Paris	P1	300
S2	Jones	10	Paris	P2	400

c.   Left (also full) outer natural join of S and SP

SNO	SNAME	STATUS	SCITY	PNO	QTY
S2	Jones	10	Paris	P1	300
S2	Jones	10	Paris	P2	400
S5	Adams	30	Athens	??	???

Fig. 1: Inner and outer natural joins (examples)

The figure is meant to be read as follows. Part a. shows sample values for the suppliers table (S) and the shipments table (SP); part b. shows the regular (or *inner*) natural join of those two tables;[3] and part c.—where the question marks represent nulls—shows a corresponding *outer* natural join. As the figure indicates, the inner join "loses information" for suppliers who supply no parts (supplier S5, in the example), whereas the outer join "preserves" that information; indeed, this distinction is the whole point of outer join. *Note:* Since every row in table SP necessarily has a matching row in table S (because SNO in table SP is a foreign key matching the key SNO in table S), the left and full outer natural joins are identical in this particular example and are as shown in part c. of

_____

[3] As far as I'm concerned (in this chapter and elsewhere), "natural" join means, by definition, join on the basis of common column names (i.e., on SNO, in the case of the examples of Fig. 1).

the figure. The right outer natural join, by contrast, degenerates to the inner natural join and is thus as shown in part b. of the figure.

A few further preliminary remarks:

- For obvious reasons, all discussions and examples in this chapter are framed in terms of SQL specifically. But the points I have to make don't apply to SQL only but rather are of general applicability.

- Second, despite my many documented reservations regarding nulls and three-valued logic, 3VL—see, e.g., reference [7]—I have to assume throughout most of this chapter that we're indeed operating within a 3VL framework. I'll examine this aspect of the outer join problem in a little more detail toward the end of the chapter. *That said, however, let me state for the record that it's not at all clear that outer join, as that term is usually understood, is really what we need anyway.* But I'm obviously not in a position yet to discuss this point in detail.

- Third, I'm going to be giving a number of examples, based on several commercially available DBMS products, of how *not* to do outer join. However, please be aware that those examples aren't intended (or at least aren't primarily intended) as criticisms of the products in question; rather, they're merely intended to illustrate some of the many different ways in which it's possible to get outer join wrong. In particular, I certainly don't mean to suggest that other products have got it right!

WHY OUTER JOIN?

As I've already indicated, I'm not sure we really need outer join at all. However, we do need a solution to the problem that outer join is supposed to address, and so I'm just going to assume, at least until further notice, that outer join is the solution we're looking for. To see what that problem might be, consider the following expression (one possible SQL formulation of the outer join of Fig. 1c):

```
SELECT  S.SNO , S.SNAME , S.STATUS , S.SCITY ,
                                        SP.PNO , SP.QTY
FROM    S , SP
WHERE   S.SNO = SP.SNO
UNION
SELECT  S.SNO , S.SNAME , S.STATUS , S.SCITY ,
                CAST ( NULL AS VARCHAR(3) ) AS PNO ,
                CAST ( NULL AS INTEGER ) AS QTY
FROM    S
WHERE   NOT EXISTS
      ( SELECT SP.SNO
        FROM    SP
        WHERE   SP.SNO = S.SNO )
```

Note: As you probably know, SQL doesn't allow the keyword NULL to be used as an element in a SELECT list. Now, this rule might seem at first to be nothing but an annoyance; in fact, however, it does make a kind of sense, because the elements in a SELECT list are supposed to denote values, and null isn't a value. But there's more ... Because null isn't a value, it doesn't have a type. And yet CAST expressions like the ones shown *are* allowed, which frankly makes no sense at all—because what those expressions apparently do is give a type to something that (by definition) can't possibly have one, thereby producing, in the example, a "null varying length character string" and a "null integer." SQL apologists please explain!

Aside: The SQL apologist par excellence is the SQL standard, of course. But what the SQL standard actually has to say about this issue is at best unclear (I'm tempted to say, characteristically unclear). First of all, it tries to pretend that null is a value after all—even though it certainly doesn't behave like one—by referring to it, frequently though not exclusively, as *the null value*. This latter term it defines as "a special value that is used to indicate the absence of any data value." (In other words, null is a value that means there isn't a value. Got that?) Then it goes on to say:

> Since the null value is in every data type, the data type of the null value implied by the keyword NULL cannot be inferred; hence NULL can be used to denote the null value only in certain contexts, rather than everywhere that a literal is permitted ... Although the null value is neither equal to any other value nor not equal to any other value ... in some contexts, multiple null values are treated together; for example, the <group by clause> treats all null values together.

Note how this text goes out of its way not to say two nulls are equal (they're merely "treated together"), but at the same time doesn't say they aren't (they're merely neither equal to nor not equal to "any other value"). Also note the qualification "in some contexts," which being interpreted means that sometimes two nulls are equal and sometimes they aren't.

Well, I don't want to get sucked any further here into the nulls quagmire. I'll just say this: If the foregoing extracts from the standard aren't sufficient to convince you that there's something deeply fishy about the whole nulls idea, then I'm sorry, but (at best) you might not be ready for some of the discussions to follow later in this chapter. *End of aside.*

In any case, even if we ignore the question of whether null is a value, the problems in the example are obvious: The expression overall is quite complicated (and it's much worse in more complex cases); it's error prone (in general, the differences between a "genuine" outer join expression and some other expression that represents some quite different outer join—or something that's not an outer join at all—can be quite subtle); and there's very little chance that the system optimizer will recognize that the user is actually trying to construct an outer join, and performance is thus likely to be poor.

Note: As the example suggests, outer join isn't a primitive operator—it can be expressed in terms of existing operators of the relational algebra (for details, see reference [3]). But a user who wishes to formulate an outer join shouldn't have to indulge in circumlocutions of the kind illustrated in the example.

WHY THIS CHAPTER?

The paper I wrote on this topic earlier [3] was an attempt to explain the basic concepts of outer join. However, it clearly failed in that attempt—maybe it wasn't widely seen—because DBMS products in turn have certainly failed to support outer join in any kind of logical and systematic fashion. How have they failed? Well, the remainder of this chapter gives a number of answers to this question. For now, let me just note that it's actually quite difficult to extend SQL to do outer join "right." Why? As a basis for answering this question, it's helpful to review the semantics of the basic SQL SELECT – FROM – WHERE construct (the GROUP BY and HAVING clauses are irrelevant and can be ignored for present purposes). Loosely speaking, what happens is the following:

- First, the cartesian product of the tables named in the FROM clause is computed.

- Next, that product is restricted to that subset of the rows that satisfy the "restriction condition" in the WHERE clause.

- Last, that subset is projected over the columns named in the SELECT clause.

So the SELECT – FROM – WHERE expression is evaluated in the order FROM, then WHERE, then SELECT, and the expression overall denotes a projection of a restriction of a product. Points arising:

- For simplicity I ignore the fact, here and throughout this chapter, that a true projection always eliminates duplicate rows, whereas the SQL SELECT clause eliminates duplicate rows only if it's explicitly requested to do so by means of the operator DISTINCT.

- I also assume for the most part that the elements of the SELECT clause are all just column names; the explanation above requires some refinement, which I ignore here for simplicity, in order to be able to deal with more complicated scalar expressions (as SQL of course does permit).

- I also ignore the fact that the boolean expression in the WHERE clause isn't necessarily a restriction condition as such (i.e., it isn't necessarily a condition that can be evaluated for a given row by examining just that row in isolation), because SQL allows it to contain a subquery. Again, this simplification is justified because it doesn't materially affect the issue at hand.

Now, the foregoing conceptual evaluation algorithm works for inner joins, because (a) the inner θ-join is indeed a restriction of a product, and (b) the inner natural join is indeed a projection of the inner equijoin.[4] When we turn our attention to outer joins, however, the algorithm doesn't work at all. *This state of affairs makes it virtually impossible to express outer joins in terms of **any** "simple" extension to the SELECT – FROM – WHERE construct as such.* The fact is, outer join possesses a number of Nasty Properties, properties that effectively undermine the assumptions underlying the original design of SQL in

---

[4] *Equijoin* is what results when the "θ" in "θ-join" is equality ("="). For simplicity, I'll usually take θ to be "=" in what follows. The extensions to handle the other comparison operators are straightforward.

the first place. I'll state those properties here for purposes of future reference, and then go on to discuss them in detail in the remainder of the chapter:

1. Outer equijoin isn't a restriction of cartesian product.

2. Restriction doesn't distribute over outer equijoin.

3. $A \leq B$ and $A < B$ OR $A = B$ aren't equivalent.

4. The comparison operators aren't transitive.

5. Outer natural join isn't a projection of outer equijoin.

6. Outer natural join isn't associative.

Note: Most of these Nasty Properties can be discussed without any loss of generality in the context of dyadic joins only. For simplicity, therefore, I'll assume henceforth that all joins involve exactly two tables, barring explicit statements to the contrary.

WHAT DOES "SUPPORT" MEAN?

Before going any further, perhaps I should give some indication as to what I'd consider to be "good" outer join support (always assuming, of course, that outer join as such is what we want to support in the first place—see the further discussion of this point toward the end of the chapter). Briefly, I'd want to see at least all of the following:

■ Explicit "one liner" outer join expressions such as S OUTER JOIN SP. *Note:* I first proposed a syntax somewhat along these lines in reference [3]. Such "one liner" support is desirable for reasons of usability, analyzability, optimizability, etc.

■ Support for:

　　a. Outer natural join (much the most important case in practice)

    b. Outer θ-joins (including outer equijoin in particular)

    c. Left, right, and full versions for both of the above

    d. Outer joins of any number of tables

- Generality (i.e., all possible outer joins systematically handled, not just an incomplete ragbag of special cases)

- Ability for the user to control the representation of the fact that information is missing (see later)

I now explain, in the next several sections, why it's not feasible to extend the SQL SELECT – FROM – WHERE construct in any straightforward manner to satisfy the foregoing requirements.

WHY WE CAN'T JUST EXTEND THE WHERE CLAUSE (1)

The first "Nasty Property" is that outer equijoin isn't a restriction of the product of the tables in question. By way of illustration of this state of affairs refer to Fig. 2 (opposite), which shows (a) the product of tables S and SP from Fig. 1a and (b) the left—which in this case is the same as the full—outer equijoin of those same tables on SNO. I've renamed the two supplier number columns in the result tables SSNO and SPSNO, respectively, to avoid confusion.

    It follows from this first Nasty Property that we can't coherently expect to be able to express an outer equijoin by merely inventing some new kind of comparison operator and then allowing that operator to appear in the boolean expression in the WHERE clause (why not, exactly?). Sybase and CA-Universe are examples of products that fail on this score. Here, for example, is the way the outer join of Fig. 1c would be expressed in Sybase (note the "*=" comparison operator in the last line):[5]

```
SELECT S.SNO , S.SNAME , S.STATUS , S.SCITY ,
                                    SP.PNO , SP.QTY
FROM   S , SP
WHERE  S.SNO *= SP.SNO
```

---

[5] That "*=" would be "=?" in CA-Universe.

a. Product of S and SP

SSNO	SNAME	STATUS	SCITY	SPSNO	PNO	QTY
S2	Jones	10	Paris	S2	P1	300
S2	Jones	10	Paris	S2	P2	400
S5	Adams	30	Athens	S2	P1	300
S5	Adams	30	Athens	S2	P2	400

b. Left (also full) outer equijoin of S and SP (on SNO)

SSNO	SNAME	STATUS	SCITY	SPSNO	PNO	QTY
S2	Jones	10	Paris	S2	P1	300
S2	Jones	10	Paris	S2	P2	400
S5	Adams	30	Athens	??	??	???

Fig. 2: Outer equijoin isn't a restriction of a product

According to reference [9], that special comparison operator "*=" in the WHERE clause means "include all rows from the first named table in the join specification [*i.e., table S, in the example*] whether or not there's a match on the [joining] column in the [second named] table [*i.e., table SP, in the example*]."

Now, it's undeniably true that the foregoing expression is much more succinct than the UNION expression shown earlier (in the section "Why Outer Join?"). However, it's also true that such an ad hoc trick won't handle the general case; what's more, it's not at all easy to state exactly which cases it *will* handle. And since the result isn't a restriction of a product (so the conceptual evaluation algorithm breaks down), how can the overall operation be explained to the user? (The "explanation" above from reference [9] isn't an explanation at all, in my opinion.) In fact, I defy anyone to produce a complete, precise, coherent, context free explanation of the semantics of the expression A *= B for arbitrary A and B. (Of course, I hope it's obvious that such an explanation certainly can be given for the much more familiar expression A = B!)

There are a few further, albeit minor, points I think I should mention in connection with the foregoing:

■ First, thanks to the projection performed by the SELECT clause, the Sybase expression shown actually produces a left outer natural join, not a left outer equijoin. However, this particular fact doesn't materially affect the discussion.

- Second, I hope I'm not to blame for the Sybase scheme! In reference [3], I used the notation R[A *= B]S to stand for the left outer equijoin of tables R and S on columns R.A and S.B. I also used "=*" and "*=*" analogously for the right and full outer equijoins. But there's a big logical difference between a mere *notation* that happens to involve the symbol "*=" and a formal syntax that actually attempts to use that symbol to denote an actual operator!

- Finally, note that Sybase supports "*=" and "=*" but not "*=*"—i.e., it doesn't support the full outer equijoin, but only the left and right versions. As for CA-Universe, that product supports "=?" only, not "?=" or "?=?"— i.e., it supports the left outer equijoin only.

WHY WE CAN'T JUST EXTEND THE WHERE CLAUSE (2)

I've shown that the idea of inventing a new comparison operator such as "*=" and allowing that operator to appear in the WHERE clause falls foul of Nasty Property No. 1—viz., that outer equijoin isn't a restriction of a product. In fact, however, it also falls foul of Nasty Property No. 2—viz., that restriction doesn't distribute over outer equijoin. Informally, what this latter statement means is that the expressions

```
( R outer equijoin S ) WHERE restriction on R
```

and

```
( R WHERE restriction on R ) outer equijoin S
```

aren't equivalent, in general. By way of example, consider the following Sybase expression (a slight extension of the example from the previous section):

```
SELECT S.SNO , S.SNAME , S.STATUS , S.SCITY ,
                                 SP.PNO , SP.QTY
FROM   S , SP
WHERE  S.SNO *= SP.SNO
AND    SP.QTY < 1000
```

This expression has two potential interpretations, depending on whether the restriction condition SP.QTY < 1000 is applied before or after the join condition S.SNO *= SP.SNO. In terms of the sample data shown in Fig. 1a (in which it so happens that every QTY value is less than 1000), performing the restriction first gives a result containing rows for both supplier S2 and supplier S5; performing the join first gives a result containing rows for supplier S2 only (because after the join, the QTY for supplier S5 is given as null, and "null < 1000" doesn't evaluate to *true*). So which interpretation is correct? And whichever it is, how can we obtain the other one? (For the record, I note that Sybase actually does the restriction first.)

You might also care to meditate on the following examples (and an infinite number of others like them):

```
SELECT  S.SNO , S.SNAME , S.STATUS , S.SCITY ,
                                     SP.PNO , SP.QTY
FROM    S , SP
WHERE   S.SNO *= SP.SNO
OR      SP.QTY < 1000

SELECT  S.SNO , S.SNAME , S.STATUS , S.SCITY ,
                                     SP.PNO , SP.QTY
FROM    S , SP
WHERE   S.SNO *= SP.SNO
AND     S.STATUS =* SP.QTY

SELECT  S.SNO , S.SNAME , S.STATUS , S.SCITY ,
                                     SP.PNO , SP.QTY
FROM    S , SP
WHERE   S.SNO *= SP.SNO
AND     SP.SNO *= S.SNO

SELECT  S.SNO , S.SNAME , S.STATUS , S.SCITY ,
                                     SP.PNO , SP.QTY
FROM    S , SP
WHERE   NOT ( S.SNO *= SP.SNO )
AND     SP.QTY < 1000
```

The meanings of such expressions are anybody's guess.

By the way, I don't mean to pick on Sybase here; analogous comments and criticisms apply to many other products also. For brevity, however, I won't usually bother from this point forward to spell out the problems in so much detail for every individual product.

HOW WE *MIGHT* EXTEND THE FROM CLAUSE

I've shown that outer equijoin isn't a restriction of the product of the tables in question. However, it *is* a restriction of the product of certain *augmented versions* of those tables—where by the term *augmented version* (of table T), I mean a table that contains all of the rows of table T together with one additional row, viz., a row of all nulls. Let me use the notation T+ to denote the augmented version of table T, and the expression T1 TIMES T2 to denote the product of tables T1 and T2. A little more precisely, then, the left outer equijoin of T1 and T2 is a restriction of T1 TIMES T2+, the right outer equijoin is a restriction of T1+ TIMES T2, and the full outer equijoin is a restriction of T1+ TIMES T2+.

The foregoing observations suggest that one possible approach to extending SQL to support outer equijoins would be to allow the FROM clause to refer to such augmented tables, and then to use the WHERE clause to express the restriction of the result of that FROM clause—in other words, the product of those augmented tables—that's needed to construct the desired outer join. And exactly such an approach was proposed by Chamberlin in reference [1]. This would be Chamberlin's formulation of the outer join of Fig. 1c:

```
SELECT S.SNO , S.SNAME , S.STATUS , S.SCITY ,
                                    XYZ.PNO , XYZ.QTY
FROM    S , SP+ AS XYZ
WHERE   S.SNO = XYZ.SNO
OR    ( NOT EXISTS
            ( SELECT SP.SNO
                FROM    SP
               WHERE   SP.SNO = S.SNO )
          AND XYZ.SNO IS NULL )
```

Note the need to introduce an explicit range variable—XYZ in the example—in order to be able to reference rows of the augmented version SP+ of table SP.

The foregoing approach certainly works, and it's not ad hoc. But it does suffer from a number of problems, of which perhaps the most significant is that it's very error prone: It requires extremely careful use of range variables (Chamberlin himself gets them wrong in his example in reference [1]), and it's not at all easy to get the restrictions in the WHERE clause right, even in simple cases such as the one illustrated. Moreover, the technique is intuitively difficult to apply, because there's no immediately obvious rule connecting the tables that need to be flagged with a plus sign and the tables for which information is to be preserved. Note too that these criticisms apply to all schemes that are based on the concept of flagging tables to be "augmented," including the schemes implemented in, e.g., Informix, Oracle, and SQLBase (see below). *Note:* If you're not convinced of the truth of these observations, then I recommend you try some examples for yourself (especially more complex examples, involving three or more tables).

A more comprehensive analysis of Chamberlin's approach, with more examples, can be found in reference [3].

WHY WE CAN'T JUST EXTEND THE FROM CLAUSE (1)

Given that it's so difficult to get the WHERE clause right in Chamberlin's approach (because the necessary restriction conditions rapidly become so complex), it's tempting to try to find a way to extend the FROM clause to augment tables appropriately *and* to do the necessary restrictions automatically, without the user having to specify those restrictions explicitly. Informix is an example of a product that attempts such an approach. Here's how the outer join of Fig. 1c would be expressed in Informix:

```
SELECT S.SNO , S.SNAME , S.STATUS , S.SCITY ,
                                    SP.PNO , SP.QTY
FROM    S , OUTER SP
WHERE   S.SNO = SP.SNO
```

An immediate criticism of this syntax is that the result includes rows for which the condition in the WHERE clause doesn't evaluate to *true*! Another is that the reference to SP in the WHERE clause must presumably be taken to denote the augmented version of that table, not table SP itself, and such syntactic trickery (punning on table names) doesn't seem to be a very sound basis on which to construct a formal language.

A rather more serious criticism is this. First, I hope we can all agree that regardless of the sequence in which the individual clauses of the overall expression are conceptually executed, the system must surely execute each one in its entirety before moving on to the next—for otherwise how can the semantics of individual clauses be defined?[6] Yet the sequence in the example has to be as follows:

---

[6] Actually SQL violates this requirement anyway (I mean, quite apart from outer join considerations). To be specific, the precise meanings in general of the SELECT, GROUP BY, and HAVING clauses aren't (as they ought to be) "context free" but are instead highly dependent on one another. In other words, those clauses aren't *orthogonal*. For a full account of this sorry state of affairs, see reference [6].

1. Augment table SP (to form "SP+")   (OUTER in FROM clause)
2. Form product S TIMES SP+   (FROM clause)
3. Apply join condition   (WHERE clause)
4. Apply "complex" restrictions   (FROM clause)

In fact, if the WHERE clause includes any "local" restrictions (such as SP.QTY < 1000) that apply to just one of the tables in the FROM clause, those local restrictions must presumably be applied either before Step 1 or after Step 4 in the foregoing sequence. Assuming for the sake of discussion that it's before Step 1—I don't know what Informix actually does—the overall execution sequence thus has to be:

1. Execute WHERE clause   (certain portions)
2. Execute FROM clause   (certain portions)
3. Execute WHERE clause   (remaining portions)
4. Execute FROM clause   (remaining portions)

And even if I have the sequence here wrong, the question remains: How can we express any other sequence? To repeat (or paraphrase) some of the criticisms I leveled at Sybase earlier: This technique definitely won't handle the general case, nor is it easy to state exactly which cases it will handle. (Like Sybase, Informix supports left and right outer equijoins, but not the full outer equijoin—at least one table in the FROM clause must be free of that OUTER qualification.) And as I've already indicated, it's difficult (to say the least) to explain the overall operation to the user. (Reference [10] says: "The table which is marked by OUTER ... will supply values ... where there are values in the table which match the values in the [other] table, and otherwise will supply nulls." This isn't an explanation, in my opinion. In fact, I defy anyone to produce a complete, precise, coherent, context free explanation of the semantics of the expression "OUTER T" for arbitrary T.)

I turn my attention now to what Oracle does.[7] Oracle's approach to the outer join problem is a kind of hybrid of Chamberlin's approach and the Informix approach. It resembles Chamberlin's approach inasmuch as it also involves flagging tables to be "augmented" by means of a plus sign; it resembles the Informix approach inasmuch as it applies the necessary restrictions automatically

---

[7] Another product, SQLBase, includes outer join support that seems to be identical to that of Oracle, as near as I can tell. For simplicity I'll limit my attention to Oracle in what follows.

and implicitly. *Note:* The plus signs are actually specified in the WHERE clause, not the FROM clause, but this is nothing but a solecism; it's the FROM clause, not the WHERE clause, whose semantics are affected by those plus signs. (I remark in passing though that this syntactic irregularity raises an additional problem of its own, which I'll discuss in just a moment.)

Here then is Oracle's version of the outer join of Fig. 1c:

```
SELECT  S.SNO , S.SNAME , S.STATUS , S.SCITY ,
                                     SP.PNO , SP.QTY
FROM    S , SP
WHERE   S.SNO = SP.SNO (+)
```

All of the Informix criticisms apply here also, mutatis mutandis, except perhaps for the criticism regarding the punning use of table names:

■ First, the result includes rows for which the condition in the WHERE clause doesn't evaluate to *true*.

■ Second, it's virtually impossible to explain exactly how query expressions are evaluated—in particular, the sequence of evaluation of the FROM and WHERE clauses is very unclear. (Reference [11] says: "Extra null columns will be created for the table with the (+) outer join operator and joined against all rows from the other table that would not have been returned in a normal join." This is not an explanation, in my opinion.)

■ Third, whatever the sequence of evaluation actually is, there's no way to specify any different sequence.

■ Fourth, the syntax definitely won't handle the completely general case, nor is it easy to state exactly which cases it will handle. (Like Sybase and Informix, Oracle definitely doesn't support the full outer equijoin.)

■ Finally, I defy anyone to produce a complete, precise, coherent, context free explanation of the semantics of the expression T.C(+) for arbitrary T and C.

In addition to all of the foregoing defects, Oracle suffers from additional problems of its own, caused by the fact that the plus signs are specified in the WHERE clause and not the FROM clause, where they more logically belong. As a consequence of this fact, it's possible to include both "plussed" and "nonplussed" references to the same table in the same WHERE clause. Some examples:

```
SELECT  S.SNO , S.SNAME , S.STATUS , S.SCITY ,
                                     SP.PNO , SP.QTY
FROM    S , SP
WHERE   S.SNO = SP.SNO (+)
AND     S.SNO < SP.SNO

SELECT  S.SNO , S.SNAME , S.STATUS , S.SCITY ,
                                     SP.PNO , SP.QTY
FROM    S , SP
WHERE   S.SNO = SP.SNO (+)
OR      SP.QTY < 1000

SELECT  S.SNO , S.SNAME , S.STATUS , S.SCITY ,
                                     SP.PNO , SP.QTY
FROM    S , SP
WHERE   S.SNO = SP.SNO (+)
AND     S.STATUS = SP.QTY
```

I have no idea what such examples will produce.

WHY WE CAN'T JUST EXTEND THE FROM CLAUSE (2)

The technique of flagging tables in the FROM clause and specifying the join condition in the WHERE clause as if it were a regular inner join (as in Informix and—more or less—in Oracle) suffers from yet another serious problem, thanks to Nasty Property No. 3 (viz., that $A \leq B$ and $A < B$ OR $A = B$ aren't equivalent, in the context of outer join). Consider the following two expressions (using, purely for definiteness, Informix-style syntax):

```
SELECT  S.SNO , S.SNAME , S.STATUS , S.SCITY ,
                              SP.SNO , SP.PNO , SP.QTY
FROM    S , OUTER SP
WHERE   S.SNO <= SP.SNO

SELECT  S.SNO , S.SNAME , S.STATUS , S.SCITY ,
                              SP.SNO , SP.PNO , SP.QTY
FROM    S , OUTER SP
WHERE   S.SNO < SP.SNO
OR      S.SNO = SP.SNO
```

Given the sample data of Fig. 1a, the first of these expressions produces a result that happens to be identical to the outer equijoin of Fig. 2b (apart from a certain nontrivial difference in column naming, which I'll leave as an exercise for you to think about). The second, however, is equivalent to the following:[8]

```
SELECT  S.SNO , S.SNAME , S.STATUS , S.SCITY ,
                                    SP.SNO , SP.PNO , SP.QTY
FROM    S , OUTER SP
WHERE   S.SNO < SP.SNO
UNION
SELECT  S.SNO , S.SNAME , S.STATUS , S.SCITY ,
                                    SP.SNO , SP.PNO , SP.QTY
FROM    S , OUTER SP
WHERE   S.SNO = SP.SNO
```

In other words, the second expression produces a result that's the union of (a) the result produced by the first expression and (b) the left outer "less than"-join of the two tables. In general, therefore, the results produced by the two expressions are certainly not the same. (Given the sample data of Fig. 1a, the "union" result includes an additional row, a row in which the supplier SNO is S2 and the shipment SNO is null.)

So we see that the user has to wrestle here with a rather counterintuitive idea. The basic problem (loosely speaking) is that the union of the outer "less than"-join and the outer "equals"-join (i.e., equijoin) isn't equivalent to the outer "less than or equals"-join (nor is there any reason why it should be), but the Informix-style syntax suggests rather strongly that it is. (Perhaps I should add that the equvalence *is* valid if "outer" is replaced by "inner" throughout; i.e., the union of the inner "less than" and "equals" joins *is* identical to the inner "less than or equals" join. This state of affairs probably serves only to compound the confusion.)

I remark in passing that the foregoing discussion ought to apply to Oracle as well as to Informix, but doesn't! That is, Oracle effectively, though incorrectly, replaces $A < B$ OR $A = B$ by $A \leq B$ in this context.

Yet another criticism applies to the approach under discussion (i.e., flagging tables in the FROM clause and specifying the join condition in the WHERE clause). This one arises from Nasty Property No. 4: The comparison operators aren't transitive. This property is a consequence of the fact that we're dealing with three-valued logic (3VL). For example, using IF ... THEN ... to denote logical implication, the following—

---

[8] At least, it should be! I haven't been able to test the example on an actual Informix system.

```
IF ( A = B AND B = C ) THEN ( A = C )
```

(which of course is valid in conventional two-valued logic, 2VL)—is *not* valid in 3VL. For instance, if A is 1 and B is null and C is 2, then (A = B) AND (B = C) is *unknown*, but (A = C) is *false*. Furthermore, analogous remarks apply if we replace "=" by "<" throughout, or by ">" throughout, or if we leave the first "=" alone but replace the other two by ">" (etc., etc.).

Such considerations become particularly relevant when we consider outer joins of more than two tables. In reference [3], I considered the case of three tables, as follows:

```
S ( SNO , SCITY )
P ( PNO , PCITY )
J ( JNO , JCITY )
```

(S is suppliers, P is parts, and J is projects). By examining a set of sample values, I showed that the natural language expression "the outer equijoin of S, P, and J on SCITY, PCITY, and JCITY" wasn't well defined. In fact, there are at least three such outer equijoins, corresponding to the three distinct join conditions

```
SCITY = PCITY AND SCITY = JCITY
SCITY = PCITY AND PCITY = JCITY
SCITY = JCITY AND PCITY = JCITY
```

(Of course, these three conditions are all equivalent in 2VL, but not in 3VL.) So if you're using a product that "supports" outer joins by simply flagging tables in the FROM clause and specifying the join condition in the WHERE clause, then you're going to have to exercise considerable caution in order to be sure you're specifying the outer join you actually want.

HOW ABOUT A NEW CLAUSE?

By now I hope you're convinced that no "simple" extension to the FROM or WHERE clause can handle outer joins satisfactorily. So how about introducing some entirely new clause? In reference [3], I proposed a new PRESERVE clause (belonging both syntactically and semantically after the WHERE clause), whose effect was to "preserve" rows from the table(s) named in that clause that didn't—

the rows, that is—otherwise contribute to the result of evaluating the preceding FROM and WHERE clauses. A version of PRESERVE was implemented in the product CA-DB (previously known variously as Enterprise:DB, IDMS/SQL, and StellaR/DB), from Computer Associates. Here's a CA-DB version of our running example (left outer natural join of S with SP on supplier numbers):

```
SELECT    S.SNO , S.SNAME , S.STATUS , S.SCITY ,
                                       SP.PNO , SP.QTY
FROM      S , SP
WHERE     S.SNO = SP.SNO
PRESERVE S
```

PRESERVE as defined in reference [3] was sufficient to deal correctly with left, right, and full outer θ-joins of exactly two tables. (Note, however, that the CA-DB implementation supports left and right outer θ-joins only, because it allows only one table to be named in the PRESERVE clause.) To deal with more than two tables, reference [3] also proposed the ability to include nested table expressions in the FROM clause, together with the addition of a column renaming operator.[9] Taken together, these facilities would be sufficient to deal with completely general outer θ-joins in a clean and systematic manner (and hence the CA-DB support is at least upward compatible with such a clean and systematic implementation). However, the PRESERVE clause as such still doesn't provide a particularly elegant solution to the outer *natural* join problem,[10] thanks to Nasty Property No. 5, as we'll see in the section immediately following.

SO WHAT ABOUT OUTER NATURAL JOIN?

Unfortunately, none of the approaches discussed so far is completely adequate to deal with the problem of outer natural join—"unfortunately," because outer natural join, like its inner counterpart, is probably the most important case in practice. And the problem is Nasty Property No. 5: viz., that outer natural join isn't a projection of outer equijoin. As a consequence, any language that's based, as SQL is, on taking projections—recall that the SQL SELECT clause

---

[9] Of course, these latter features are needed anyway for reasons having nothing to do with outer join as such, and they've now been incorporated, albeit not very elegantly, into the SQL standard. But that didn't happen until well after the original version of this chapter was first written.

[10] Despite the fact that the CA-DB example shown above does happen to produce an outer natural join.

corresponds to relational projection, loosely speaking—is going to be awkward to extend to support outer natural join. Take a look at Fig. 3 below.

a.　S

SNO	SNAME	STATUS	SCITY
S2	Jones	10	Paris
S5	Adams	30	Athens

SP

SNO	PNO	QTY
S2	P1	300
S6	P2	400

b.　Full outer equijoin of S and SP (on SNO)

SSNO	SNAME	STATUS	SCITY	SPSNO	PNO	QTY
S2	Jones	10	Paris	S2	P1	300
S5	Adams	30	Athens	??	??	???
??	?????	??	??????	S6	P2	400

c.　Full outer natural join of S and SP (on SNO)

SNO	SNAME	STATUS	SCITY	PNO	QTY
S2	Jones	10	Paris	P1	300
S5	Adams	30	Athens	??	???
S6	?????	??	??????	P2	400

Fig. 3: Illustration of Nasty Property No. 5

Explanation: The figure is basically a revised version of Fig. 1, but now I'm assuming for the sake of the example that SNO in table SP isn't a foreign key after all, and so it's possible for a supplier number to appear in table SP that doesn't appear in table S. Part a. of the figure gives a slightly revised set of sample values for the tables (I've changed S2 to S6 in one row of SP); part b. shows the full outer equijoin of the two tables on supplier numbers;[11] and part c. shows the corresponding full outer natural join. Observe in particular that the table in part c. isn't a projection of the one in part b.

Here now is one possible way to formulate a query that will yield the outer natural join of Fig. 3c:

---

[11] As you can see, I've named the two supplier number columns in the result SSNO and SPSNO, respectively, in order to avoid a naming ambiguity that would otherwise occur.

```
SELECT     COALESCE ( S.SNO , SP.SNO ) AS SNO ,
           S.SNAME , S.STATUS , S.SCITY , SP.PNO , SP.QTY
FROM       S , SP
WHERE      S.SNO = SP.SNO
PRESERVE S , SP
```

Explanation: First, the FROM, WHERE, and PRESERVE clauses together construct the outer *equi*join shown in Fig. 3b; the SELECT clause then derives the outer natural join. The element COALESCE (S.SNO, SP.SNO) AS SNO in the SELECT clause is interpreted as follows: First, the COALESCE operator (originally introduced in reference [3]) returns a value equal to the value of its first nonnull argument, or null if both arguments are null; then the specification AS SNO assigns the name SNO to the resulting column.

So it's at least possible to use PRESERVE, plus certain related mechanisms, to formulate an outer natural join. But such formulations are hardly very succinct, and it's unfortunate, to say the least, that such a commonly required operator should be so cumbersome to express.[12] Of course, analogous remarks apply to inner joins in SQL also; in fact, as I've remarked elsewhere, the real reason SQL is so hard to extend to support outer join is that it doesn't directly support inner join, but uses that "projection of a restriction of a product" circumlocution instead.

Which brings me, finally, to my preferred solution to this problem: Extend SQL to provide direct ("one liner") support for inner join first; extending it to support outer join will then be straightforward. I first proposed such an approach in reference [3], and I'm glad to report that the SQL standard does now support it, more or less [8]. Here's an SQL formulation of the outer natural join of Fig. 3c using features of the standard:

```
SELECT *
FROM   S NATURAL FULL OUTER JOIN SP
```

Not quite as elegant as S OUTER JOIN SP, perhaps, but a considerable improvement on most of what we've seen previously in this chapter.

Mind you, we're still not quite out of the woods yet, thanks to Nasty Property No. 6: Outer natural join (full outer natural join, that is) isn't associative.[13] For brevity, let's agree to use the keywords OUTER JOIN to mean

---

[12] If it truly is "commonly required," I suppose I should add—which as I keep saying is something I'm far from convinced about.

[13] By contrast, inner natural join is; that is, the expressions (A JOIN B) JOIN C and A JOIN (B JOIN C), where the keyword JOIN represents inner natural join (on common columns, by definition) *are* equivalent.

full outer natural join specifically, and consider the example shown in Fig. 4. Part a. of that figure shows three sample tables A, B, and C, and parts b. and c. show the tables resulting from evaluation of the expressions (A OUTER JOIN B) OUTER JOIN C and A OUTER JOIN (B OUTER JOIN C), respectively. Those two result tables are clearly not the same.

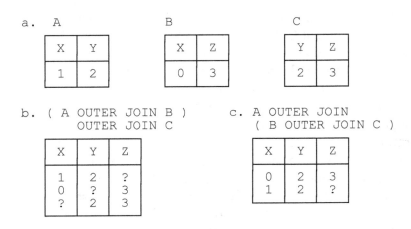

Fig. 4: Nasty Property No. 6 (example)

Of course, Nasty Property No. 6 has implications for such matters as language design, transformation of expressions, and optimizability. *Note:* On the other hand, it is at least true (as is shown in reference [3]) that in the special case where tables A, B, and C have just one common column, then the expressions (A OUTER JOIN B) OUTER JOIN C and A OUTER JOIN (B OUTER JOIN C) are equivalent after all.

DO WE REALLY WANT OUTER JOIN?

I come now to the point that I touched on very briefly near the beginning of this chapter: *Is outer join really the right operator anyway?* In my opinion, "outer join," as that operator is usually understood, is really much too simplistic, because of the well known "nulls interpretation" problem [7]. The basic point is this: There are many possible reasons for generating nulls in the result of an outer join; hence, generating just a single kind of null ("value unknown") in every case is clearly not the right thing to do. Let me illustrate. Suppose we're given the following tables:

```
EMP  ( EMPNO , DEPTNO , SALARY )
DEPT ( DEPTNO , BUDGET )
PGMR ( EMPNO , LANG )
```

PGMR ("programmer") is intended to represent employees who are programmers (if employee *e* is a programmer, then *e* will be represented in both the EMP and PGMR tables). All other aspects of the three tables are meant to be self-explanatory.

Now let's consider some possible outer joins involving these three tables:

1. The left outer natural join of EMP with PGMR on EMPNO will generate null LANG values for any employee who isn't a programmer. Those nulls should clearly be of the "value not applicable" variety.

2. The left outer natural join of DEPT with EMP on DEPTNO will generate null EMPNO and SALARY values for any department with no employees. The EMPNO nulls are clearly of the "value doesn't exist" variety. The SALARY nulls also mean "value doesn't exist," but they're at least arguably different from the EMPNO nulls, because such a SALARY value fails to exist solely and precisely because no corresponding employee exists.

3. The left outer natural join of EMP with DEPT on DEPTNO will generate null DEPTNO and BUDGET values for any employee with an unknown department. The DEPTNO nulls are thus clearly of the "value unknown" variety. The BUDGET nulls also mean "value unknown," but they're at least arguably different from the DEPTNO nulls, because such a BUDGET value is unknown solely and precisely because the corresponding department is unknown.

4. Suppose EMP.DEPTNO isn't a foreign key, and there exists at least one employee with a DEPTNO value that doesn't appear in table DEPT. Then the left outer natural join of EMP with DEPT on DEPTNO will generate a null BUDGET value for any such employee, but such a null seems to me to be different in kind yet again; it doesn't have the same meaning as any of the nulls mentioned in paragraphs 1, 2, and 3 above.

So suppose we now construct "the" (or "a"?) full outer natural join of EMP and DEPT and PGMR. What kinds of nulls should be generated? It looks to me as if the user is going to need to be able to ask for distinct kinds of nulls to be generated on an individual column by column basis. It's even conceivable that different kinds of nulls might need to be generated in the same column in different rows; suppose, for example, that some employees have an unknown department, others have a department that isn't represented in the DEPT table, and still others have no department at all. What kinds of nulls should be generated for the BUDGET column?

DO WE REALLY WANT NULLS AT ALL?

This is clearly the appropriate place to repeat my conviction that "nulls" per se—meaning the nulls of three- or higher-valued logic—aren't what we want anyway [7]. I'd greatly prefer a DBMS that provides a (systematic) "default values" mechanism as sketched in references [4] and [7], and a version of outer join that generated default values instead of nulls. (All discussions in previous sections of this chapter should thus be reinterpreted accordingly!) Reference [2] contains a specific proposal for such an outer join that supports only certain many to one left (or right) outer natural joins. In terms of the example of the previous section, it would support Cases 1 (EMP with PGMR), 3 (EMP with DEPT), and 4 (likewise), but not Case 2 (DEPT with EMP). It would also not support our running example (left outer natural join of S with SP). I refer you to the paper for specific details of the proposal, also for a detailed justification of the apparent limitations. However, I'll give part of that justification here in order to allay (perhaps, and only somewhat) any curiosity you might have in that connection.

The basic point is that outer join isn't a good model to follow for certain real world situations anyway. To return to Case 2 for a moment (left outer natural join of DEPT with EMP on DEPTNO): As indicated in the previous section, this outer join should generate "value doesn't exist" nulls for EMPNO and SALARY for departments with no employees. Note, therefore, that if the result contains n rows for department d, it means that department d has n employees—unless n is one, in which case it means *either* that department d has one employee *or* that it has no employees at all!

Let's examine this example a little more carefully. In general, a table of p columns can be thought of as representing a certain p-place *predicate*, or in other words a certain truth valued function with p parameters. Moreover, the rows of that table can be thought of as *propositions*, or in other words assertions to the effect that substituting certain arguments—viz., the pertinent column values—for the parameters make the predicate evaluate to *true*. For example, the appearance of the row (E1,D1,50K) in the EMP table is an assertion that the predicate or truth valued function EMP (EMPNO, DEPTNO, SALARY) evaluates to *true* for the arguments EMPNO = E1, DEPTNO = D1, and SALARY = 50K. More generally, the row (*e,d,s*) appears in the EMP table if and only if *e* is the employee number of some employee who works in department *d* and earns salary *s*; this is the *criterion for membership* for a given row to appear in the EMP table. It's what the EMP table "means."

What then is the "meaning" of the table produced by the outer join of Case 2 (left outer natural join of DEPT with EMP on DEPTNO)? The columns of that table are DEPTNO, BUDGET, EMPNO, and SALARY. What is the criterion of membership in this table for some candidate row (*d,b,e,s*)? It has to be something like the following:

> There exists some department with department number *d* and budget *b*, and *either* (a) *e* is the employee number of some employee who works in that department and *s* is that employee's salary, *or* (b) that department has no employees at all and *e* is null and *s* is null.

This criterion of membership is not only difficult to state, it's quite difficult to understand as well. And any misunderstanding is likely to lead to incorrect query formulations and wrong answers out of the database. As a trivial example, consider the difficulty already touched on above that arises in connection with counting the number of employees in each department.

For reasons such as the foregoing, I think it's worth exploring alternative approaches to the problem that outer join is supposed to solve, but doesn't. In this connection, there's just one point I'd like to mention here: namely, that *outer join as usually understood would be completely unnecessary if relation valued attributes were supported* (which I think they should be anyway, for other reasons). See reference [5] for a detailed examination of this issue.

ACKNOWLEDGMENTS

I'd like to thank Hugh Darwen, Nat Goodman, and Adrian Larner for numerous helpful discussions, and Hugh Darwen, Nat Goodman, and Colin White for their careful reviews of earlier drafts of this chapter. I'd also like to thank the following for helping me with information regarding the indicated DBMS products: Valerie Anderson (Sybase); Ron Landers (CA-Universe); David McGoveran (CA-DB and NonStop SQL); and Colin White (Oracle, ShareBase, and SQLBase).

REFERENCES

1. Donald D. Chamberlin: "A Summary of User Experience with the SQL Data Sublanguage," Proc. International Conference on Databases, Aberdeen, Scotland, July 1980.

2. Hugh Darwen: "Outer Join with No Nulls and Fewer Tears," in C. J. Date, *Relational Database Writings 1989-1991* (Addison-Wesley, 1992).

3. C. J. Date: "The Outer Join," in C. J. Date, *Relational Database: Selected Writings* (Addison-Wesley, 1986).

4. C. J. Date: "Null Values in Database Management," in C. J. Date, *Relational Database: Selected Writings* (Addison-Wesley, 1986). See also reference [7].

5. C. J. Date: "What First Normal Form Really Means," in C. J. Date, *Date on Database: Writings 2000-2006* (Apress, 2006).

6. C. J. Date: "Some SQL Criticisms," in *Fifty Years of Relational, and Other Database Writing: More Thoughts and Essays on Database Matters* (Technics Publications, 2020).

7. C. J. Date: "NOT Is Not 'Not'!" (in two parts), Chapters 12 and 13 of the present book.

8. C. J. Date and Hugh Darwen: *A Guide to the SQL Standard*, 4th edition (Addison-Wesley, 1997).

9. Sandra L. Emerson, Marcy Darnovsky, and Judith S. Bowman: *The Practical SQL Handbook: Using Structured Query Language* (Addison-Wesley, 1989).

10. Jonathan Leffler: *Using Informix-SQL* (Addison-Wesley, 1989).

11. Oracle Corporation: *SQL Language Reference Manual* (Oracle RDBMS Version 6.0 with the Transaction Processing Subsystem), Oracle Part No. 778-V6.0 (October 1988).

Chapter 7

Some Principles of

Good Language Design

The purpose of this short chapter is simply to pull together a list of language design principles in order to serve as a reference for, specifically, database language designers (and any others who might be interested, of course). The list isn't taken from any one place but rather is culled from a variety of sources, including computer science folklore and "conventional wisdom."
Publishing history: This is a heavily revised version of, and supersedes, a paper that first appeared in ACM SIGMOD Record 14, No. 3 (November 1984) and was later republished in my book Relational Database: Selected Writings (Addison-Wesley, 1986). This version copyright © C. J. Date 2022.

I'll begin with a position statement. It's my opinion that:

1. Database languages (also known, not very appropriately, as "query languages") are nothing but special purpose programming languages.

2. Therefore the same design principles apply.

3. There are well established (though not always well documented) principles for the design of programming languages in general.

4. There's little evidence that database languages in particular (including SQL, I'm sorry to say) were designed in accordance with any such principles.

As noted in the preamble, therefore, my aim in what follows is to pull together a list of such principles, to serve as a reference for database language designers in particular and any others who might be interested.

One general point that I think is worth stating at the outset is the following (from reference [11], lightly edited here):

> Most languages are too big and intellectually unmanageable. The problems arise in part because the language is too restrictive; the number of rules needed to define a language increases when a general rule has additional rules attached to constrain its use in certain cases. (Ironically, these additional rules usually make the language *less* powerful.) ... *Power through simplicity, simplicity through generality, should be the guiding principle.*

ORTHOGONALITY

The guiding principle espoused in the foregoing quote is usually referred to in language design circles as *the principle of orthogonality*—where the term *orthogonality* denotes what might better be called "concept independence," meaning distinct concepts should always be cleanly separated and never bundled together. To amplify:

■ An example of orthogonality is provided in the language PL/I by the rule that says that wherever a scalar value is required, then that scalar value can be specified by means of an arbitrarily complex scalar expression (of the appropriate type, of course). One consequence of this rule is that scalar expressions can be nested to any depth. Thus, for example, the subscript in a subscripted variable reference can consist of an arbitrarily complex expression—it can even contain further subscripted variable references— just so long as the expression in question is integer valued. Here are a couple of examples to illustrate this particular point:[1]

```
A [ ROUND ( ( X + Y ) / 2 ) ]
A [ Q [ I ] - 1 ]
```

---

[1] Note, however, that PL/I uses parentheses to enclose subscripts, not brackets as in these examples.

By contrast, a rule to the effect that subscripts must be specified by integer literals or simple integer variable references would be a clear violation of the orthogonality principle.

■ A good example of lack of orthogonality is the "owner coupled set" construct of DBTG [3]. (I deliberately use the term "owner coupled set"—introduced by Codd in reference [1]—rather than the official DBTG term "set," simply in order to make it very clear that the construct in question isn't a set in the mathematical sense.) The owner coupled set construct bundles together at least three different concepts and arguably as many as six: viz., (a) a relationship between an owner record and a set of member records; (b) a relationship among a set of member records; (c) certain integrity rules; (d) a set of access paths; (e) a scope for concurrency control purposes; and (f) a scope for authorization purposes. As a result, it might be impossible to drop an owner coupled set that was originally introduced purely for integrity reasons but is no longer needed for that purpose, because some program might now be using it as an access path. This example is just one of the many kinds of problems that lack of orthogonality can lead to.

The advantage of orthogonality is that it leads to *a coherent language.* What do I mean by "a coherent language"? I mean a language that displays, in both its syntax and its semantics, a simple, clean, and consistent structure, one that's easy for users to grasp. If a language is coherent in this sense, users will be able (perhaps without realizing the fact) to build a simple mental model of its behavior, from which they can make extrapolations and predictions with confidence. There won't be any exceptions or unpleasant surprises. In a nutshell: The manuals will be thinner, and the training courses will be shorter. As reference [14] puts it (possibly a little tongue in cheek):

> Orthogonal design maximizes expressive power while avoiding deleterious superfluities [*slightly edited*].

A number of related points arise from the notion of orthogonality:

1. *Small number of concepts*: The number of concepts should be small (though not necessarily minimal), in order that the language might be easy to describe, teach, learn, implement, and use. *Note:* As an example of the distinction between "small" and "minimal," consider the operators of

ordinary arithmetic. Given the operators "infix plus," "prefix minus," and "reciprocal," the operators "infix minus," "times," and "divide by" are all strictly speaking unnecessary—but we wouldn't think much of a language that excluded them.

As another example of the same distinction, more directly relevant to database languages per se, consider the natural join operator of relational algebra. Natural join isn't primitive[2] (it's equivalent to a projection of a restriction of a product), and so it might legitimately be excluded from a minimal set of relational operators. For that reason, in fact, it was indeed excluded from the earliest versions of SQL, including the first two versions of the SQL standard in particular [10]. However, it's of such overwhelming practical—not to mention theoretical—utility that a strong case can be made for supporting it directly (which presumably accounts for the fact that SQL does now support it directly, albeit belatedly).

2. *Syntactic consistency*: A given syntactic construct should have the same semantics everywhere it appears. *Counterexample*: Consider the following two DBTG FIND statements:

```
FIND EMP WITHIN DEPT-EMP USING SALARY

FIND DUPLICATE EMP USING SALARY
```

In the first of these statements, "USING SALARY" refers to the SALARY field in the User Work Area; in the second, it refers to the SALARY field in the current EMP record. Error potential is high.

3. *Syntactic consistency bis*: A given semantic construct should have the same syntax everywhere it appears. *Counterexamples*: (a) In SQL, the SALARY field of the EMP table is referred to as EMP.SALARY in some contexts, as SALARY FROM EMP in others, and as EMP (SALARY) in still others; (b) in SQL again, rows of tables are designated as "*" in SELECT and COUNT but as blank in INSERT and DELETE (e.g., why is the syntax not DELETE * FROM *T* ?).

---

[2] At least, it's possible to define a set of primitives for the algebra that doesn't include it; one such set consists of the operators product, union, difference, restrict, and project. However, my own preference would be to define product in terms of natural join instead of the other way around, in which case natural join would be a primitive after all.

4. *Statement atomicity*: Statements should be either executed or not—there should be no halfway house (i.e., it shouldn't be possible for a statement to fail in the middle and leave the database or other variables in an undefined state). *Counterexamples*: In SQL—at least, SQL as implemented in the IBM product SQL/DS at the time the first version of this chapter was written—the set level INSERT, DELETE, and UPDATE statements aren't atomic in the foregoing sense.

5. *Symmetry*: To quote Polya [12], albeit writing in a different context:

> Try to treat symmetrically what is symmetrical, and do not destroy wantonly any natural symmetry.

Counterexamples: In SQL, (a) a GRANT of UPDATE authority can be column specific but the corresponding REVOKE can't, and neither can a GRANT of SELECT authority; (b) in a table that permits duplicate rows, the INSERT and DELETE operations aren't inverses of each other.

The following rule is another aspect of symmetry: Default assumptions should always be explicitly specifiable. *Counterexample*: In SQL, "nulls not allowed" can be explicitly specified (via the NOT NULL clause), but "nulls allowed" (the default) can't be. It's difficult even to talk about a linguistic construct if there's no explicit syntax for it.

6. *No arbitrary restrictions*: While it's understood that the implementer might have to impose implementation-specific restrictions for a variety of pragmatic reasons, such restrictions shouldn't be built into the fabric of the language. *Counterexamples*: DBTG doesn't allow the owner and member records in an owner coupled set to be of the same type; DL/I supports exactly ten distinct "lock classes" A, B, ..., J; the keyword DISTINCT can appear at most once in an SQL SELECT statement.[3]

7. *No side effects*: No amplification necessary. *Major counterexample*: Currency indicators in the DBTG data manipulation language (which in fact constitute the absolute linchpin of that language!).

---

[3] This observation regarding SQL was true when first written but is so no longer.

8. *Expressions recursively defined*: "Recursively defined" here doesn't mean the language should support recursion per se (it might or it might not)—it merely means there should be no artificial restrictions on the nesting of expressions. (I touched on this point earlier, but it bears repetition.) *Counterexamples*: In SQL, (a) the argument to an aggregate operator invocation can't itself be another aggregate operator invocation, and so for example it's impossible to write an SQL expression to compute the sum of a set of averages; (b) a subquery can't involve a union[4] (and this state of affairs has numerous repercussions, beyond the scope of this short chapter).

LANGUAGE DEFINITION

The language should possess a rigorous formal definition that's independent of any particular implementation. The purposes of such a definition include the following:

1. To provide precise, definitive answers to technical questions, and hence to act as the arbiter in disputes

2. To prevent—or attempt to prevent, at any rate—the possibility of divergent and incompatible implementations

3. Generally to serve as *the* reference source for users, manual writers, teachers, implementers, and anyone else concerned with the details of the language at any time

Counterexamples: Just about every database language in existence at the time this chapter was first written! In strong contrast to most of those languages, SQL does have a formal definition, viz., the SQL standard [10]; unfortunately, however, that definition wasn't produced until well after the first few SQL implementations had been done, and to say the least it leaves a lot to be desired. In my opinion, many of the problems with SQL today could and would have been avoided if only a formal and precise definition had been produced first.[5]

---

[4] The previous footnote applies here also.

[5] In fact, I believe the standard itself would have been far less of a mess than it actually is if it had been defined first. As it is, it's the horrendous mess it is (at least in part) precisely because it had to start out by reflecting what had already been implemented, in all of its gory detail.

EXPRESSIONS

The kinds of data objects supported by a given language typically fall into a natural hierarchy (or set of hierarchies).[6] For example, SQL supports tables, rows, and scalars, and these various kinds of objects can be hierarchically ordered as indicated in the following diagram:

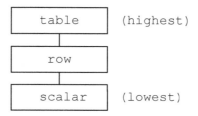

Now, completeness dictates that for each kind of object it supports, a language should provide at least all of the following:

■ An operator for selecting a particular object of the given kind by specifying values for objects of the next lower kind in the hierarchy

   Examples: It should be possible to select a particular table—meaning, more precisely, a particular table *value*—by specifying the pertinent set of rows, where the rows in question are specified in turn by means of row expressions. Likewise, it should be possible to select a particular row—i.e., a particular row value—by specifying the pertinent set of component (column) values, where the component values in question are specified in turn by means of appropriate expressions.

■ An operator for extracting the values of component objects of the next lower kind from an object of the given kind

---

[6] My use of the term *object* here and elsewhere in this chapter is not intended to refer to objects in the OO sense (whatever that sense might be, I'm tempted to add).

Examples: It should be possible to extract the value of a given row from a given table value, and the value of a given column component from a given row value.

- Operators for comparing objects of the given kind—certainly to test for equality, and possibly to test for comparative rank according to some defined ordering

  Examples: It should be possible to test (a) whether two tables *A* and *B* are equal and (b) whether one table *A* is a "subtable" of another table *B*, in the sense that every row of *A* is also a row of *B*.

- A means for assigning a value of the given kind to a variable of the same kind

  Example: It should be possible to assign a given table value (denoted by some table expression) to a given table variable.

- A general, recursively defined syntax for expressions representing values of the given kind that exploits to the full any closure properties that might apply

  Example: If "+" is an operator that applies to numbers, then the operands to an invocation of that operator should be specifiable by means of numeric expressions of (in turn) arbitrary complexity.

It is instructive to examine a language such as SQL to see how and to what extent it meets the foregoing "expressive completeness" requirements.

SYNTACTIC SUBSTITUTION

Note: This section is new—it had no counterpart in the original paper on which the present chapter is based. It consists primarily of a rewrite of a brief discussion that previously appeared in reference [6].

There's one extremely important design principle I haven't mentioned in this chapter so far, and that's *syntactic substitution*. In fact, it's my opinion that syntactic substitution is "the right and proper way" to build a language, be it a database language specifically or any other kind. It works like this. Suppose we're trying to design some new language from scratch. Then the way to go about it is as follows:

- First we need to decide what basic concepts our language needs to support. The concepts in question, or *primitives*, need to be chosen very carefully: Ideally, they should be (a) few in number; (b) mutually independent (i.e., orthogonal), as far as is reasonably possible; (c) agreed upon by all parties concerned; and of course (d) agreeable, not disagreeable, in nature.

  Note: This collection of primitives might reasonably be called a *model*. Certainly the relational model provides an appropriate collection of primitives if the language we're supposed to be defining is a database language specifically.

- Next we need to choose some good syntax for those basic or primitive concepts.

- And now we have a language!—in fact, a *complete* language, in the sense that it supports everything in our model. But if that's it in its entirety (i.e., if that's *all* we have), then our language will probably be quite hard to use; that is, in all but the simplest cases the statements and expressions needed to solve problems will probably be quite difficult or tedious to formulate.

  Example: The only update operator that's included in the relational model as such—in other words, the only updating *primitive*—is relational assignment, which assigns a specified relation value to a specified relation variable, lock, stock, and barrel. However, I for one would certainly prefer not to have to formulate all relational update operations in terms of explicit relational assignment alone.

- So the next step is to define some good syntactic shorthands. The trick here is to recognize commonly occurring patterns—combinations of concepts and/or operations that occur over and over again—and then come up with some well thought out and well defined shorthands for those patterns.

  Examples: In the case of a database language, examples of such shorthands include INSERT, DELETE, and UPDATE; foreign key constraints; the MATCHING and NOT MATCHING operators; image relations; and many, many others. In each of these examples, the syntax commonly used to express them is basically just shorthand for something that provides the same functionality but is typically much more longwinded.

■ Such shorthands obviously save a great deal of writing. More to the point, they effectively *raise the level of abstraction*, by allowing the user to think about those commonly occurring bundles of concepts as single things (a bit like macros in a conventional programming language). What's more, they also offer the chance of improved performance, because they allow the implementation to recognize those bundles of concepts more readily and give them some kind of special-case treatment. And, of course, they can be used as the basis for defining further, still higher level shorthands. In other words, development of the language should proceed where possible by defining new language constructs in terms of ones already defined. That's what syntactic substitution is all about [2].

Example: The language **Tutorial D** [9], by Hugh Darwen and myself, illustrates the foregoing approach very nicely. Certainly it supports the various shorthands already mentioned (INSERT, DELETE, and UPDATE, foreign keys, MATCHING and NOT MATCHING, and image relations), as well as many, many others. As a fairly striking example, reference [5] proposes a new **Tutorial D** operator called IS_NTH_LARGEST, which is defined in terms of another such operator called QUOTA, which is defined in terms of still another such operator called RANK, which is defined in terms of the existing operators EXTEND, RENAME, and restriction. (And as a matter of fact RENAME isn't primitive either, though EXTEND and restriction are.)[7]

MISCELLANEOUS POINTS

I conclude this short chapter by listing some additional design principles and objectives, taken from a variety of sources, with little by way of additional commentary—except to say that, to be honest, I'm not entirely sure myself in one

---

[7] Even this statement isn't entirely true. In our book on *The Third Manifesto* [8], Hugh Darwen and I define a primitive relational algebra we call **A**, consisting of just two operators (one a simplified version of the conventional relational projection operator and the other a relational analog of either of the logical operators NOR and NAND), and we go on to show how all of the operators of the conventional relational algebra—including both EXTEND and restriction in particular—can be defined in terms of those two operators.

or two of the cases mentioned exactly what the writer(s) originally had in mind! Perhaps you can make better sense of those cases than I can.

From the definition of Algol 68 [14]:

- *Security*: The writers elaborate on this point thus: "Most syntactical and many other errors [should be easily detectable] before they lead to calamitous results. Furthermore, the opportunities for making such errors [should be] greatly reduced."

- *Efficiency*: This point includes:

  a. Static type checking

  b. Type-independent parsing

  c. Independent compilation

  d. Loop optimization

  e. Representation (support for a variety of character sets)

From an evaluation of a number of proposals for incorporating database functionality into COBOL [13]: [Any COBOL database language should:]

- Be a natural extension of COBOL

- Be easy to learn

- Conform to a standard

- Support relations, hierarchies, and networks

- Promote quality programming

- Be usable as a query language

- Provide set level access

- Have a stable definition

- Increase programmer productivity

- Be data independent

- Reflect user input in its design

From a proposal of my own for extending the conventional high level ("host") languages to include database functionality [4]:

- [The language] should be designed from the user's point of view rather than the system's.

- It should fit well with the host language. Wherever possible it should exploit existing language features rather than introducing new ones.

- It should transcend and outlive all features of the underlying hardware and software that are specific to those systems.

- It should provide access to as much of the function of the underlying systems as possible without compromising on the first three objectives.

- It should establish a stable long-range design that can be gracefully subset for short-range implementation.

- It should be efficiently implementable.

And last but not least, of course, we mustn't forget the following [7]:

- *The Principle of Cautious Design*: Given a design choice between options *A* and *B*, where *A* is upward compatible with *B* and the full consequences of going with *B* aren't yet known, the cautious decision is to go with *A*.

REFERENCES

1. E. F. Codd: "Interactive Support for Nonprogrammers: The Relational and Network Approaches," Proc. 1974 ACM SIGMOD Workshop on Data Description, Access, and Control, Vol. II, Ann Arbor, Michigan (May 1974). Republished in C. J. Date, *Relational Database: Selected Writings* (Addison-Wesley, 1986). See also the detailed analysis of and commentary on this paper in Chapter 6 of my book *E. F. Codd and Relational Theory, Revised Edition: A Detailed Review and Analysis of Codd's Major Database Writings* (Technics Publications, 2021).

2. Hugh Darwen: "Valid Time and Transaction Time Proposals: Language Design Aspects," in Opher Etzion, Sushil Jajodia, and Suryanaryan Sripada (eds.): *Temporal Databases: Research and Practice* (Springer Verlag, 1998).

3. Data Base Task Group of CODASYL Programming Language Committee: *Report* (April 1971).

4. C. J. Date: "An Introduction to the Unified Database Language (UDL)," Proc. 6th International Conference on Very Large Data Bases, Montreal, Canada (September/October 1980). Republished (in considerably revised form) in C. J. Date, *Relational Database: Selected Writings* (Addison-Wesley, 1986).

5. C. J. Date: "Quota Queries," Chapter 14 of my book *Logic and Relational Theory: Thoughts and Essays on Database Matters* (Technics Publications, 2020).

6. C. J. Date: "Fifty Years of Relational: A Personal View Part II," Chapter 2 of my book *Fifty Years of Relational, and Other Database Writings* (Technics Publications, 2020).

7. C. J. Date: "*The Principle of Cautious Design*," Chapter 2 of the present book.

8. C. J. Date and Hugh Darwen: *Databases, Types, and the Relational Model: The Third Manifesto* (3rd edition). Addison-Wesley (2007). See also the website *www.thethirdmanifesto.com*.

9. C. J. Date and Hugh Darwen: "**Tutorial D**" (standalone version), in *Database Explorations: Essays on The Third Manifesto and Related Topics.* Trafford Publishing (2010). See also the website *www.thethirdmanifesto.com*.

10. International Organization for Standardization (ISO): *Database Language SQL*, Documents ISO/IEC 9075:1987 ("SQL/86"); ISO/IEC 9075:1989 ("SQL/89"); ISO/IEC 9075:1992 ("SQL:1992"); and subsequent versions.

11. R. Morrison: *S-Algol Reference Manual.* Internal Report CSR-80-81, Dept. of Computer Science, University of Edinburgh (February 1981).

12. G. Polya: *How To Solve It* (2nd edition). Princeton University Press (1971).

13. SHARE DBMS Language Task Force: "An Evaluation of Three COBOL Data Base Languages—UDL, SQL, and CODASYL," Proc. SHARE 53 (August 1979).

14. A. van WijnGaarden et al (eds.): *Revised Report on the Algorithmic Language Algol 68.* Springer-Verlag (1976).

Chapter 8

A Critique of SQL/86

Part 1

The name "SQL/86" refers to the first version of the SQL standard, which appeared in 1986 (I don't think it has anything to do with the slang meaning of "86"). SQL/86 was essentially identical in all major respects to the dialect of SQL supported by the System R prototype (developed in IBM Research in the late 1970s). I wrote the paper on which this chapter and the next two are based as a critique of that IBM / System R dialect, in order to draw attention to a series of what seemed to me to be rather major defects in the language (in that dialect of the language, at any rate). My aims were twofold. First, I wanted the database community at large to think very hard about whether SQL was suitable as a basis for a standard at all. Second, if that community decided to standardize on SQL anyway, then at least I wanted the problems I'd identified to be fixed if at all possible, and preferably as soon as possible as well.

Of course I was unsuccessful in those aims—the standardizers essentially took the System R dialect of SQL and elevated it to the status of a standard, warts and all. These chapters are thus possibly only of historical interest. Nevertheless, I think they can still serve a useful purpose, or rather two such purposes. First, although some of my complaints have been addressed in subsequent versions of the standard, many of them haven't[1]—and even when they have, what Hugh Darwen has called "The Shackle of Compatibility" has guaranteed that the fixes have generally left something to be desired, to say the least. As I've had occasion to write elsewhere, languages do live forever, even bad ones—which is why it's so important to get them right first time, of course.

---

[1] I'll leave it as an exercise to determine which have and which haven't.

Second, even where the problems have been fixed, I think it can still be useful to see what those problems were and why those fixes were needed.

Two final preliminary points: First, for obvious reasons, the unqualified name "SQL" should be taken throughout what follows as referring to SQL/86 specifically, unless the context demands otherwise (likewise, unqualified references to "the standard" or "the SQL standard" should also be taken as referring to SQL/86 specifically). Second, both SQL as such and my own critique of it would have been greatly improved if the crucial logical difference between values and variables—between table values and variables in particular—had been recognized and acted upon at the time. But it wasn't. I considered revising the text (with 20:20 hindsight, of course) in order to take that particular logical difference into account, but eventually decided not to (it smacked too much of rewriting history). As a consequence, however, the text does still display a few awkward phrasings, circumlocutions, and imprecisions here and there that might otherwise have been avoided, and for that state of affairs I apologize.

Publishing history: This is a heavily revised version of, and supersedes, a paper that first appeared (along with a companion paper, "Some Principles of Good Language Design," which now forms Chapter 7 of the present book) under the title "A Critique of the SQL Database Language" in ACM SIGMOD Record 14, No. 3 (November 1984) and was later republished in my book Relational Database: Selected Writings (Addison-Wesley, 1986). I've divided this revised version into three parts in order, I hope, to make it a little more digestible. This version (all three parts) copyright © 2022 C. J. Date.

The preamble to the original 1984 version of the paper on which this chapter and the next two are based ran more or less as follows:

The ANSI Database Language Committee X3H2 is currently at work on a proposed standard relational database language, codenamed RDL [14],[2] and it has

---

[2] All references for this chapter and the next two are listed at the end of Chapter 10.

adopted the "Structured Query Language" SQL from IBM as a basis for that activity. Moreover, several other hardware and software vendors in addition to IBM have already released, or at least announced, products that are based to a greater or lesser extent on SQL as defined by IBM. There can thus be little doubt that the importance of that language will increase significantly over the next several years. Yet SQL is very far from perfect. The purpose of this paper is to present a critical analysis of the language's major shortcomings, in the hope that it might be possible to remedy some of the deficiencies before their influence becomes too all pervasive. The paper's standpoint is primarily that of formal computer languages in general, rather than that of database languages specifically.

Now, it did appear back in 1984 that the X3H2 committee was indeed in the process of making a number of improvements to SQL along the lines I was proposing. However, the version of the language that was eventually accepted as a standard failed to include those improvements; in fact, SQL/86 was virtually identical to IBM SQL in all but a few minor respects. The criticisms documented in that 1984 paper thus apply virtually unchanged to that standard version also (i.e., SQL/86).

OVERVIEW

The language SQL (the name was originally pronounced "sequel" but is now—at least officially—pronounced just S-Q-L)[3] was pioneered in the IBM prototype System R [1] and subsequently adopted by IBM and others as the basis for numerous commercial implementations. It represents a major advance over older database languages such as the DL/I language of IMS, or the DML and DDL of the Data Base Task Group (DBTG) of CODASYL; in particular, it's much easier to use than those older languages. As a result, users in an SQL system—both end users and application programmers—can be far more productive than they used to be in those older systems (improvements of up to 20 times have been reported). Among the strongpoints of SQL that have led to such improvements are the following:

■ Simple data structure

---

[3] In fact the IBM version of the language was originally known not as SQL but as SEQUEL, which stood for "Structured *English* Query Language." The name was subsequently changed for legal reasons.

- Powerful operators

- Short initial learning period

- Improved data independence

- Integrated data definition and data manipulation

- Dual mode of use

- Integrated catalog

- Compilation and optimization

However, the language does have its weak points too. In fact, it can't be denied that SQL in its present form leaves rather a lot to be desired—even that, in some important respects, it fails to realize the full potential of the relational model. Thus, the purpose of this critique is to describe and examine some of those weakpoints. It's divided into the following major sections:

- Lack of orthogonality: expressions

- Lack of orthogonality: aggregate operators

- Lack of orthogonality: miscellaneous

- Formal definition

- Mismatch with host languages

- Missing functionality

- Mistakes

- Relational features not supported

Reference [9] gives some background material—specifically, a set of principles that apply to the design of programming languages in general and database languages in particular. The criticisms that follow have been formulated with those principles very much in mind. *Note:* A few of the points I'll be making apply to interactive SQL only and a few to embedded SQL only, but most apply to both. I haven't bothered to spell out the distinctions, since the context makes it clear in every case. Also, the structure of the critique is a little arbitrary, in the sense that it's not always clear which heading a particular point really belongs under. There's also some repetition (I hope not too much), for essentially the same reason.

LACK OF ORTHOGONALITY: EXPRESSIONS

It's convenient to begin by introducing some terminology (terminology of my own, I hasten to add; I think I'm right in saying that none of the terms in question is used in the standard as such—not in the way I'm using them, at any rate):

- A *table expression* is an SQL expression that yields a table—for example, the expression

```
SELECT  *
FROM    EMP
WHERE   DEPTNO = 'D3'
```

- A *row expression* is an SQL expression that yields a row—for example, the expression

```
SELECT  *
FROM    EMP
WHERE   EMPNO = 'E2'
```

Note: It would be more correct to regard the foregoing example as a table expression that just happens to yield a table containing exactly one row. In certain contexts, however (not all!), SQL effectively coerces the table that results from evaluating such an expression to the single row it contains, in which case the table expression in question can be thought of, albeit not entirely logically. as a row expression.

- A *scalar expression* is an SQL expression that yields a scalar value—for example, the expression

```
SELECT AVG ( SALARY )
FROM   EMP
```

Here's another example:

```
SELECT SALARY
FROM   EMP
WHERE  EMPNO = 'E2'
```

Note: It would be more correct to regard each of the foregoing examples as a table expression that just happens to yield a table containing exactly one row and one column. In certain contexts, however (not all!), SQL effectively coerces the table that results from evaluating such an expression to the single value it contains at that row and column intersection, in which case the table expression in question can be thought of, again not entirely logically, as a scalar expression.[4]

Of course, these three kinds of expressions correspond to the three kinds of data objects (tables, rows, scalars) supported by SQL.[5] As pointed out in reference [9], moreover, those three kinds of objects can be hierarchically arranged as follows:

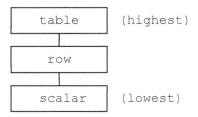

It follows that, as reference [9] also points out, there are five crucial features, or pieces of functionality, that the language needs to provide for each of these three kinds of objects:

---

[4] Two points here: First, note the tacit assumption that the value at a given row and column intersection is always a scalar value specifically. That assumption was valid (at least to a first approximation) in the first few versions of the standard but has since ceased to be so. Second, it would be more correct to describe the coercion involved in examples like the ones shown as a *double* coercion—first (a) the table denoted by the expression in question is coerced to the single row that table contains; and then (b) that row in turn is coerced to the single scalar value that row contains.

[5] To repeat something I said in reference [9], my use of the term *object* here and elsewhere in this chapter is not intended to refer to objects in the OO sense.

1. An operator for selecting a particular object of the given kind by specifying values for objects of the next lower kind in the hierarchy

2. An operator for extracting the values of component objects of the next lower kind in the hierarchy from an object of the given kind

3. Operators for comparing objects of the given kind—certainly to test for equality, and possibly to test for comparative rank according to some defined ordering

4. A means for assigning a value of the given kind to a variable of the same kind

5. A general, recursively defined syntax for expressions representing values of the given kind that exploits to the full any closure properties that might apply

Does SQL measure up to these requirements? Well, no, not entirely; in fact, it hardly does so at all. Here's a brief summary of the situation:

■ *For tables:* 1. No. 2. Yes. 3. No. 4. No explicit table assignment, but INSERT, DELETE, and UPDATE are supported. 5. No (see further discussion below).

■ *For rows:* 1. Only via INSERT and UPDATE (and component values must be specified only by means of literals or host variable references). 2. Yes. 3. No. 4. Same as 1. 5. No.

■ *For scalars:* 1. Not applicable. 2. Not applicable. 3. Yes. 4. Only via INSERT and UPDATE. 5. No.

The foregoing state of affairs, it seems to me, serves among other things to highlight what can happen if a language is designed as unsystematically as SQL seems to have been. I mean, the numerous omissions identified above would surely never have occurred if only the hierarchic structure (tables vs. rows vs. scalars) and those five crucial features, or requirements, had been recognized and acted upon right at the outset. That's what I think, anyway.

Be that as it may, let's now take a closer look at table expressions specifically. SELECT – FROM – WHERE expressions, which—despite the remarks made earlier about those row and scalar expression special cases—can generally be regarded as table expressions, have the following broad structure (simplifying considerably for the purposes of the present discussion):

```
SELECT scalar expression commalist
FROM   table name commalist
WHERE  boolean expression
```

Note in particular that it's specifically table *names* that appear in the FROM clause, not more general table expressions. However, completeness strongly suggests that it should be the latter (as Jim Gray once memorably said to me [12], "anything in computer science that's not recursive is no good"). This isn't just an academic consideration, by the way. On the contrary, there are several practical reasons as to why such recursiveness is desirable:

■ First, consider the relational algebra. Relational algebra possesses the important property of *closure*—that is, relations form a closed system under the operators of the algebra, in the sense that the result of applying any of those operators to any given relation (or relations, plural) is itself another relation. As a consequence, the operands to any given operator aren't constrained to be base relations only, but rather can be any relation that can be derived by evaluating some algebraic expression. Thus, the relational algebra allows the user to write nested relational expressions—and this feature is useful for precisely the same kinds of reasons that nested expressions are useful in ordinary arithmetic.

■ Now consider SQL. SQL does support, at least indirectly, all of the operators of the relational algebra.[6] However, the table expressions of SQL (which are the SQL analog of the expressions of the relational algebra) *can't* be arbitrarily nested. Let's consider the question of exactly which cases of nesting SQL does support. Simplifying matters slightly, an SQL SELECT – FROM – WHERE expression is the SQL analog of a nested algebraic expression of the form

---

[6] But it doesn't support relations of degree zero. See reference [5] for further discussion of some of the logical consequences of this unfortunate omission.

```
projection
   ( restriction
      ( product
         ( table1 , table2 , ... ) ) )
```

The product corresponds to the FROM clause; the restriction corresponds to the WHERE clause; the projection corresponds to the SELECT clause; and *table1*, *table2*, ... are the tables identified in the FROM clause (and note that, as remarked earlier, they must be identified by simple table names, not more general expressions). Likewise, the expression

```
SELECT ... FROM ... WHERE ...
UNION
SELECT ... FROM ... WHERE ...
```

is the SQL analog of the nested algebraic expression

```
union ( tabexp1 , tabexp2 , ... )
```

where *tabexp1*, *tabexp2*, ... are table expressions of the form shown earlier (i.e., projections of restrictions of products of named tables). But it isn't possible to formulate direct SQL equivalents of any other nested algebraic expressions. For example, it isn't possible to write a direct SQL equivalent of the nested expression

```
restriction ( projection ( table ) )
```

Instead, the user has to recast the expression into a semantically equivalent but syntactically different form in which the restriction is applied before the projection:

```
projection ( restriction ( table ) )
```

What this means in practical terms is that the user might have to spend time and effort transforming the "natural" formulation of a given query into some different, and arguably less "natural," representation (see example below). What's more, the user must therefore also understand exactly when such transformations are valid and when they're not. For example, is it intuitively obvious that a projection of a union is always equivalent to the union of two projections? (Is it even true?)

Example: Given the tables

```
NYC ( EMPNO , DEPTNO , SALARY )
SFO ( EMPNO , DEPTNO , SALARY )
```

(representing New York and San Francisco employees, respectively), list EMPNO for all employees. "Natural" formulation (projection of a union):

```
SELECT EMPNO FROM ( NYC UNION SFO )
```

SQL formulation (union of two projections):

```
SELECT EMPNO FROM NYC
UNION
SELECT EMPNO FROM SFO
```

Note that allowing both formulations of the query would enable different users to perceive and express the same problem in different ways. (Of course, both formulations should ideally translate to the same internal representation, for otherwise the choice between the two would no longer be arbitrary.)

■ The foregoing example tacitly makes use of the fact that a simple table reference (i.e., a table name, syntactically speaking) ought to be just a special case of a general table expression (and indeed would be, in a properly designed language). Thus I wrote

```
NYC UNION SFO
```

instead of

```
SELECT * FROM NYC
UNION
SELECT * FROM SFO
```

(which is what SQL would actually require). More generally, it would be highly desirable for SQL to allow the expression SELECT * FROM *T* to be replaced by simply *T* wherever it appears, in the style of more conventional languages. In other words, SELECT should be regarded as an *operator* whose function is to retrieve a table (represented by some more conventionally defined table expression), and table expressions per se—

nested table expressions in particular—shouldn't require that "SELECT * FROM" prefix. Among other things this change would improve the usability of the EXISTS operator (see the next chapter). It would also help to clarify the fact that INTO and ORDER BY are clauses of the SELECT *statement* (not the SELECT operator), and hence not part of a table expression. The question of whether they can appear in a nested expression would then simply not arise, thus avoiding the need for a language rule that might look arbitrary but in fact isn't.

■ An SQL-style table expression is permitted—in fact required—in SQL as the argument to EXISTS (but strangely enough not as the argument to the aggregate operators such as COUNT; this point too is discussed in the next chapter). Such expressions are also

  a. *Required* with the ANY and ALL operators (including the IN operator, which is just a different spelling for =ANY), and

  b. *Permitted* but not required with the scalar comparison operators ("=", "<", ">", etc.),

if and only if the table expression in question yields a table of just one column and additionally (for case b.) just one row.[7] Moreover, the table expression is allowed to include GROUP BY and HAVING clauses in case a. but not in case b. Why?

■ In fact, SQL does already support nested table expressions in a kind of "under the covers" sense. Consider the following example:

Base table S ("suppliers"):

```
S ( SNO , SNAME , STATUS , CITY )
```

---

[7] Actually *at most* one row—but if it's not exactly one, then we get into the murky business of nulls, and I don't want to discuss nulls just yet.

View definition LS ("London suppliers"):

```
CREATE VIEW LS AS
    SELECT SNO , SNAME , STATUS
    FROM   S
    WHERE  CITY = 'London'
```

"Query" (Q):

```
SELECT *
FROM   LS
WHERE  STATUS > 50
```

Resulting SELECT expression (Q'):

```
SELECT SNO , SNAME , STATUS
FROM   S
WHERE  STATUS > 50
AND    CITY = 'London'
```

The expression Q' is obtained from the original expression Q by a process usually described as "merging"—Q is "merged" with the SELECT expression in the definition of view LS to produce Q'. To the naive user this looks a little bit like magic. But in fact what's going on is simply that the *reference* to LS in the FROM clause in Q is being replaced by the expression that *defines* LS, as follows:

```
SELECT *
FROM ( SELECT SNO , SNAME , STATUS
       FROM   S
       WHERE  CITY = 'London' )
WHERE  STATUS > 50
```

However, this explanation, though both easy to understand and accurate, can't conveniently be used in describing or teaching SQL, precisely because SQL doesn't support nesting in the FROM clause at the external or user's level. I mean, the expression just shown isn't a legal SQL expression.

■ UNION isn't permitted in a subquery[8] and hence (among other things) can't be used in the definition of a view (although strangely enough it *can* be used to define the scope for a cursor in embedded SQL). So a view can't be any arbitrary derived table, and the relational closure property breaks down. Likewise, INSERT ... SELECT can't be used to assign the union of two tables to another table. Yet another consequence of the special treatment given to UNION is that it's not possible to apply an aggregate operator such as AVG to a union (see the next chapter).

To conclude this discussion of table expressions in SQL, here are a few more apparently arbitrary restrictions:

■ The boolean expresion "*column comparison subquery*" must be written in the order shown and not the other way around (i.e., the syntax "*subquery comparison column*" is illegal).[9]

■ If we regard SELECT, INSERT, DELETE, and UPDATE all as special kinds of assignment statement—in each case, the value of some expression is being assigned to some variable (a newly created and temporary variable, perhaps, in the case of SELECT)—then source values for those assignments can be specified by means of general scalar expressions (involving database columns, host variables, literals, and various scalar operators) for SELECT and UPDATE, but must be specified by means of simple host variables or literals for INSERT. (Of course, there aren't any source values that need to be specified in the case of DELETE.) Thus, for example, the following is valid:

```
SELECT :X + 1
FROM   T
```

And so is:

```
UPDATE T
SET C = :X + 1 ;
```

---

[8] A *subquery* in SQL is a table expression enclosed in parentheses that's nested inside another table expression.

[9] In this connection, see the discussion of "Darwen's last straw" in Chapter 2 ("Fifty Years of Relational: A Personal View Part II") in my book *Fifty Years of Relational, and Other Database Writings* (Technics Publications, 2020).

But the following isn't:

```
INSERT INTO T ( C )
VALUES ( :X + 1 ) ;
```

■ Suppose we're given the tables (S = suppliers, P = parts):

```
S ( SNO , SNAME , STATUS , CITY )
P ( PNO , PNAME , COLOR , WEIGHT , CITY )
```

Then the following is valid:

```
SELECT COLOR
FROM   P
WHERE  CITY =
       ( SELECT CITY
         FROM   P
         WHERE  PNO = 'P1' )
```

But the following isn't:

```
UPDATE P
SET    COLOR = 'Blue'
WHERE  CITY =
       ( SELECT CITY
         FROM   P
         WHERE  PNO = 'P1' ) ;
```

Worse, neither is this:[10]

```
UPDATE P
SET    CITY =
       ( SELECT CITY
         FROM   S
         WHERE  SNO = 'S1' )
WHERE  ... ;
```

Even worse, given tables as follows—

```
EMP     ( EMPNO , SALARY )
BONUSES ( EMPNO , BONUS )
```

---

[10] I assume for simplicity and for the sake of the example that a row for supplier S1 does appear in table S.

—the following (potentially very useful) UPDATE is also not valid:

```
UPDATE EMP
SET     SALARY = SALARY + ( SELECT BONUS
                            FROM   BONUSES
                            WHERE  EMPNO = EMP.EMPNO ) ;
```

Note: Actually there's a slight problem in this last example. Suppose a given employee number *e* appears in EMP but not in BONUSES. Then the parenthesized expression will evaluate to null for employee *e*, and the UPDATE will therefore set that employee's salary to null as well—whereas what we wanted is surely for that salary to remain unchanged. To fix this problem, we'd need to be able to replace the parenthesized expression by (say)

```
COALESCE ( ( SELECT BONUS ... EMP.EMPNO ) , 0 )
```

where COALESCE is a hypothetical operator[11] that returns the first of its arguments that isn't null, or null if they all are. Note that COALESCE is different in kind from the aggregate operators currently provided in SQL, in that its arguments are scalar values, represented by scalar expressions.

To be continued.

---

[11] Hypothetical in 1984, that is.

Chapter 9

A Critique of SQL/86

Part 2

For a description of the background to this chapter, please see the preamble to Chapter 8. This version copyright © 2022 C. J. Date.

LACK OF ORTHOGONALITY: AGGREGATE OPERATORS

The term "aggregate operator" as used here—it's not an official SQL term—refers to an operator that effectively reduces an entire column of scalar values to a single such value. SQL supports the well known aggregate operators COUNT, SUM, AVG, MAX, and MIN. [1] However, that support is, frankly, so much of a mess that it's hard to criticize it coherently. But I'll do my best.

First of all, then, observe that (to repeat) the argument to such an operator is a column of scalar values and the result is a single scalar value. Orthogonality would therefore dictate that:

a. Any expression that evaluates to a column should be allowed to appear as the expression denoting the argument, and

b. The expression—i.e., the *aggregate operator reference*—denoting the operator invocation should be allowed to appear in any context where a scalar literal makes sense (i.e., wherever a scalar value is required).

Unfortunately, however:

a. The argument is actually specified in a most unorthodox manner, which means in turn that

---

[1] The special case of COUNT(*) is discussed later.

b. Aggregate operator references can actually appear only in a rather small set of special contexts. In particular, they can't appear nested inside other such references.

In addition to the foregoing, aggregate operators in general are subject to a large number of peculiar, annoying, and apparently arbitrary restrictions, as we'll see.

Syntactically, aggregate operator references in SQL look something like function invocations in a conventional language—that is, they take the form *agg* (...), where *agg* is the name of the aggregate operator in question. But as for that "(...)" ... Well, as already noted, the argument to an aggregate operator invocation is specified in a most unconventional manner. By way of example. consider the following database (suppliers and parts; SP is shipments of parts by suppliers):

```
S  ( SNO , SNAME , STATUS , CITY )
P  ( PNO , PNAME , COLOR , WEIGHT , CITY )
SP ( SNO , PNO , QTY )
```

Consider also the following SQL expression (or "query"):

```
SELECT SUM ( QTY )
FROM   SP
```

The argument to SUM in this example is in fact the entire column of QTY values in table SP, and a more conventional syntax would accordingly be:

```
SUM ( SELECT QTY
        FROM   SP )
```

Once again, however, that SELECT seems unnecessary, and in fact intrusive; just QTY FROM SP, or—even better—simply SP.QTY, would surely be more orthodox:

```
SUM ( SP.QTY )
```

As another example, the expression

```
SELECT SUM ( QTY )
FROM   SP
WHERE  PNO = 'P2'
```

would more conventionally be written

```
SUM ( SELECT QTY
      FROM   SP
      WHERE  PNO = 'P2' )
```

or (better)

```
SUM ( SP.QTY WHERE SP.PNO = 'P2' )
```

As it is, the argument to such invocations has to be determined (fully determined, that is) by context. An immediate consequence of this state of affairs is that a query such as "Find parts supplied in a total quantity of more than 1000" can't be expressed in a natural style. First, the syntax:

```
SELECT PNO
FROM   SP
WHERE  SUM ( QTY ) > 1000
```

clearly doesn't work, neither with SQL's rules for argument scope nor with any others. A more logical formulation (but still retaining an SQL-like style) would be:

```
SELECT SPX.PNO
FROM   SP SPX
WHERE  SUM ( SELECT QTY
             FROM   SP SPY
             WHERE  SPY.PNO = SPX.PNO ) > 1000
```

Or rather, albeit annoyingly:

```
SELECT DISTINCT SPX.PNO
FROM   SP SPX
WHERE  SUM ( SELECT QTY
             FROM   SP SPY
             WHERE  SPY.PNO = SPX.PNO ) > 1000
```

(The DISTINCT is needed because of SQL's rules concerning duplicate elimination.) However, a more typical SQL formulation would be:

```
SELECT PNO
FROM   SP
GROUP  BY PNO
HAVING SUM ( QTY ) > 1000
```

Note carefully that we aren't really interested in grouping per se in this example; in effect, by writing GROUP BY (and HAVING), *we're telling the system what steps it has to go through in order to obtain the result*, instead of simply telling it the result that we want (which is what a truly nonprocedural language would let us do). In other words, the expression overall begins to look more like a prescription for solving the problem, rather than a simple description of what the problem is.

More important, that grouping in turn makes it necessary to introduce the HAVING clause, the justification for which isn't immediately apparent("Why can't I just use a WHERE clause?"). *The HAVING clause—and the GROUP BY clause also, come to that, as we'll see later—are required in SQL merely and purely as a consequence of the syntax SQL uses to express aggregate operator arguments.*

As a matter of fact, it *is* possible to produce an SQL formulation of the example that doesn't use GROUP BY or HAVING at all, and is thereby fairly close to "the most logical formulation" suggested earlier:

```
SELECT DISTINCT PNO
FROM   SP SPX
WHERE  1000 <
     ( SELECT SUM ( QTY )
       FROM   SP SPY
       WHERE  SPY.PNO = SPX.PNO )
```

(As mentioned in the previous chapter, SQL requires the boolean expression in the outer WHERE clause to be written as shown—i.e., in the order "1000 < subquery"— instead of the other way around, "*subquery* > 1000.").

One important consequence of all of the above is that *SQL can't support arbitrary retrievals on arbitrary views.* Consider the following example. First, here's a view definition:

```
CREATE VIEW PQ ( PNO , TOTQTY )
   AS SELECT PNO , SUM ( QTY )
      FROM   SP
      GROUP  BY PNO ;
```

"Query" (?):

```
SELECT  *
FROM    PQ
WHERE   TOTQTY > 1000
```

But this expression fails, because the "merging" process described in the previous chapter leads to something like the following—

```
SELECT  PNO , SUM ( QTY )
FROM    SP
WHERE   SUM ( QTY ) > 1000
GROUP   BY PNO
```

—which isn't a legitimate SELECT expression. Likewise, the "query"

```
SELECT  AVG ( TOTQTY )
FROM    PQ
```

also fails, for similar reasons.

The following is another striking example of the unobviousness of SQL's syntax for aggregate arguments. Consider these two expressions:

```
SELECT  SUM ( QTY )              SELECT  SUM ( QTY )
FROM    SP                       FROM    SP
                                 GROUP   BY PNO
```

The expression on the left returns a single scalar value (the argument to the SUM invocation is the entire QTY column). By contrast, the expression on the right returns n scalar values—the aggregate operator SUM is invoked n times, where n is the number of groups created by the GROUP BY clause.[2] Notice how the meaning of the syntactic construct SUM (QTY) depends on context! (Likewise for the entire SELECT clause, of course.) In the GROUP BY example, in fact, SQL is moving out of what might be called the strict tabular framework of the relational model and introducing a new kind of data object, viz. *a set of tables* (which is of course not the same thing as a table as such). What GROUP BY does is convert a given table into such a set of tables (and the SUM operator is then applied in the example to each member of that set in turn—or,

---

[2] These two sentences are both somewhat sloppy. It would be more correct to say: The expression on the left returns a table of one column and one row; the one on the right returns a table of one column and n rows (some of which might be duplicates of one another).

rather, to a column within each member of that set in turn). Thus, a more logical formulation of the second example might look something like this:

```
APPLY ( SUM , SELECT QTY
               FROM ( GROUP SP BY PNO ) )
```

Here "GROUP SP BY PNO" produces the set of tables; "SELECT QTY FROM (...)" extracts a corresponding set of columns; and APPLY applies the operator specified as its first argument to each column in the set of columns specified as its second argument, thereby producing a set of scalars, or in other words another column. (I'm not suggesting a concrete syntax here, only indicating a possible direction for systematic development of such a syntax.)

As a matter of fact, GROUP BY would be logically unnecessary in the example anyway if only aggregate operator references were more systematic and could be used more orthogonally:

```
SELECT DISTINCT SPX.PNO , SUM ( SELECT QTY
                                FROM   SP SPY
                                WHERE  SPY.PNO = SPX.PNO )
FROM    SP SPX
```

This formulation also shows, incidentally, that it might be preferable to declare "aliases" (more precisely, *range variables*) such as SPX and SPY by means of separate statements before they're used. As it is, the use of such variables may well precede their definition, possibly by a considerable amount. Although there's nothing logically wrong with this state of affairs, it does make SQL code difficult to read (and write) on occasion.

Yet another consequence of SQL's aggregate operator syntax is that as already mentioned it's not possible to nest aggregate operator references. Extending the earlier example of generating the total quantity per part (i.e., a column of values, each of which is a total quantity), suppose we now wanted to find the *average* total quantity per part—i.e., the average of that column of values. The logical formulation would look something like this:

```
AVG ( APPLY ( SUM ,
              SELECT QTY FROM ( GROUP SP BY PNO ) ) )
```

As already noted, however, SQL can't currently formulate this problem as a single expression at all.

There are several further points to be made regarding SQL's lack of orthogonality with respect to aggregate operators, all of them having to do with the interaction between such operators and SQL's DISTINCT operator:

■ First of all, the expression denoting the column argument to SUM and AVG can optionally include a DISTINCT invocation, as in this example.

```
SELECT SUM ( DISTINCT QTY )
FROM   SP
```

Moreover, the expression denoting the column argument to COUNT *must* include such an invocation, though there doesn't seem to be any logical justification for such a requirement. As for MAX and MIN, specifying DISTINCT in this way is legal but has no semantic effect.

■ If and only if DISTINCT is omitted, the column argument can be a "computed" column—in other words, it can be specified by means of some (scalar) operational expression. For example:

```
SELECT AVG ( X + Y )
FROM   T
```

(But X and Y here must be specifically column names and/or literals, not arbitrary scalar expressions.)

■ Also if and only if DISTINCT is omitted, the aggregate operator reference can be used to provide an operand in some (scalar) operational expression. For example:

```
SELECT AVG ( X ) * 3
FROM   T
```

■ Nulls are always eliminated from the column argument to an SQL aggregate operator invocation, regardless of whether DISTINCT is specified. However, this behavior is better considered a property of the existing operators specifically, rather than as a necessary property of all such operators. In fact, it would be better not to ignore nulls in such operators at all but rather to introduce a new operator whose effect is to reduce a given column to another in which nulls have been eliminated—

and, of course, to allow that new operator to be used completely orthogonally.[3]

COUNT(*) and EXISTS

The SQL operators COUNT(*) and EXISTS do at least resemble aggregate operators as previously discussed, inasmuch as they each reduce their nonscalar argument to a single scalar value (an integer for COUNT(*), a truth value for EXISTS). However, the argument in these two cases isn't just a single column, it's an entire table, with any number of columns. To elaborate:

- COUNT(*) is basically very similar to the aggregate operators already discussed. Thus, most of the comments made above apply here also. For example,

  ```
  SELECT COUNT(*)
  FROM   SP
  ```

  would more logically be expressed as

  ```
  COUNT ( SELECT * FROM SP )
  ```

  or (much better!) as just

  ```
  COUNT ( SP )
  ```

  Note: Just to remind you, the "regular" aggregate operators simply ignore any nulls in their argument. But COUNT(*) doesn't. To be specific, if the argument contains a row with nulls in every position, then that row is included in the count.

- Interestingly, EXISTS does use a more logical syntax.[4] For example:

---

[3] Of course, this whole paragraph does assume that nulls are supported in the first place, which in my opinion they shouldn't be.

[4] Probably because it wasn't supported in SQL as originally defined but was added later.

```
SELECT  *
FROM    S
WHERE   EXISTS
      ( SELECT  *
        FROM    SP
        WHERE   SP.SNO = S.SNO )
```

Of course, I think the EXISTS reference here would look much better if that "SELECT * FROM" could be dropped, like this—

```
SELECT  *
FROM    S
WHERE   EXISTS ( SP WHERE SP.SNO = S.SNO )
```

—and it would be better still if the outer "SELECT * FROM" could be dropped as well:

```
S WHERE EXISTS ( SP WHERE SP.SNO = S.SNO )
```

Note: To repeat, EXISTS takes a table as its argument (though that table must be specified by means of a SELECT expression, not just by a simple table name). It returns the value TRUE if that table is nonempty, FALSE otherwise. (A table that contains nothing but nulls is considered to be nonempty.) However, because there's currently no BOOLEAN data type in SQL, EXISTS can be used only in a WHERE or HAVING clause, not in (e.g.) a SELECT clause. Lack of orthogonality once again.

DISTINCT and UNION

DISTINCT and UNION aren't usually regarded as aggregate operators as such. However, they do resemble the operators COUNT(*) and EXISTS inasmuch as they take an entire table as their operand—though, in contrast to those two operators, the result they return is a table as well. In any case (i.e., whether or not you agree with putting these operators all in the same box, as it were), there are a couple of points I want to make in connection with DISTINCT and UNION that do seem to fit, somewhat, with the other points I've been making in the present section. To elaborate:

■ DISTINCT takes a table as input and returns another table that's identical to the first except that redundant duplicate rows have been removed. (Rows containing nothing but nulls are considered as duplicates of one

another in this context; thus, the result will contain at most one such row.)
Once again, however, the syntax is unconventional. For example, the
expression

```
SELECT DISTINCT SNO
FROM    SP
```

would more logically be written as

```
DISTINCT ( SELECT SNO FROM SP )
```

or (much better!) just as

```
DISTINCT ( SP.SNO )
```

- ■ UNION takes two tables as input (each of which must be specified by
  means of a SELECT expression, not just by a simple table name) and
  produces their union as another table. It's written as an infix operator.
      Note: I consider UNION, alone of the operators of the relational
  algebra, as (at least somewhat) resembling an aggregate operator in SQL
  merely because of the special syntax SQL uses to express it. For example,
  it's not possible in SQL (as mentioned in the previous chapter) to apply an
  operator such as AVG to the union of two columns, precisely because of
  that special syntax.[5]

LACK OF ORTHOGONALITY: MISCELLANEOUS ITEMS

Indicator Variables

Let C be a database column for which nulls are allowed, and let HC be a
corresponding host variable, with associated indicator variable HN. Then

```
SELECT C INTO    :HC:HN ... ;
```

---

[5] Strictly speaking, SQL's UNION operator doesn't correspond to true relational union anyway but rather to
an operator which I'll call *union plus*. Here's a loose definition: Let row *r* appear *n1* times in table *t1* and
n2 times in table *t2*; then the "union plus" of *t1* and *t2* contains *n1+n2* copies of *r* (and it doesn't contain any
other rows). For further explanation, see Chapter 15, "The Theory of Bags: An Investigative Tutorial," of
my book *Logic and Relational Theory* (Technics Publications, 2020).

is legal, and so are

```
INSERT ... VALUES ( :HC:HN ... ) ;
```

and

```
UPDATE ... SET C = :HC:HN ... ;
```

But the following isn't:

```
SELECT ... /* or UPDATE or DELETE */ ...
WHERE  C = :HC:HN
```

References to Current Data

Let X be a cursor that currently identifies a row of table T. Then it's possible to designate the "CURRENT OF X"—i.e., the row currently identified by X—as a DELETE or UPDATE target, using syntax as shown in this example:

```
UPDATE  T
SET     ...
WHERE   CURRENT OF X ;
```

I remark in passing that a formulation such as the following would be more logical:

```
UPDATE CURRENT OF X
SET     ... ;
```

Specifying the table name T is redundant (this point is recognized in the syntax of FETCH, see later), and in any case WHERE CURRENT OF X doesn't make logical sense—CURRENT OF X isn't a boolean expression (it doesn't return a truth value), and hence it's different in kind from what normally does appear in a WHERE clause. As a consequence, it can't be combined with the kind of thing that usually appear (e.g., WHERE CURRENT OF X AND SALARY > 80000 is illegal).

But to return to my main point: Although the first of the UPDATEs shown above is legal, the following SELECT isn't:

```
SELECT  ...
FROM    T
WHERE   CURRENT OF X
```

In other words, columns within the "CURRENT OF X" can't be simply referenced without being retrieved. For example, the following is illegal a fortiori:

```
SELECT  *
FROM    EMP
WHERE   DEPTNO =
      ( SELECT DEPTNO
        FROM    DEPT
        WHERE   CURRENT OF X )
```

Turning now to the FETCH statement, we have here an example of bundling. The statement "FETCH X INTO ..." is effectively a shorthand for a sequence of two separate (but hypothetical) statements—

```
STEP X TO NEXT ;
SELECT * INTO ... WHERE CURRENT OF X ;
```

—the first of which (STEP) advances X to the next row of T in accordance with the ordering associated with X, and the second of which (SELECT) then retrieves that row. (Of course, I'm assuming here that SELECT ... WHERE CURRENT OF X is legal after all, although we saw a moment ago that it isn't. But it should be! Note, incidentally, that any FROM clause in such a SELECT would be redundant.)

Replacing the FETCH statement by two separate and more primitive statements in this way would have a number of advantages:

a. It would be clearer.

b. It would be more logical. Note in particular that FETCH X doesn't really make sense—it's not the cursor as such that's being fetched, it's the row the cursor identifies.

c. It would allow SELECTs of individual columns of the current row (as in e.g., SELECT *column* WHERE CURRENT OF X).

d. It would allow selective and repeated access to the same row (e.g., SELECT C1 followed by SELECT C2, both selecting column values from the same row, viz., the row that's CURRENT OF X).

e. It could easily be extended to other kinds of STEP operation—e.g., STEP X TO PREVIOUS (say).

In fact we could go further. Note first that CURRENT OF X is really a row expression—it denotes a particular row. So we could introduce a new FETCH *rx* statement whose purpose is to fetch the row identified by the row expression *rx*. Then we could outlaw SELECT where this new FETCH is really intended. Next, we could introduce scalar expressions of the form *rx.C*, where *rx* is a row expression and *C* is a column name. Finally, we could and should support all of these constructs orthogonally. Then, e.g., all of the following would be legal:

```
FETCH CURRENT OF X INTO ... ;

FETCH ( CURRENT OF X ).C INTO ... ;

SELECT *
FROM    EMP
WHERE   DEPTNO = ( CURRENT OF X ).DEPTNO

UPDATE CURRENT OF X
SET     ... ;

DELETE CURRENT OF X ;
```

Incidentally, these examples illustrate the point that CURRENT OF X is really a very cumbersome notation, but an improved syntax is beyond the scope of this chapter. See reference [2] for a preferable alternative.

ORDER BY in Cursor Declarations

Specifying ORDER BY in the declaration of cursor X means the statements UPDATE ... WHERE CURRENT OF X and DELETE ...WHERE CURRENT OF X are illegal (in fact, the declaration of X isn't allowed to include a FOR UPDATE clause if ORDER BY is specified). The rationale for this restriction is that the ORDER BY might mean the application has to operate (via cursor X) on a copy of the data instead of the actual data as such, and hence that updates and deletes (again, via cursor X) would be meaningless—but the restriction is unfortunate, to say the least. For example, consider a program that needs to process employees in department number order and needs to update some of them as it goes. Then the code has to look something like this:

```
EXEC SQL DECLARE X CURSOR FOR
                   SELECT EMPNO , DEPTNO , ...
                   FROM   EMP
                   ORDER  BY DEPTNO ;

EXEC SQL OPEN X ;
DO WHILE more to come ;
   EXEC SQL FETCH X INTO :EMPNO , :DEPTNO , ... ;
   if this row needs updating, then
   EXEC SQL UPDATE EMP
           SET    ...
           WHERE  EMPNO = :EMPNO
     /* not WHERE CURRENT OF X */ ;
END ;
EXEC SQL CLOSE X ;
```

The UPDATE statement here is an "out of the blue" (also called "searched") UPDATE, not the CURRENT form. Problems:

a. The update will be visible through cursor X if and only if X is running through the real data, not a copy.

b. If cursor X is running through the real data and the UPDATE changes the DEPTNO value, the effect on the positioning of cursor X appears to be undefined.

I can't help pointing out too that the FOR UPDATE clause is a little mysterious (its real significance isn't immediately apparent); it's also logically unnecessary. This whole area smacks of a most unfortunate loss of physical data independence.

Empty Tables

Let *tx* be a table expression. If *tx* evaluates to an empty table, then what happens depends on the context in which it (i.e., that table expression *tx*) appears. For example, consider these two table expressions:

```
SELECT SALARY              vs.        SELECT AVG ( SALARY )
FROM   EMP                            FROM   EMP
WHERE  DEPTNO = 'D3'                  WHERE  DEPTNO = 'D3'
```

Note that the second of these expressions represents the application of the AVG function to the result of the first. As pointed out earlier, therefore, it would more logically be written as follows:

```
AVG ( SELECT  SALARY
      FROM    EMP
      WHERE   DEPTNO = 'D3' )
```

(and this fact might help you make sense of what follows). Suppose now that department D3 currently has no employees. Then:

■ The statement[6]

```
EXEC SQL SELECT SALARY
         INTO   :SAL:SALN
         FROM   EMP
         WHERE  DEPTNO = 'D3' ;
```

gives "not found" (SQLCODE = +100, host variables SAL and SALN unchanged).

■ The statement

```
EXEC SQL SELECT AVG ( SALARY )
         INTO   :SAL:SALN
         FROM   EMP
         WHERE  DEPTNO = 'D3' ;
```

sets host variable SALN to an unspecified negative value to indicate that the AVG invocation has returned a null. The effect on host variable SAL is undefined.

■ The statement

```
EXEC SQL SELECT ...
         INTO   :V:VN
         FROM   ...
         WHERE  something IN
                ( SELECT  SALARY
                  FROM    EMP
                  WHERE   DEPTNO = 'D3' ) ;
```

---

[6] Note that it is indeed a statement, not an expression (note the INTO clause and the semicolon terminator).

gives "not found" (but, somewhat illogically, at the *outer* level).

■ The statement

```
EXEC SQL SELECT ...
         INTO    :V:VN
         FROM    ...
         WHERE   something = /* note "=", not IN */
                 ( SELECT  SALARY
                   FROM    EMP
                   WHERE   DEPTNO = 'D3' ) ;
```

also gives "not found" at the outer level, though there's a good argument for treating this case as an error, as follows: First, the parenthesized expression "(SELECT ... WHERE DNO = 'D3')" should really be understood as shorthand for an expression of the form "UNIQUE (SELECT ... WHERE DNO = 'D3')." Second, that hypothetical operator UNIQUE should be understood as s a quantifier (analogous to EXISTS) that means *there exists exactly one*; equivalently, it should be understood as an operator whose effect is to extract the single member from a singleton set, and to raise an error if that set doesn't in fact contain exactly one member.[7]

■ The statement

```
EXEC SQL SELECT ...
         INTO    :V:VN
         FROM    ...
         WHERE   something =
                 ( SELECT  AVG ( SALARY )
                   FROM    EMP
                   WHERE   DEPTNO = 'D3' ) ;
```

also gives "not found" at the outer level.

---

[7] Note that SQL will certainly raise an error in the example if the expression SELECT ... WHERE DNO = 'D3' returns a table having two or more rows—so why doesn't it do so if that table contains no rows at all?

"Long Fields" (i.e., LONG VARCHAR, or VARCHAR(n) with n > 254)

"Long fields" are subject to numerous restrictions. Here are some of them (this is probably not an exhaustive list). A long field:

- Can't be referenced in a WHERE or HAVING clause

- Can't be referenced in DISTINCT

- Can't be referenced in GROUP BY

- Can't be referenced in ORDER BY

- Can't be referenced in COUNT, MAX, or MIN (note that SUM and AVG wouldn't make any sense anyway)

- Can't be involved in a UNION

- Can't be involved in a subquery

- Can't be INSERTed into from a literal or a SELECT expression

- Can't be UPDATEd from a literal (UPDATE from NULL is legal, but strictly speaking NULL isn't a literal anyway, because it doesn't have a defined data type)

UNION Restrictions

Union isn't permitted on long fields or in a subquery (in particular, in a view definition). Also, the data types of corresponding items in a union must be exactly the same. To be specific:

- If the data type is DECIMAL(p,q), then p must be the same for both items and q must be the same for both as well

- If the data type is CHAR(n), then n must be the same for both items

- If the data type is VARCHAR(n), then n must be the same for both items

■   If NOT NULL applies to either item, then it must apply to both

Given these restrictions, incidentally, it's particularly unfortunate—not to say perverse—that a character string literal such as 'ABC' is treated as type VARCHAR (of maximum length 3, in the example), with nulls allowed (!).[8]

Note too that UNION always eliminates duplicates—there's no DISTINCT vs. ALL option as there is with SELECT, and if there were, the default would have to be DISTINCT (for compatibility reasons), whereas the default for SELECT is ALL.

GROUP BY Restrictions

GROUP BY:

■   Only works to one level (it can construct a "set of tables" but not a "set of sets of tables," etc.)

■   Can only have individual columns as arguments (unlike ORDER BY)

The fact is (as indicated earlier, in the discussion of aggregate operators), a fully orthogonal treatment of GROUP BY would require a thorough treatment of an entirely new kind of data object (namely, "set of tables")—presumably a major undertaking.

NULL Anomalies

Note: When I wrote the original paper on which these three chapters are based, back in the 1980s, I didn't fully appreciate just how disastrously bad nulls are as a "solution" to the missing information problem. In fact, I've published several critiques since that time—critiques of the whole nulls idea, that is—that are far more searching and extensive than the one contained in the present subsection (see, for example, references [3], [10], and [11]). However, I decided to retain the following points from the original paper nevertheless, because they're still

---

[8] At this distance it's hard to say whether the remarks of this paragraph were really true of SQL/86. They don't seem to be true of later versions of the standard. Maybe they were true of System R? Or maybe I just got it wrong.

valid as far as they go—but please be aware that nulls suffer from problems far worse than the ones identified here.

■ To test in a WHERE clause whether some column position (within some row) contains a null, SQL provides the special comparison "*column* IS NULL." However, it's not immediately obvious why the user has to write "*column* IS NULL" and not "*column* = NULL"—especially since (a) the syntax "*column* = *expression*" is legal in general, even if *expression* evaluates to null,[9] and (b) the syntax "*column* = NULL" is used in the SET clause of the UPDATE statement to set a column to null.

■ Two nulls are considered to be duplicates for the purposes of DISTINCT and ORDER BY but not for the purposes of WHERE and GROUP BY. Nulls are also considered as greater than all nonnull values for the purposes of ORDER BY but not for the purposes of WHERE. There's simply no logical justification for these arbitrarinesses and inconsistencies—and precisely because there's no justification for them, the rules aren't easy to remember, either.

■ As noted earlier, nulls are always eliminated from the argument to an aggregate operator such as SUM or AVG, regardless of whether DISTINCT is specified—except for the case of COUNT(*), which counts all rows, including both duplicates and rows containing nothing but nulls. Thus, e.g., given the following—

```
SELECT AVG ( STATUS ) FROM S    --    Result: x

SELECT SUM ( STATUS ) FROM S    --    Result: y

SELECT COUNT(*)       FROM S    --    Result: z
```

—there can be no guarantee in general that $x = y/z$.

■ Similarly, the expression SUM (*C*) can't be guaranteed to be equivalent to the expression

---

[9] If you see what I mean, I suppose I should add (after all, nothing can ever "evaluate to null," because the whole point about null is that it's not a value). The truth is, it's impossible even to talk about nulls without spouting nonsense like "evaluates to null." So I apologize; but please don't blame me—it wasn't me that invented this stuff.

$$c1 + c2 + ... + cn$$

where *c1*, *c2*, ..., *cn* are all of the values[10] appearing in column *C* (duplicates and nulls not eliminated) at the time the SUM operator is invoked. Perhaps even more counterintuitively, the expression

```
SUM ( C1 + C2 )
```

can't be guaranteed to be equivalent to the expression

```
SUM ( C1 ) + SUM ( C2 )
```

Host Variables

Host variable references are permitted wherever literals are permitted, also in the INTO clause of SELECT and FETCH, but nowhere else. In particular, table names and column names can't be specified by means of such references.

Introduced Names

The user can introduce names ("aliases"—actually range variables) for tables, as in, e.g., FROM T TX, but not for columns. Note that this latter could easily be supported by means of the SELECT clause, as in, e.g., SELECT C CX. Such a facility would be particularly useful when the column is "computed" or derived, as in, e.g., SELECT C1 + C2 CX, C3 * C4 CY (etc.), The names CX and CY (etc.) could then be used in WHERE or ORDER BY or GROUP BY or as an inherited name in CREATE VIEW (and so on).

Legal INSERTs, DELETEs, and UPDATEs

Certain INSERT, DELETE, and UPDATE statements aren't allowed. For example, consider the requirement "Delete all suppliers with a status less than the average," for which the following might seem a reasonable formulation:

---

[10] The previous footnote applies here also, mutatis mutandis.

```
DELETE
FROM    S
WHERE   STATUS <
        ( SELECT AVG ( STATUS )
          FROM    S ) ;
```

But this statement is illegal—the FROM clause in the subquery isn't allowed to refer to the table against which the DELETE is being done. Likewise, the UPDATE statement:

```
UPDATE S
SET     STATUS = 0
WHERE   STATUS <
        ( SELECT AVG (STATUS)
          FROM    S ) ;
```

is also illegal, for analogous reasons.

Third, the statement

```
INSERT INTO T
        SELECT * FROM T ;
```

(which might be regarded as a perfectly natural way to "double up" on the contents of table T) is also illegal, again for analogous reasons.

To be continued.

Chapter 10

A Critique of SQL/86

Part 3

For a description of the background to this chapter, please see the preamble to Chapter 8. This version copyright © 2022 C. J. Date.

FORMAL DEFINITION

SQL does have a formal definition—that's what reference [13] is (at least in principle). Unfortunately, however, that definition was produced "after the fact." As a consequence, it effectively defines the way existing implementations (especially IBM implementations) already work, not the way a "pure" language ought to work. And in any case there appear to be areas where the definition still isn't fully precise (examples to follow).

Cursor Positioning

Let cursor X be associated with some specific collection of rows, and let the ordering associated with X be defined in terms of values of column C within those rows. If X is positioned on row *r* and *r* is deleted, X goes into the "before" state—i.e., it's now positioned "before" row *r'*, where *r'* is the immediate successor of *r* with respect to the pertinent ordering—or, if there's no such successor, then it goes into the "after" state—i.e., it's "after" the last row in the collection . (Note that the "after" state is possible even if the collection is empty.) Questions:

    a. If X is "before" *r'* and a new row *r''* is inserted with a value for C such that *r''* logically belongs between *r'* and the predecessor of *r'* (if any), what happens to X? [*Answer:* Implementation defined.]

b. Does it make a difference if the new row *r''* logically precedes or follows the old row *r* that X was positioned on before that row was deleted? [*Answer:* Implementation defined.]

c. Does it make a difference if X was actually running through a copy of the real data? [*Answer:* Implementation defined.]

   Note that for cases a.-c. it's at least guaranteed that (so long as no other updates occur that could affect the situation) the next FETCH on cursor X will retrieve row *r'*.

d. What if *r''* is produced by some UPDATE, not some INSERT? [*Answer:* Undefined.]

e. If C is positioned on row *r* and the value of column C in that row is changed (not via cursor X, of course), what happens to X? [*Answer:* Undefined.]

Name Resolution

Consider these two expressions:

```
SELECT  SNO
FROM    S
WHERE   CITY = 'London'

SELECT  PNO
FROM    P
WHERE   CITY = 'London'
```

Clearly, the meaning of the unqualified column name CITY depends on context—it stands for S.CITY in the first of these examples and P.CITY in the second. But now suppose those columns are renamed SCITY and PCITY, respectively (so now the names are "globally unique"), and consider the query "Find suppliers located in cities in which no parts are stored." The obvious formulation is:

```
SELECT  SNO
FROM    S
WHERE   NOT EXISTS
        ( SELECT *
          FROM    P
          WHERE   PCITY = SCITY )
```

But this formulation fails on a syntax error!—SQL assumes that "SCITY" stands for "P.SCITY," and then complains that no such column exists. The following, by contrast, succeeds:

```
SELECT  SNO
FROM    S
WHERE   NOT EXISTS
        ( SELECT *
          FROM    P
          WHERE   PCITY = S.SCITY )
```

So too does:

```
SELECT  SNO
FROM    S SX
WHERE   NOT EXISTS
        ( SELECT *
          FROM    P
          WHERE   PCITY = SX.SCITY )
```

Is the following ("suppliers who supply P1 and P2") valid?

```
SELECT  *
FROM    S
WHERE   EXISTS ( SELECT *
                 FROM    SP SPX
                 WHERE   SPX.SNO = S.SNO
                 AND     SPX.PNO = 'P1'
                 AND     EXISTS ( SELECT *
                                  FROM    SP SPX
                                  WHERE   SPX.SNO = S.SNO
                                  AND     SPX.PNO = 'P2' ) )
```

What if "FROM SP SPX" is replaced by "FROM SP" (twice) and all other occurrences of "SPX" are replaced by "SP"? And is the following valid?

```
SELECT  *
FROM    S
WHERE   EXISTS ( SELECT *
                 FROM    SP SPX
                 WHERE   SPX.SNO = S.SNO
                 AND     SPX.PNO = 'P1' )
AND     EXISTS ( SELECT *
                 FROM    SP SPX
                 WHERE   SPX.SNO = S.SNO
                 AND     SPX.PNO = 'P2' )
```

(etc., etc.). In a nutshell: What *are* the name scoping rules?

There's another point to be made while on the subject of name resolution, incidentally. Consider the expression

```
SELECT  S.SNO , P.PNO
FROM    S , P
WHERE   S.CITY = P.CITY
```

(reverting now to just CITY for the two column names). This expression is conceptually evaluated as follows (simplifying somewhat):

1. Form the product of S and P; call the result TEMP1.

2. Restrict TEMP1 according to the boolean expression S.CITY = P.CITY; call the result TEMP2.

3. Project TEMP2 over the columns S.SNO and P.PNO.

But how can this procedure possibly make sense? The restriction condition on TEMP1 in Step 2 (viz., S.CITY = P.CITY) doesn't refer to columns of TEMP1—it refers to columns of S and P, obviously. Similarly, the projection of TEMP2 in Step 3 is on columns S.SNO and P.PNO, but these columns aren't columns of TEMP2.

In order for these various column references to be interpreted appropriately, therefore, certain *name inheritance rules* are needed, indicating how result tables inherit their column names from the pertinent source tables—which might of course be (intermediate) result tables themselves, with inherited column names of their own. Such rules are currently defined only very informally, if at all. Such rules become even more important if SQL is to provide proper support for nested expressions, as suggested in Chapter 8.

Base vs. Copy Data

When exactly does a cursor iterate over the real "base data" and when over a copy?

*Binding of "SELECT *"*

When exactly does "*" become bound to a specific set of column names? [*Answer:* Implementation defined—but this seems an unfortunate aspect to leave to the implementation, especially as the binding is likely to be different for different uses of the feature (e.g., it may depend on whether the "*" appears in a program or in a view definition).]

MISMATCH WITH HOST LANGUAGES

The general point here is that there are far too many frivolous distinctions between SQL and the host language in which it happens to be embedded—also that in some cases SQL has failed to benefit from lessons learned in the design of such host languages in general. After all, orthogonality suggests rather strongly that what's useful on one side of the interface for "permanent" (i.e., database) data is likely to be useful on the other side for "temporary" (i.e., local) data also; thus, a distinct sublanguage is the wrong approach, and a two-level store is wrong too (fundamentally so!). Some specific points:

- SQL fails to exploit the exception handling capabilities of the host (e.g., "ON conditions" in PL/I). This point and (even more so) the following one mean that SQL doesn't exactly encourage the production of well structured, quality application programs, and that in some respects SQL programming is at a lower level than that of the host.

- SQL fails to exploit the control structures of the host (loop constructs in particular).

- SQL objects (tables, cursors, etc.) aren't known and can't be referenced in the host environment.

- Host objects can be referenced in the SQL environment only if:

a. They're specially declared (might not apply to all hosts);

b. They're scalars or certain limited kinds of structures (in particular, they're not arrays);

c. The references are marked with a colon prefix (admittedly only in some contexts—but in my opinion "some" is worse than "all");

d. The references are constrained to certain limited contexts (e.g., they can appear in a SELECT clause but not in a FROM clause); and

e. The references are constrained to certain limited formats (e.g., no subscripting, only limited dot qualification, etc.).

Moreover, host procedures can't be referenced in the SQL environment at all.

■ SQL object names and host object names are independent and can clash. SQL names don't follow the scoping rules of the host.

■ SQL keywords and host keywords are independent and can clash (e.g., PL/I SELECT vs. SQL SELECT).

■ SQL and host can have different name qualification rules (e.g., T.C in SQL vs. C OF T in COBOL—and note that the SQL form must be used even for host object references in the SQL environment).

■ SQL and host can have different data type conversion rules.

■ SQL and host can have different expression evaluation rules (e.g., SQL division operations and varying string comparisons differ from their PL/I analogs, at least in the IBM product SQL/DS).

■ SQL and host can have different boolean operators (e.g., AND, OR, and NOT in SQL vs. "&", "|", and "¬" in PL/I).

■ SQL and host can have different comparison operators—e.g., COBOL has IS NUMERIC, SQL has BETWEEN.

■ SQL imposes statement ordering restrictions that are alien to the host.

■ SQL DECLARE can't be abbreviated to DCL, unlike PL/I DECLARE.

■ Nulls are handled differently on the two sides of the interface.

■ Function invocations (aggregate operator invocations in SQL) have different formats on the two sides of the interface.

■ SQL name resolution rules are different from those of the host.

■ Cursors are a clumsy way of bridging the gap between the database and the application. A much better method would be to associate an SQL expression ("query") with a sequential file in the host, and then let the application use conventional host file access operators on that file.

■ The "structure declarations" in CREATE TABLE should use the standard COBOL or PL/I (etc.) syntax. As it is, it's doubtful whether they can be elegantly extended to deal with minor structures ("composite columns") or arrays, should such extensions ever prove desirable (they will).

■ The SQL parameter mechanism is regressive, clumsy, ad hoc, restrictive, and different from that of the host.

MISSING FUNCTIONALITY

The functionality I'm talking about in this section is, primarily, functionality that's missing from the embedded (programming) version of SQL. (Other missing function is discussed in the section "Relational Features Not Supported," later.) Of course, the list of desirable extensions for any given language is probably always endless; however, the items listed below are (at least arguably) fairly obvious omissions from the SQL programmer's standpoint.

- Ability to override WHENEVER NOT FOUND at the level of an individual statement

- "En bloc" row replacement

- Procedure call instead of GO TO on WHENEVER

- Cursor stepping other than "next"

- Cursor comparison and assignment

- Generally, cursors as "first class objects," thereby permitting, e.g., cursor arrays, dynamically created cursors and cursor stacks, reusable cursors, and so on

- Ability to access a specific row and keep a cursor on it without having to go through separate DECLARE, OPEN, and FETCH (e.g., "FETCH UNIQUE (EMP WHERE EMPNO = 'E2') SET (X);")

And so on.

MISTAKES

Nulls

I've argued against nulls at length elsewhere (see, e.g., references [3], [10], and [11] among others), and I don't intend to repeat those arguments here. In my opinion the whole business of nulls is far more trouble than it's worth. Certainly it hasn't been properly thought through in SQL specifically (see the various criticisms of nulls already mentioned in Chapters 8 and 9). As a specific case of that lack of thinking through, consider the fact that functions such as AVG simply ignore nulls in their argument. That state of affairs clearly violates what should surely be a fundamental principle, viz.: *The system should never produce a (spuriously) precise answer to a query when the data involved in that query is itself imprecise.* At least the system should offer the user the explicit option to ignore nulls, or to treat their presence as an exception.

Unique Indexes

Note: In the early days of SQL, IBM used "unique indexes" to enforce key uniqueness. Nothing wrong with that, I hasten to add—but IBM then went on, in effect, to expose those indexes to the user, which is something that should never have happened. Fortunately, SQL/86 did fix this particular problem, and the paragraph below therefore doesn't apply to SQL/86 as such. I've retained it, though, if only on account of the well known principle that those who don't know history are doomed to repeat it.

Key uniqueness is a logical property of the data, not a physical property of an access path. Accordingly, it should be specified on CREATE TABLE, not on CREATE INDEX.[1] Specifying it on CREATE INDEX is an unfortunate bundling, and could lead to a loss of data independence (dropping the index could put the integrity of the database at risk). Indeed, the fact that it was specified on CREATE INDEX suggests rather strongly, at least to me, that the original designers of SQL in IBM didn't really understand the relational model in the first place.

FROM Clause

The only function of the FROM clause that's not actually redundant is to allow the introduction of range variables, and that function would be better provided in some more elegant manner. (The normal use, as exemplified by the expression SELECT C FROM T, could better be handled by the expression SELECT T.C, especially since this latter expression—albeit with an accompanying but redundant FROM clause—is already legal in SQL anyway.)

Punning

SQL doesn't make a clear distinction between tables, rows, and range variables. Instead, it allows a single symbol to stand for any one of those objects, and leaves the interpretation to depend on context. Conceptual clarity would dictate that it at least always be possible to distinguish among these different constructs

---

[1] Two points here: First, CREATE INDEX as such shouldn't even be part of the normal application programming interface anyway (and it isn't, in SQL/86). Second, I've recently begun to think that, like other integrity constraints, even key definitions should be stated separately from table definitions (i.e., they shouldn't be bundled in with CREATE TABLE either, let alone with CREATE INDEX).

(i.e., syntactically), even if there are rules that allow such punning games to be played when intuitively convenient. Otherwise it might be possible that—for example—extendability might suffer, though I have to admit that I can't at the time of writing point to any concrete problems. (But it shouldn't be necessary to have to defend the principle of a one to one correspondence between names and objects!)

While on the subject of punning, I might also mention the point that SQL is ambivalent as to the meaning of the term *table*. Sometimes it means a base table specifically, as in CREATE TABLE; at other times it means either a base table or a view, as in GRANT.[2] Since the crucial point about a view is, first and foremost, that it's a table (just as the crucial point about a subset is that it's a set), I would vote for the following changes:

a.   Replace the terms "base table" and "view" by "real table" and "virtual table," respectively.

b.   Use the term "table" generically to mean "real table or virtual table."

c.   In concrete syntax, use the expressions [REAL] TABLE and VIRTUAL TABLE (where it's necessary to distinguish them, as in CREATE), with REAL as the default.

*SELECT **

This is an example (possibly) of a situation in which the needs of the end user and those of the application programmer might be slightly at odds. "SELECT *" is fine for the interactive user (it saves keystrokes). However, it's dangerous for the application programmer, because the meaning of that "*" might change at any time in the life of the application. The use of "ORDER BY *n*" (where *n* is an integer instead of a column name) in conjunction with "SELECT *" could be particularly unfortunate. Similar remarks apply to the use of INSERT without an explicit list of column names.

Note: At this point the original paper on which these chapters are based went on to say the following (lightly edited here as always):

---

[2] I'm embarrassed to have to note here that when I wrote the original paper these three chapters are based on I didn't even mention the worst aspect of SQL's ambivalence with respect to the meaning of the term *table*—viz., that it uses one and the same term to mean sometimes a table *value*, sometimes a table *variable*. See the preamble to Chapter 8.

I believe the foregoing are the only situations in SQL in which the user is dependent on the left to right ordering of columns in a table. It would be nice to eliminate that dependence entirely.

Well, I certainly agree with the second sentence here—but as for the first, I couldn't have been more wrong! See my book *SQL and Relational Theory* [5] for an extensive discussion of further situations in which that left to right column ordering rears its ugly head and causes further problems.

=ANY (etc.)

The comparison operators =ANY, >ALL, etc., are totally redundant and in many cases actively misleading (error potential is high). The following example, which is taken from the IBM manual "IBM Database 2 SQL Usage Guide" (IBM Form No. GG24-1583), illustrates the point very nicely. The query is "Get employees who are younger than any member of department E21." Proposed SQL formulation (irrelevant details omitted):[3]

```
SELECT  EMPNO , LASTNAME , WORKDEPT
FROM    TEMPL
WHERE   BRTHDATE >ANY
      ( SELECT BRTHDATE
        FROM   TEMPL
        WHERE  WORKDEPT = 'E21' )
```

This expression does *not* yield "employees who are younger than any employee in E21"!—at least, not in the sense that this requirement would normally be understood in normal colloquial English. Rather, it gives employees who are younger than *at least one* employee in E21.[4]

As for the redundancy, consider the query "Get supplier names for suppliers who supply part P2." This is a very simple query, and yet it's not difficult to find no less than seven formulations for it, all of them at least

---

[3] I believe I'm right in saying that SQL identifiers in DB2 at the time were limited to a maximum of eight characters, which accounts for the proposed SQL expression's slightly awkward use of BRTHDATE instead of BIRTH_DATE, LASTNAME instead of LAST_NAME, etc.

[4] See reference [5] for an extended discussion of the interpretation problems like this one that comparison operators such as >ANY can give rise to (and how to avoid them).

superficially distinct (see below).[5] Of course, the differences would be unimportant if all formulations worked equally well, but that's unlikely.

```
1. SELECT  SNAME
   FROM    S
   WHERE   SNO IN
           ( SELECT  SNO
             FROM    SP
             WHERE   PNO = 'P2' )

2. SELECT  SNAME
   FROM    S
   WHERE   SNO =ANY
           ( SELECT  SNO
             FROM    SP
             WHERE   PNO = 'P2' )

3. SELECT  SNAME
   FROM    S
   WHERE   EXISTS
           ( SELECT  *
             FROM    SP
             WHERE   SNO = S.SNO AND PNO = 'P2' )

4. SELECT  DISTINCT SNAME
   FROM    S , SP
   WHERE   S.SNO = SP.SNO AND SP.PNO = 'P2'

5. SELECT  SNAME
   FROM    S
   WHERE   0 <
           ( SELECT  COUNT(*)
             FROM    SP
             WHERE   SNO = S.SNO AND PNO = 'P2' )

6. SELECT  SNAME
   FROM    S
   WHERE   'P2' IN
           ( SELECT  PNO
             FROM    SP
             WHERE   SNO = S.SNO )
```

---

[5] I've revisited this example elsewhere [7] and shown that, at least in the version of the standard that's been current ever since 1992, this simple query can be expressed in at least *fifty* different ways (!), and arguably many more than that.

```
7. SELECT  SNAME
   FROM    S
   WHERE   'P2'  =ANY
          ( SELECT PNO
            FROM   SP
            WHERE  SNO = S.SNO )
```

In fact the comparison operators =ANY (etc.) need never be used. If we assume for simplicity that no nulls are involved anywhere (as I would strongly recommend), then (a) the WHERE clause

```
WHERE  x  $ANY  ( SELECT  y  FROM  T  WHERE  bx )
```

(where $ is any one of "=", ">", etc.) is logically equivalent to

```
WHERE  EXISTS  ( SELECT  *  FROM  T  WHERE  ( bx )  AND  x $ T.y )
```

And (b) the WHERE clause

```
WHERE  x  $ALL  ( SELECT  y  FROM  T  WHERE  bx )
```

is logically equivalent to

```
WHERE  NOT  EXISTS  ( SELECT  *  FROM  T  WHERE  ( bx )
                                          AND  NOT  ( x $ T.y ) )
```

Note: Actually it's not just the comparison operators =ANY (etc.) that are redundant—the entire "IN *subquery*" construct could be deleted with no loss of functionality! This state of affairs is somewhat ironic, since that construct was the justification for the "Structured" in "Structured Query Language" in the first place. I mean, that was the "structure" that the name referred to.

RELATIONAL FEATURES NOT SUPPORTED

There are numerous features of the full relational model as defined in, e.g., reference [6] that SQL doesn't currently support. A few of them are listed below. Of course, most if not all of these features can be added to SQL at some later time—the sooner the better, in most cases. However, their omission now leads to a number of situations in current SQL that are extremely ad hoc and might be difficult to remedy later on for compatibility reasons.

Keys

Note: Keys in general are extremely important. However, I'm much less certain now than I was when I wrote the paper on which these chapters are based that primary keys in particular are more important than keys in general are. As a result, I've rewritten this subsection to talk in terms of keys in general instead of primary keys in particular (which is what it originally did).

Keys provide the sole row level addressing mechanism in the relational model. That is, the only system guaranteed method of identifying an individual row wthin a base table or a view (or any other named table, come to that) is via the combination (*T,k*), where *T* is the name of the table concerned and *k* is a value for the pertinent key for the desired row within that table. Thus, every named table—including in particular every base table and every view—is required to have at least one key.

Now, SQL does provide mechanisms that allow users to apply the foregoing key discipline for themselves if they choose, but it doesn't insist on it, nor does it understand the semantics associated with that discipline. As a consequence, its support for certain other relational features is either deficient or lacking entirely, as I now explain:

- Key support is prerequisite to foreign key support (see the subsection following this one).

- Consider this SQL expression:

```
SELECT  P.PNO , P.WEIGHT, AVG ( SP.QTY )
FROM    P , SP
WHERE   P.PNO = SP.PNO
GROUP   BY P.PNO , P.WEIGHT
```

  The reference to P.WEIGHT in the GROUP BY clause here is logically unnecessary, but must be included because SQL doesn't understand that each part has just one weight. (This requirement on SQL's part might only be a minor annoyance, but it could be puzzling to the user.)

■ An understanding of keys is required in order to support the updating of views correctly.[6] SQL's rules for the updating of views are disgracefully ad hoc. I'll consider projection, restriction, and join views briefly here; a detailed discussion of this topic can be found in reference [4]. *Note:* I assume for simplicity that in each case the table or tables underlying the view can themselves be successfully updated in turn.

a. Projections are logically updatable if they preserve a key of the underlying table. However, SQL supports updates, not on projections per se, but on what might be called *column subsets* (where a "column subset" is any subset of the columns of the underlying table for which duplicate elimination isn't requested, via DISTINCT). If such a subset doesn't in fact include some key, though, then the user might be in for a few surprises.

b. Restrictions are always logically updatable. However, SQL prohibits such updates if DISTINCT is specified, even though that DISTINCT can have no effect if the underlying table has a key. What's more, even when it does allow updates, SQL doesn't always check that updated rows satisfy the restriction condition; hence, an updated (or inserted) record can instantaneously vanish from the view. And there are concomitant security exposures (e.g., a user restricted to accessing employees with salary less than $100K might nevertheless create a salary greater than that value via INSERT or UPDATE).[7] However, these latter deficiencies are nothing to do with SQL's lack of knowledge of keys per se.

c. A key-based join of two tables is logically updatable. So too is a join of one table on one of its keys to another on a matching foreign key (though the details aren't totally straightforward). But SQL doesn't allow joins to be updated at all.

---

[6] I was tempted to rewrite this sentence to say it's an understanding of *functional dependencies*, rather, that's required in order to support the updating of views correctly. Which is perfectly true—but it's not stretching the truth too much to say that it's the functonal dependencies that are consequences of keys that are the most important ones in practice, in this context. See reference [4] for a detailed analysis of the entire question of view updating.

[7] The SQL CHECK option is intended to prevent such abuses but suffers from several rather severe problems of its own. See reference [8] for a detailed discussion of such matters.

Foreign Keys

SQL currently provides no support for foreign keys at all.

Domains

Note: I vastly prefer the term "type" (or "data type") to the unnecessarily confusing term "domain," and I'll talk in terms of types here.

SQL currently provides no support for types at all apart from a few rather primitive, system defined, scalar ones such as INTEGER, FLOAT, etc. (And even that support is muddled. For example, SQL is very unclear as to whether CHAR(2) and CHAR(3) are two types or just one). There's no proper support for nonscalar types at all, nor for user defined types.

Table Assignment

A very limited form of table assignment is supported via INSERT ... SELECT, but that operation doesn't overwrite the previous content of the target table as a true table assignment (i.e., one of the form "*table := table expression*") would do. Moreover, the source for INSERT ... SELECT can't be specified by means of an arbitrarily complex table expression.

Explicit INTERSECT and DIFFERENCE

These omissions are perhaps not all that serious, since equivalent SELECT expressions exist in both cases; however, symmetry would suggest that, since UNION is explicitly supported, INTERSECT and DIFFERENCE ought to be explicitly supported as well—especially since some problems are more "naturally" formulated in terms of explicit intersections and differences. On the other hand (as indicated in the discussion of =ANY etc. earlier), it might not be a good idea to provide a multiplicity of different but equivalent ways of formulating the same problem, unless it can be guaranteed that the implementation will recognize the equivalences and treat all formulations in the same way, which it probably won't.

Explicit JOIN

Explicit support for (natural) join is highly desirable for both practical and theoretical reasons. Indeed, the case for such support is much stronger than the case for explicit intersection and difference support.

CONCLUDING REMARKS

I've discussed a large number of deficiencies and shortcomings in SQL as originally defined, and indicated in some cases (certainly not all) how matters might be improved. My primary aim has been to identify problems and thereby to try to contribute to the solution of those problems, before their influence becomes too irrevocably widespread.[8]

Of course, I realize that many of the deficiencies I've been discussing will very likely be dismissed by many as academic, trivial, or otherwise unimportant, especially as SQL is so clearly superior to older languages such as the DDL and DML of DBTG. However, experience shows that "academic" considerations have a nasty habit of becoming horribly practical a few years further down the road. The mistakes we make now will come back to haunt us in the future. Indeed, SQL in its present form is already proving difficult to extend in some (desirable) ways because of limitations in its present structure.

I also realize there are those who'll dismiss my criticisms on the grounds that many of the problems I've mentioned have now been fixed. But that misses the point! The point is, the problems should never have been allowed to occur in the first place (not to mention the fact that some of them aren't fixable anyway, sometimes but not always because of that *Shackle of Compatibility* I mentioned in the preamble to Chapter 8). And it's my contention that the reason the problems occurred in the first place is because the language was designed without any attention being paid to the principles spelled out in this chapter's companion piece [9]. Language design needs to be done by people who possess the appropriate background knowledge and skills.

In conclusion, let me say that I do understand that most other proposed relational (or would-be relational) languages suffer from deficiencies similar to those discussed in these three chapters; SQL certainly isn't alone in this regard. For reasons we all know only too well, however, SQL is likely to be the most

---

[8] A pious hope, perhaps. I'll leave it to you to judge whether and to what extent the problems have been fixed in later versions of the standard.

influential of those languages—and if it's adopted on a wide scale in its present form, then to some degree I think we'll have missed the relational boat, or at least failed to capitalize to the fullest extent on the potential of the relational model. That would be a shame, because we do have an opportunity to do it right, and with a little effort we could do so. The question is whether it's now too late. I sincerely hope not.

ACKNOWLEDGMENTS

I'm pleased to acknowledge the helpful comments and criticisms I received on previous drafts of the original paper (i.e., back in the 1980s) from my friends and colleagues Ted Codd, Phil Shaw, and Sharon Weinberg.

REFERENCES

1. M. M. Astrahan et al: "System R: Relational Approach to Database Management," *ACM Transactions on Database Systems 1*, No. 2 (June 1976).

2. C. J. Date: "An Introduction to the Unified Database Language (UDL)," Proc. 6th International Conference on Very Large Data Bases, Montreal, Canada (September/October 1980). Republished (in considerably revised form) in C. J. Date, *Relational Database: Selected Writings* (Addison-Wesley, 1986).

3. C. J. Date: "Why Three- and Four-Valued Logic Don't Work," in *Date on Database: Writings 2000-2006.* Apress (2006).

4. C. J. Date: *View Updating and Relational Theory: Solving the View Update Problem.* O'Reilly (2013).

5. C. J. Date: *SQL and Relational Theory: How to Write Accurate SQL Code* (3rd edition). O'Reilly (2015).

6. C. J. Date: "The Relational Model Defined," in Appendix A ("The Relational Model") of reference [5].

7. C. J. Date: "Redundancy in SQL," in *Stating the Obvious, and Other Database Writings: Still More Thoughts and Essays on Database Matters* (Technics Publications, 2020).

8, C. J. Date: "View Assignment in SQL," in Chapter 2 ("Assignment") of *Stating the Obvious. and Other Database Writings: Still More Thoughts and Essays on Database Matters* (Technics Publications, 2020).

9. C. J. Date: "Some Principles of Good Language Design," Chapter 7 of the present book.

10. C. J. Date: "NOT Is Not 'Not'!" (in two parts), Chapters 12 and 13 of the present book.

11. C. J. Date: "EXISTS Is Not 'Exists'!", Chapter 14 of the present book.

12. J. N. Gray: Private communication (undated).

13. International Organization for Standardization (ISO): *Database Language SQL*, Documents ISO/IEC 9075:1987 ("SQL/86"). See also C. J. Date: *A Guide to the SQL Standard* (first edition), Addison-Wesley (1987).

14. X3H2 (American National Standards Database Committee): *Draft Proposed Relational Database Language*, Document X3H2-83-152 (August 1983).

Chapter 11

A Type Is a Type Is a Type

Chapter 2 ("What Is a Domain?") of my book Relational Database Writings 1985-1989 (Addison-Wesley, 1990) included a short appendix on the logical differences between system defined and user defined types. This short chapter consists of a revised and greatly expanded version of that appendix. This version copyright © 2022 C. J. Date.

I'm on record in many places—see, e.g., my book *SQL and Relational Theory: How to Write Accurate SQL Code* (3rd edition, O'Reilly, 2015)—as arguing that a domain is nothing more than a data type (which I usually prefer to abbreviate to just *type*), possibly system defined, possibly user defined. However, E. F. (Ted) Codd, the originator of the relational model, never really agreed with me on this issue. For example, in his paper "Domains, Keys, and Referential Integrity in Relational Databases" (*InfoDB 3*, No. 1, Spring 1988)—referred to throughout this chapter as just *the domains and keys paper*—he says, in effect, that if a domain is a data type at all,[1] then it's an "extended" one and not merely a "basic" one:

> Each domain is declared as an extended data type (not as a mere basic data type) ... The distinction between extended ... and basic data types is NOT that the first is user defined and the second is built into the system.

Note in particular the emphasis he lays on his claim that the distinction between "extended" and "basic" types isn't that the first is user defined and the second system defined. In fact, he goes on to say in his paper that basic and extended types can both be either system defined (built in) or user defined—though it's not at all clear what a "user defined basic type" might look like, since

---

[1] I believe he did eventually come round to agreeing (after many years of debate between us!) that domains and types did at leasr have a lot in common, but I don't think he ever accepted the idea that they were really just the same thing by different names.

he doesn't give any examples of such in the paper (nor does he do so anywhere else in his writings either, at least so far as I'm aware).

In response to these statements of Codd's, I have to say I don't find the distinction he draws, or tries to draw, between basic and extended types a particularly useful one; in fact, I don't think it's even meaningful, as I believe the rest of this short chapter makes quite clear. By contrast, I do think the distinction between system defined and user defined types is a useful one, at least to some extent. Of course, I agree that one user *U1* might define a type *T* which, despite being (obviously) user defined, subsequently becomes, in effect, built-in or system defined from the point of view of some other user *U2*; thus, the system vs. user defined distinction does, in effect, have to be interpreted with respect to some particular user. Nevertheless, it still seems to me a distinction worth making, because it does have operational meaning for the user doing the defining, at least. By contrast, I don't see how the basic vs. extended type distinction has any significant meaning at all as far as any user is concerned.

Let's examine Codd's position in a little more detail. Later in the domains and keys paper, in a section with the title "Extended Data Types: Built-in and User Defined," he requires the system (i.e., the DBMS) to support "calendar dates, clock times, and decimal currency as built-in extended data types." Well, I think this requirement as stated raises a few obvious questions:

1. What does that "built-in" add? Is it there just to stress the point that—in Codd's opinion—a type can be "extended" but also "built in" (i.e., supported by the system")? But then, if the system has to support these types, aren't they "built in" by definition?

2. What does that "extended" add? How exactly would matters be different if it was replaced by "basic"? Or if it was simply dropped?

3. If as Codd claims "the distinction between extended and basic types isn't that the first is user defined and the second is system defined," then what exactly *are* the criteria for distinguishing between extended and basic types?

4. Are those criteria subjective or objective ?

5. By way of a concrete example, the IBM product DB2 supports the following built-in types among others: CHAR; VARCHAR; GRAPHIC;

DATE; TIME; TIMESTAMP. So which of these do you, the reader, think are basic and which extended? (Justify your answer!) Note that only one of these types (viz., CHAR) is directly representable by the underlying IBM machine architecture, and further that for *none* of them does that underlying architecture support all of the pertinent operators (e.g., substring, concatenate, etc., in the case of CHAR).[2]

The domains and keys paper also gives a table that summarizes what Codd claims to be the differences (but are they *operational* differences?) between basic and extended types. That table looks more or less as follows:

#	Basic Data Type	Extended Data Type
1	property-oriented name	object-oriented name
2	a property of an object	an object
3	not independently declarable	independently declarable
4	range of values NOT specifiable	range of values specifiable
5	applicability of >, < not specifiable	applicability of >, < specifiable
6	two database values with the same basic data type need not have the same extended data type	

Let's examine the points in this table one by one.

NAMING

All types have names (e.g., the name of the type INTEGER is "INTEGER"). But some of those names are prescribed by the system (for built-in or system defined types) and some are chosen by the user (for user defined types). Codd explains what he calls the "property-oriented vs. object-oriented" naming distinction thus:[3]

---

[2] As a matter of fact I would argue that several of these so called types, including CHAR in particular, aren't types at all anyway, but rather type *generators*—but this observation isn't all that relevant to the discussion at hand. (Again see my book *SQL and Relational Theory: How to Write Accurate SQL Code*, 3rd edition, O'Reilly, 2015, for an explanation of the difference between types as such and type generators.)

[3] It's not clear what the explanation in question has to do with naming as such, but let's agree to overlook that point.

[Unless it is built in] ... an extended data type must be declared as an object itself prior to any use being made of it. In contrast, a basic data type is normally a property associated with an object at the time of the object's declaration.

But surely an "extended" data type is also "associated with an object [*i.e., of the type in question*] at the time of the object's declaration"? I fail to see any fundamental distinction here, other than the system- vs. user-defined one. See the next two sections for examples and further discussion.

PROPERTY vs. OBJECT

One problem with this second point is that there's no precise, objective definition of what a property is or what an object is. Indeed, I've argued myself (in a different context, but repeatedly) that "one person's entity is another person's property"—see, for example, Chapter 8 ("Thinking Clearly about Decapsulation") of my book *Stating the Obvious, and Other Database Writings* (Technics Publications, 2020)—and:

a. First, the term *entity* could be replaced in that quote of mine by the term *object* without making any logical difference, and

b. Second, I know from numerous private conversations with Codd that he completely agreed with what I was saying in this connection. In fact, I'm pretty sure he said the exact same thing himself (quoting me) in some of his own writings.[4]

Suppose I create a user defined data type called RECTANGLE, with the intuitively obvious semantics, and suppose further that I also declare a variable ("VAR") of that type:

```
VAR R RECTANGLE ;
```

---

[4] On page 7 of his book *The Relational Model for Database Management Version 2* (Addison-Wesley, 1990) he says "One person's entity is another person's relationship." Yes, I know this quote talks about relationships, not properties, but *all* of these terms are hopelessly fuzzy and imprecise, and my general point still stands.

Well, it seems to me that RECTANGLE here is performing exactly the same function with respect to the variable R as INTEGER is performing with respect to the variable I in the declaration

```
VAR I INTEGER ;
```

Both RECTANGLE and INTEGER surely represent "properties" of the variable (or "object"?) in whose declaration they're referenced.

Furthermore, both RECTANGLE and INTEGER are "objects" in their own right, with corresponding "properties" of their own (for example, rectangles have length and width, integers have sign and magnitude). The difference between them is simply that, in the case of built-in types like INTEGER, it's the system that defines those properties, whereas in the case of user defined data types like RECTANGLE it's the user who does (the user doing the defining, I mean).

Of course, I realize that (a) the user who actually defines a particular "user defined" type and (b) the user who merely makes us of that type (e.g., in the declaration of some variable) might not actually be the same person. Indeed, they often won't be, if only because defining a new type surely requires certain specialized skills that the average user probably doesn't possess. But that's not the point. The point is, there'll surely always be types in general that, like type RECTANGLE in the example, can't and won't be built in (system defined) ahead of time but instead have to be provided by some appropriately skilled human user.

DECLARABILITY

Of course, it's true that type INTEGER (assuming it's built in, which in practice it surely will be) isn't "independently declarable" and type RECTANGLE is. To state the matter a little more precisely, no human user can define the type INTEGER, because that type already exists—it's part of the package, as it were; it comes out of the same box the system itself came out of. By contrast, some human user not only can but must define the type RECTANGLE (if it's needed), precisely because it *doesn't* already exist. In other words: What else is "independent declarability vs. the lack of same," other than just another way of saying that RECTANGLE is user defined and INTEGER is built in or system defined?

RANGE OF VALUES

In the final analysis, any type is basically just a set of values. For example, type INTEGER is the set of all integers, and type RECTANGLE is the set of all rectangles.[5] So when a given type is defined (or "declared"), one of the things that has to be specified is the set (or "range") of values that go to make up the type in question. That specification in turn constitutes what I've referred to elsewhere[6] as the *type constraint* for the type in question.

Now, there are several different syntactic mechanisms, in general, by which the type constraint might be specified for a given type; those details aren't important here. What's important for our purposes is that, obviously enough, the type constraint (or "range of values") for a system defined type is specified by the system, while the type constraint (or "range of values") for a user defined type is specified by the user doing the defining. For the person who's merely using the type in question (e.g., in the definition of a variable), it comes to the same thing. So once again, the only significant difference between what Codd calls "basic" and "extended" types is neither more nor less than that the former are system defined and the latter are user defined.

APPLICABILITY OF ">" AND "<"

Every type *T* has associated with it a set of operators that can be used with values and variables of type *T*, because types without operators are useless (obviously enough). So what do I mean by "associated with" here? I mean precisely the following, no more and no less:

■ Let *Op* be an operator.

■ Let *Op* have a parameter *P*.

■ Let *P* be declared (as part of the definition of *Op*) to be of type *T*.

---

[5] Well ... not *all* integers or rectangles, because those sets are infinite, and we're dealing here with finite computing systems. So certain limitations do have to be imposed in practice, and that, in part, is precisely what that business of "range of values" does.

[6] See in particular the book *Databases, Types, and the Relational Model: The Third Manifesto*, by Hugh Darwen and myself (3rd edition, Addison-Wesley, 2007), or the book I've mentioned a couple of times already, *SQL and Relational Theory: How to Write Accurate SQL Code* (3rd edition, O'Reilly, 2015). The treatment in this latter book is less formal than that in the other one.

■   Then *Op* is associated with *T*.

In other words, a given type is "associated with" just those operators that have a parameter of the type in question—no more and no less.

Here by way of example is the definition of an operator called AREA_OF that's associated in the foregoing sense with type RECTANGLE:

```
OPERATOR AREA_OF ( R RECTANGLE ) RETURNS AREA ;
   RETURN ( HEIGHT ( R ) × WIDTH ( R ) ) ;
END OPERATOR ;
```

And here's another example (pseudocode) to illustrate the point that, in general, an operator can have any number of parameters:

```
OPERATOR INSIDE ( R RECTANGLE , P POINT ) RETURNS BOOLEAN ;
   RETURN ( if P is inside R then TRUE else FALSE ) ;
END OPERATOR ;
```

Operate INSIDE is "associated with" both type RECTANGLE and type POINT. [7]
All of that being said, I now observe that ">" and "<" aren't special—they're just operators in the foregoing entirely conventional sense. Thus, whether or not they apply to values and variables of a given type *T* (or are "associated with" that type *T*) depends 100% on whether or not they've been defined for that type *T*. Here's such a definition for the operator ">" and type INTEGER:

```
OPERATOR ">" ( I1 INTEGER , I2 INTEGER ) RETURNS BOOLEAN ;
   RETURN ( if I1 is greater than I2 then TRUE else FALSE ) ;
END OPERATOR ;
```

If INTEGER is a system defined type (which of course it probably is), then the foregoing definition will presumably be provided by the system; if it's a user defined type, the definition will be provided by some human user. Thus, the only significant difference in this connection between what Codd calls "basic" and "extended" types is simply that the former are system defined and the latter are user defined.

---

[7] As this example demonstrates, therefore, a given operator *Op* can be "associated with" any number of different types *T1*, *T2*, ..., *Tn*. Thus, I do *not* subscribe to the object-oriented dogma (sometimes called "selfish methods") according to which every operator is associated with—in fact, tightly bound to—exactly one type.

Note: For reasons of brevity I'm deliberately ignoring various issues that arise in connection with this last example (viz., the definition of the ">" operator specifically). The issues in question include the following:

a. In practice, we'd surely want to be able to use ">" in connection with many other types, both system and user defined, in addition to type INTEGER.

b. In practice again, we'd surely want to use the familiar infix notation for invocations of that operator.

Such issues are interesting and important, but they have little to do with the primary topic of this chapter.

REPRESENTATION

Here again is point 6 from Codd's table:

> Two database values with the same *basic* data type need not have the same *extended* data type [*Codd's words, my italics*].

To my mind, remarks of this nature—many similar ones can be found elsewhere in Codd's writings—demonstrate a serious confusion on Codd's part over the logical difference between types and representations.[8] To spell the point out:

■ *Type* is a model level concept. The user has to know about types. It's the type of a given value or variable that dictates what the user can do with that value or variable, because (as explained in the previous section) it's the type that dictates what operators are available for the value or variable in question.

■ *Representation* is an implementation level concept. The user doesn't have to know about representations. The representation merely specifies how

---

[8] It's not just Codd, though—a confusion over types vs. representations is, regrettably, all too common in the database community, and indeed in the SQL language. See Chapter 10 ("Types, Units, and Representations: A Dialog, of a Kind") of my book *Stating the Obvious, and Other Database Writings* (Technics Publications, 2020) for an illustration of this point and much further explanation

values and variables of the type in question are physically stored and implemented inside the system.

Note very carefully, therefore, that (to say it again) the operators that apply to values and variables of type *T* are the operators associated with type *T* as such—*not* the operators associated with the representation of type *T*. For example, just because (a) the representation for type ENO ("employee numbers") happens to be CHAR, say, and (b) an operator is available for concatenating two CHAR strings, it doesn't follow that (c) we can concatenate two employee numbers; we can do that only if a concatenation operator has been defined for type ENO.

So I hope you can see by now, if you didn't already, that the quote from the opening of this section—

> [Two] database values with the same basic data type need not have the same extended data type.

—would much better be replaced by the following:

> [Two] database values with the same representation need not be of the same type.

For example, with reference to the usual suppliers-and-parts database, the character string (e.g.) '004' might simultaneously be the representation of both a valid supplier number (type SNO) and a valid part number (type PNO)—but those two values (the SNO value and the PNO value) would nevertheless not be considered equal.[9] But such a situation is hardly unfamiliar! Forget about "extended" types like SNO and PNO for the moment; consider "basic" types instead. The fact is, two values of different "basic" types could both have the same representation inside the machine. For example, the bit string '1111000111110010'B might—and in fact does—simultaneously represent both a valid binary integer and a valid character string. In other words, it's all just a matter of levels of abstraction.

Here's another quote from the domains and keys paper that I think shows clearly (again) that Codd was confused over types vs. representations:

---

[9] Not only would they not "compare equal, in fact, but any attempt to perform such a comparison would fail on a type error (and fail, moreover, at compile time).

With special authorization ... a user may employ the DOMAIN CHECK OVERRIDE qualifier in his [*sic*] command, if a special need arises to "compare apples with oranges."

The "apples and oranges" comparisons Codd is referring to here are comparisons involving types (though he calls them domains) that are logically distinct by definition but share the same representation—for example, a comparison to see whether the representation of a certain supplier number is the same as that of a certain part number.

Note: Perhaps I should state for completeness how I think the "apples and oranges" requirement (if requirement it truly is) should be handled. Suppose we want to do a "domain check override" equality comparison on a supplier number variable called SNO and a part number variable called PNO. Then what we need is (a) an operator—I'll call it STOC—that takes a supplier number and returns the character string representation for that supplier number, and (b) another operator—I'll call it PTOC—that performs the analogous function for part numbers. Then the following comparison does the necessary:

```
STOC ( SNO ) = PTC ( PNO )
```

Now there's no need whatsoever for any such nasty piece of adhocery (to coin an ugly but convenient term) as "domain check override."

CONCLUDING REMARKS

"Basic types" vs. "extended types" isn't a useful distinction. "System defined types" vs. "user defined types" is—though not very. So I would revise Codd's table of differences (see earlier) to look something like this:

#	System Defined Type	User Defined Type
1	named by system	named by user
2	system defined property type	user defined property type
3	declared by system	declared by user
4	type constraint system defined	type constraint user defined
5	some ops system defined	all ops user defined
6	same representation doesn't imply same type	same representation doesn't imply same type

Chapter 12

NOT Is Not "Not"!

Part 1

SQL's approach to missing information supported is based on nulls and three-valued logic (3VL). It's disastrously bad, and all the worse for being, by now, so deeply and thoroughly entrenched. I originally wrote the paper on which this chapter and the next are based in the mid 1980s, before SQL was standardized, (a) with the aim of describing and analyzing the approach as it then was and raising some pertinent questions, and (b) in the hope that wiser heads might prevail and we could get the standard to avoid the quagmire while there was still time. Of course this latter didn't happen—and I suppose I might be partly to blame, since I didn't manage to get my paper into print until 1989 or 1990, by which time it was, I suppose, too late. So what follows, though heavily revised, might (like certain other chapters in this book) be largely just of historical interest. But the questions raised are still pertinent and have still never been satisfactorily answered in the literature; moreover, the treatment of the topic overall is rather different from what's usually found in that same literature, and so the original paper does seem worth polishing up and reviving. Well, I think so, anyway.

Publishing history: This is a major revision of, and supersedes, a paper that first appeared under the same title—but with the addition of the subtitle "Notes on Three-Valued Logic and Related Matters"—as Chapter 8 of my book Relational Database Writings 1985-1989 (Addison-Wesley, 1990). I've divided this revised version into two parts to make it a little more digestible. This version (both parts) copyright © 2022 C. J. Date.

I'm a little embarrassed to be dredging up the somewhat hackneyed topic of nulls and missing information yet one more time; there are far too many articles and papers on the subject out there already, including one by myself [4].[1] However, the emphasis of the present treatment is different—to be specific, it's more concerned with the underlying ideas, ideas that have their origin in a paper of Codd's [1]. In writing it, I had two principal objectives in mind:

- First, I remain far from convinced regarding the suitability of three-valued logic (3VL) as a basis for dealing with missing information. I've conveyed my concerns to Codd [5] and discussed them with him, but now it seems appropriate to air those concerns in front of a wider audience. Of course, it might be that I just don't understand the 3VL scheme properly; if so, however, I know I'm not alone in that position, and what follows can therefore be seen as a request for clarification (and for reassurance that we're not all marching off down the wrong path).[2]

- Second, given that DBMSs probably will support 3VL sooner or later,[3] it seemed a good idea to try to explain in semiformal, semitutorial style, with nontrivial examples, just what 3VL is all about and what problems it's trying to solve (also, I must add, what problems it gives rise to).

Now, I did say in that early paper of mine, reference [4], that I regard the missing information problem as an important one, one for which a systematic solution is highly desirable. I still subscribe to that position. I also indicated that SQL-style nulls (which are based on 3VL, of course) are *not* a satisfactory solution to that problem—so much so, in fact, that my general recommendation has to be to avoid them altogether. It's true that nulls do possess a superficial attractiveness, but I firmly believe they cause far more problems than they solve, as reference [4] and other writings amply demonstrate. The discussions that follow aren't primarily concerned with SQL per se, however (though they do point out a few specific SQL anomalies), but rather with the more fundamental

---

[1] All references for this chapter and the next are listed in a section toward the end of that next chapter.

[2] I was bending over backward to be diplomatic here. The fact is, I believe I did understand the 3VL scheme only too well, even at the time, and what I've learned since has just served to strengthen my position.

[3] Of course, by now they all do (all SQL systems, at any rate), But that's not to say everyone understands that support, even today, and there's plenty to evidence to show they don't.

question of whether it's possible to use 3VL as a satisfactory basis for dealing with the missing information problem at all.

As I've said, the idea of using 3VL for this purpose is due to Codd, who introduced it in reference [1] under the heading "Extensions of the [Relational] Algebra for Null Values" and elaborated on it in references [2] and [3]. In fact, Codd now appears to regard those extensions no longer as extensions as such but rather as part of the relational model per se. Nevertheless, it seemed to me at the time (and seems to me now even more so, all these years later) that there were some serious questions—both logical questions and psychological ones—that should have been asked (and satisfactorily answered, of course) before we committed ourselves too heavily to the 3VL scheme. Some of those questions are raised again in these two chapters.

The plan for those chapters is as follows. The section immediately following opens the discussion by examining some of the many reasons why information might be missing—value unknown, value not applicable, and so on. The rest of the discussion then homes in on the "value unknown" case specifically. It begins by giving a careful description of how the 3VL scheme is supposed to handle that case, and then goes on to discuss some consequences of that scheme. Subsequent sections (in this chapter and the next) contain (a) a series of detailed examples, using them to highlight the counterintuitive behavior of 3VL; (b) a couple of important and fundamental questions, and (c) some miscellaneous issues. The final section (in the next chapter) offers a few concluding remarks. And there's also an appendix, describing one possible approach to avoiding 3VL altogether.

KINDS OF MISSING INFORMATION

Conventional usage in this context (which I'll adhere to for present purposes) is to say something "is null" as a convenient shorthand to mean the something in question is missing for some reason. For example, the statement "Joe's salary is null" would typically be used to mean that (a) there's certainly a position (or "slot") in the database for recording Joe's salary, but (b) there's no value recorded at that position at this time. Note immediately, therefore, that *null isn't a value*; rather, it's a representation of the fact that there isn't a value. It might be thought of as a kind of flag, or marker, on the pertinent position or slot.

Because null isn't a value, the term "null value" is deprecated.[4] Indeed, in reference [2], Codd talks in terms of "marks," not nulls, in an attempt among other things to avoid any suggestion that such things might be regarded as values.[5] Thus, for example, the fact that Joe's salary is missing might be expressed as "Joe's salary is marked"—meaning that the slot that would normally hold Joe's salary in the database is marked somehow to show the information is missing. (As an aside, I note that SQL products do typically represents nulls in precisely this manner, i.e., by, in effect, marking the storage location appropriately on the disk.) I tend to agree with Codd that some systematic kind of "mark" terminology would be preferable to the more usual "nulls" terminology, but for reasons of familiarity I'll stay with the latter. For the most part, at any rate.

Of course, there are many reasons why a given piece of information might be missing—i.e., many possible interpretations of the assertion that "*X* is null" for some *X*. In other words, there are many distinct kinds of nulls. Some of them are identified below.

- Value not applicable

  Suppose the database includes an employee table EMP, with columns EMPNO, DEPTNO, JOB, SALARY, and COMMISSION, and suppose too that the property COMMISSION applies only to employees in the sales department. Also, let Joe be an employee, but not an employee in that department. Then the statement "Joe's commission is null" means Joe doesn't have a commission, because the property of having a commission doesn't apply to him.

  Note: In reference [2], Codd calls this kind of null an "I-mark" (I for inapplicable).

---

[4] Despite the fact that I used it myself in the title of reference [4]! I'm kind of embarrassed about that now. Be that as it may, it's worth noting for the record that some of the problems with nulls in SQL arise precisely because in some contexts—though not in all—SQL does treat nulls as if they were values.

[5] Though he does also repeatedly use the term "marked value," which seems to nullify that attempt (I choose my words carefully). I mean, a "marked value," whatever else it might be, certainly sounds like it's some kind of value. To spell the point out: It's not values as such, it's positions—i.e., positions, or slots, that are capable of *holding* values—that might or might not be "marked."

■ Value unknown

In contrast to the previous example, the statement "Joe's salary is null" presumably means Joe does have a salary (because all employees have a salary), but we don't know what it is.

Note: In reference [2], Codd calls this type of null an "A-mark" (A for applicable—the property of having a salary does apply to Joe, even though the actual value is unknown).

■ Value doesn't exist

Consider the property "social security number." In the U.S., at least, this property applies to employees in general—in fact, it applies to U.S. residents in general—but not everyone actually has a social security number.[6] Thus, the statement "Joe's social security number is null" could simply mean no social security number exists for Joe. Note the difference between this case and the first case above ("value not applicable"). In the example, the property of having a social security number is certainly applicable to Joe (because it's applicable to everyone); it's just that Joe doesn't actually happen to have one at this time.

■ Value undefined

Certain items are explicitly undefined: for example, the result of dividing something by zero, or the maximum value in an empty set. Thus, for example, in a table T with columns A, B, C, and D, where A stands for "person," B for "number of payments made," C for "total payment made," and D for "average payment made," D will be undefined—another type of null—for anyone who has made no payments at all.[7]

---

[6] I know this can happen because it happened to me—I was a U.S. resident for well over two years before I acquired a social security number.

[7] More problems arise in SQL here, because SQL considers the AVG (also the MAX and the MIN and the SUM) of an empty set to be unknown, not undefined. A more appropriate approach, if the system doesn't support "undefined" (and SQL doesn't), would be to allow an optional second argument to be specified for such operator invocations, representing the value to be returned if the first argument is empty. It would then be an error if that second argument were omitted and the first argument were indeed empty.

Incidentally, the result in the specific case of SUM should be zero anyway, not undefined (SQL is doubly wrong in this particular instance). After all, in the example, if B (number of payments) is zero, then C (total payment) should clearly be zero as well.

■ Value not valid

During data entry, it might be discovered that some value is invalid—e.g., employee age = 80, when employees are required to retire at 65. There might be good reasons for entering the employee into the database anyway, but marking the employee's age as invalid, if for no other reason than to permit subsequent analysis in order to discover, precisely, which values in the original data were in fact not valid.

■ Value not supplied

"Refused to answer" or "no comment" are perfectly legitimate responses to certain questions in census operations and the like. Again, there might be very good operational reasons for distinguishing such cases appropriately in the database, instead of just marking them as "unknown."

■ Value is the empty set

Let table XDE be the left outer natural join of departments and employees over department number. Suppose department *d* has no employees at this time. Then there'll be exactly one row in table XDE for department *d*, with a null in the employee number position. That null means that the set of employees in department *d* is empty set. (Note, moreover, that the SQL expression

```
SELECT DEPTNO , COUNT(*)
FROM   XDE
GROUP  BY DEPTNO
```

will return a count of one, not zero, for department *d*. This result is at best counterintuitive, at worst plain wrong.)

And there are certainly other possibilities also (for example, the nulls generated by outer union seem to be different in kind from *all* of the nulls discussed above). The overall point, however, is that each kind of null has its own special properties and its own special behavior; thus, representing and manipulating them all in the same way is clearly not the right thing to do.

By the way, this latter remark raises another point. In a system that supports—or tries to support—just one kind of null, say "value unknown," there's a strong likelihood that users will be use that null for purposes for which it's not appropriate. In other words, the fact that "null support" is provided is likely to lull users into a false sense of security ("missing information?—don't worry about it, the system can handle it"). As a concrete example of such misuse, it's quite likely in such a system that Joe's commission (see above) would erroneously be represented by means of a "value unknown" null, whereas it should of course be a "value doesn't apply" null. One consequence of this mistake is that, in attempting to compute Joe's total compensation (salary plus commission), the system will give "unknown" (see later), whereas of course it should be equal to just Joe's salary.[8]

What's more, the foregoing argument will always apply, mutatis mutandis, so long as the system supports fewer kinds of nulls than are logically necessary. In other words, simply adding support for a "value doesn't apply" null might solve the specific problem mentioned in the previous paragraph, but it won't solve the general problem. In fact, a system that does support nulls, but not at the 100% level (whatever that level might be, I suppose I should say), is just as open to abuse—perhaps even more so, perhaps even dangerously more so—than a system that provides no such support at all.

Now, in Codd's approach, the introduction of a single kind of null (his A-mark) requires an extension of the traditional two-valued logic (2VL) to a logic of three values (3VL), and the introduction of a second kind (his I-mark) requires a further extension to a logic of four values (4VL). Thus, to deal with the seven (or eight?) kinds of nulls identified above will presumably need a logic of nine (or ten?) values! In general, in fact, it seems that N kinds of nulls will require an $(N+2)$-valued logic. This fact alone should at least give us pause, I believe. But matters are worse than that ... In fact, it's easy to see that (in principle, at any rate) the number of different kinds of nulls required is quite literally infinite. For consider:

■ Again let table EMP have columns EMPNO, DEPTNO, JOB, SALARY, and COMMISSION, and let COMMISSION apply only to employees in the sales department.

---

[8] In reference [2] Codd says that the sum (i.e., "+", meaning arithmetic addition) of a "value does not apply" null or I-mark and a genuine numeric value should yield "value does not apply." But (to pursue the "salary plus commission" example a little further) the total compensation for an employee for whom the commission property is inapplicable should clearly be just that employee's salary; in other words, despite what Codd says, "$v+i$" (where v is a genuine value and i is an I-mark) should surely give v, not i.

■ Suppose now that employee Joe's DEPTNO slot is "A-marked," meaning Joe does have a department but we don't know what it is.

■ All right—so what do we do about employee Joe's commission? It surely must be null—the information is surely missing—*but we don't know whether that null should be an A-mark or an I-mark.* If Joe is in the sales department it should be an A-mark; otherwise it should be an I-mark. But *we don't know* whether Joe is in the sales department! So we don't know what kind of null we need for Joe's commission.

■ So it looks as if need a new kind of null (or mark, if you prefer), meaning "either an A-mark or an I-mark, but we don't know which." Call this new kind of null "null-3" (A- and I-marks being null-1 and -2, respectively).

■ Now we need a new kind of null to represent "either null-1 or null-2 or null-3, but we don't know which." Call this one "null-4."

■ Now we need a new kind of null to represent "either null-1 or null-2 or null-3 or null-4, but we don't know which." Call this one "null-5."

And so on, ad infinitum.

Well ... despite the somewhat depressing nature of the foregoing state of affairs, I'll focus throughout the remainder of this discussion (as Codd did in reference [1]) on just one case, viz., the "value unknown" case. (Because if we can't adequately handle the case of just one kind of null, there seems little point on attempting to deal with many different kinds, especially if that "many" really means "an infinite number of.") Moreover, from this point forward I'll refer to that one kind of null as UNK (for unknown), just to make it a little more explicit which kind it is. Note, thefore, that my UNK is Codd's A-mark.

UNK AND 3VL

The rest of this chapter consists of an extended and systematic description of an approach to dealing with UNK-type nulls based on three-valued logic (3VL). The approach is intended to be essentially the same as that proposed by Codd in references [1], [2], and [3], except that I've spelled out a few details that weren't explicitly discussed in those references. The description is intended to be reasonably rigorous, as far as it goes. *Note:* Portions of this material previously appeared in reference [4].

Scalar Comparisons

Let θ denote any of the scalar comparison operators "=", "≠", "<", "≤", ">", and "≥", and let x and y denote scalar values such that $x \theta y$ is a syntactically valid expression. What does that comparison evaluate to if x or y evaluates to UNK, or if they both do?[9] Since by definition UNK represents "value unknown," we define the result in every case to be, not *true* or *false*, but rather *unknown*. In other words (as you already know), we adopt a three-valued logic, 3VL, in place of the more usual two-valued logic 2VL. The three truth values are *true*, *false*, and *unknown* ("the third truth value," abbreviated in what follows to *unk*). Note that *unk* might intuitively be interpreted as "maybe."

Points arising:

■ An anomaly that should strike you immediately is the following: Given the foregoing definition, the comparison $x = x$ evaluates to *unk*, not *true*, if x happens to evaluate to UNK. The full implications of this anomaly aren't clear—but one thing that certainly is clear is that the scheme under consideration is going to display some fairly counterintuitive behavior, to say the very least.

■ (*Important!*) Note clearly that *unk* is not the same as UNK!—i.e., the value *unknown* is not the same as "value unknown" (if you see what I mean). For consider: Let b be a boolean variable, i.e., a variable of type boolean (or type "truth value," if you prefer). If the value of b happens to be *unk*, then the value of b is known (specifically, it's known to be *unk*, "the third truth value")—and knowing its value is *unk* is certainly not the same as its value not being known. If on the other hand b is UNK (i.e., the value of b isn't known), then it isn't known whether the value of b is *true* or *false* or *unk*.

To put it another way: If b is *unk*, then $b = b$ gives *true*; if b is UNK, then $b = b$ gives *unk*.

---

[9] Of course, if x and y do denote *values* as stated, then they can't possibly "evaluate to UNK," since as explained earlier the whole point about UNK (or null) is that it's not a value. Indeed, the very phrase "evaluate to UNK" is a contradiction in terms. The trurh is, it's just about impossible to talk about this stuff coherently, because none of it really makes sense. Never mind, let's just soldier on ...

Incidentally, in reference [1], Codd says (paraphrasing slightly):

> We use the same symbol to denote [both null and] the *unknown* truth value, because truth values can be stored in databases and we want the treatment of all unknown or null values to be uniform.

This remark seems to suggest that Codd thinks *unk* is the same as UNK after all. In a later paper (reference [2]), however, he says (again paraphrasing slightly):

> The *unknown* truth value can be thought of as a value-oriented counterpart for the A-mark [*i.e.,* UNK] when focusing on the domain of truth values.

Codd's use of the word *counterpart* here seems to suggest that now (a) he thinks that *unk* and UNK aren't the same, but that (b) there might be certain parallels between them. So which is it—are they the same or aren't they? (Of course, it's tempting to say the answer is unknown, but that would very naughty of me, so I won't.)

Scalar Operations Apart from Comparisons

Let α denote any dyadic (infix) scalar operator that's not a comparison—e.g., "+", "−", "×", "||" (concatenation), etc.—and let x and y denote scalar values such that $x \alpha y$ is a valid expression. What does that expression evaluate to if x or y evaluates to UNK, or if they both do? Since by definition UNK represents "value unknown," we define the result in every case to be UNK, rather than some definite known value. Monadic (prefix) operators are treated analogously—e.g., if x is a scalar value such that $+x$ and $-x$ are valid expressions, and if x evaluates to UNK, then those expressions do so too.
Points arising:

■ One anomaly that arises immediately is this: Let x be of some numeric type; then the expression $x - x$ evaluates to *unk*, not *true*, if x happens to evaluate to UNK. The full implications of this anomaly aren't clear.

Duplicate Scalars

We've seen that the comparison $x = x$ evaluates to *unk* if x is UNK. According to Codd, however, two UNKs still need to be considered as duplicates of one

another for purposes of duplicate elimination (e.g., when taking a projection) ...
The rather obvious contradiction involved in this situation is defined away—
rather airily, it seems to me—by Codd thus [1]:

> Identification for duplicate removal is at a lower level of detail than equality
> testing in the evaluation of retrieval conditions. Hence, it is possible to adopt a
> different rule.

Well, if we accept this position, then we have to define the notion of
duplicate scalar values (duplicate scalars for short) as follows: Scalars *x* and *y*
are *duplicates* of one another if and only if (a) they're both nonnull (i.e., not
UNK) and *x* = *y* is *true*, or (b) they're both null (i.e., UNK). Given this
definition, we can, and indeed must, define a new boolean operator DUP_OF, as
follows: The expression

```
x DUP_OF y
```

(where *x* and *y* are expressions of the same scalar type) returns *true* if the values
denoted by *x* and *y* are duplicates of one another, *false* otherwise.

Testing for Null (UNK)

We also need an operator, which I'll call IS_UNK, for testing whether a given
scalar is UNK. IS_UNK takes an arbitrary scalar expression as its argument and
returns *true* if that argument evaluates to UNK, *false* otherwise. Thus, e.g., the
expression

```
IS_UNK ( EMP.DEPTNO )
```

returns *true* if EMP.DEPTNO is UNK, *false* otherwise.

NOT, AND, OR

The boolean operators NOT, AND, and OR—3VL versions of those operators,
that is—are defined by the following truth tables (where for convenience *true*,
false, and *unk* are abbreviated to just *t*, *f*, and *u*, respectively):

```
NOT |             AND | t  u  f       OR | t  u  f
-----+----          ----+--------       ---+--------
  t  | f              t | t  u  f        t | t  t  t
  u  | u              u | u  u  f        u | t  u  u
  f  | t              f | f  f  f        f | t  u  f
```

Points arising:

■ Let *b* be a boolean variable. Note carefully, then, that the statements

   1. *b* is not *true*

and

   2. *b* is NOT *true*

aren't equivalent! (Hence my title for these two chapters, of course.) The first means the value of *b* is either *false* or *unk*. The second means the value of *b* is *false*. There are clearly rich possibilities for confusion in this field.

■ As we already know, "*unk* is not UNK." So suppose the value of boolean variable *b* is unknown (I mean it's UNK, not *unk*). What's the result of applying one of the boolean operators NOT or AND or OR to *b*? We might agree that *true* OR UNK yields *true*, and *false* AND UNK yields *false*; but it seems to me that all other cases can only yield UNK (for example, NOT UNK must surely evaluate to UNK). So is UNK another truth value? Are we really dealing with *four* truth values? In other words, are we already in the realm of four-valued logic, 4VL? (Is this problem just the problem of an infinite number of different kinds of nulls rearing its head again in a different guise?)

MAYBE

We also need a new boolean operator MAYBE, defined as follows:

```
MAYBE |
------+----
   t  | f
   u  | t
   f  | f
```

Points arising:

- Like NOT, MAYBE is a monadic operator—but whereas the purpose of NOT (loosely speaking) is to convert a *false* into a *true*, the purpose of MAYBE (again loosely speaking) is to convert an *unk* into a *true*. In other words, just as we might write (e.g.)

      NOT (EMP.JOB = 'Programmer')

  so we might write (e.g.)

      MAYBE (EMP.JOB = 'Programmer')

  The first of these expressions returns *true* if EMP.JOB does have the value 'Programmer', the second returns *true* if it "might" have that value (in other words, if it's UNK).
  Note: I'm departing slightly from Codd's scheme here; Codd's scheme doesn't include a MAYBE operator as such—instead, it includes a MAYBE option, or qualifier, on "queries" (i.e., table expressions). It also includes MAYBE versions of some—not all— of the relational algebra operators (see later).

- You might be thinking that SQL's IS NULL operator provides the functionality of the MAYBE operator as just defined. Well, it's probably correct to say that for any invocation of MAYBE there's a logically equivalent SQL expression that uses IS NULL. But using IS NULL instead of MAYBE is clunky—it can easily require an unreasonable amount of work on the part of the user—and is somewhat error prone besides. By way of example, consider the following sample query:

    Get employee numbers for employees who might be programmers born prior to August 17th, 1972, with a salary less than $80,000.[10]

---

[10] Note that this query is ambiguous as stated! What's more, it's difficult to make it precise without (in effect) making use of some kind of MAYBE operator. A precise formulation would be something like the following: "Get employee numbers for employees for whom it might be the case, but isn't definitely known to be the case, that all three of the following are true—(a) they're programmers; (b) they were born prior to August 17th, 1972; (c) they have a salary less than $80,000."

In a hypothetical version of SQL that supported MAYBE this query could be expressed quite succinctly as follows:

```
SELECT  EMP.EMPNO
FROM    EMP
WHERE   MAYBE ( EMP.JOB = 'Programmer' AND
                EMP.DOB < DATE ('1972-8-17') AND
                EMP.SALARY < 80000.00 )
```

However, in conventional SQL it would have to look more like this:

```
SELECT  EMP.EMPNO
FROM    EMP
WHERE            ( EMP.JOB = IS NULL AND
                   EMP.DOB < DATE ('1972-8-17') AND
                   EMP.SALARY < 80000.00 )

OR               ( EMP.JOB = 'Programmer' AND
                   EMP.DOB IS NULL AND
                   EMP.SALARY < 80000.00 )

OR               ( EMP.JOB = 'Programmer' AND
                   EMP.DOB < DATE ('1972-8-17') AND
                   EMP.SALARY IS NULL )

OR               ( EMP.JOB IS NULL AND
                   EMP.DOB IS NULL AND
                   EMP.SALARY < 80000.00 )

OR               ( EMP.JOB = 'Programmer' AND
                   EMP.DOB IS NULL AND
                   EMP.SALARY IS NULL )

OR               ( EMP.JOB IS NULL AND
                   EMP.DOB < DATE ('1972-8-17') AND
                   EMP.SALARY IS NULL )

OR               ( EMP.JOB IS NULL AND
                   EMP.DOB IS NULL AND
                   EMP.SALARY IS NULL )
```

■ In practice we'd probably want a TRUE_OR_MAYBE operator instead of (or as well as) the MAYBE operator. TRUE_OR_MAYBE would yield *true* if its operand is either *true* or *unk*, *false* otherwise. The reason such an operator would be useful is that it seems likely, or at least plausible, that users would more often want to see both true and maybe cases, not just the maybe cases alone. For example, consider the query "List all people who have been, or might have been, in contact with employee Joe" (who has just been diagnosed as suffering from COVID).

■ You might be thinking that if MAYBE is supported, then we don't need IS_UNK. After all, it's certainly true that (e.g.) the expressions

```
IS_UNK ( EMP.JOB )
```

and

```
MAYBE ( EMP.JOB = 'Programmer' )
```

always return the same value (either *true* or *false*, never *unk*). Logically, therefore, we could always replace the first expression by the second. But to do so does smack a little bit of trickery (to me, at any rate). Note in particular that it would absolutely no difference to the value of the second expression if we replace 'Programmer' by 'Engineer', or 'Salesperson', or 'King Arthur', or indeed anything at all, except UNK.

Rows and Tables

Clearly, any thorough (and systematic) treatment of a scheme involving UNK ("null") and *unk* ("the third truth value") for dealing with missing information needs to deal with the implications of these concepts for rows and tables as well as for scalars. I don't propose to discuss those implications here, however (at least, not in detail) because I'm not attempting any such thorough treatment.[11] I will, however, make the following points:

■ A row with at least one UNK component doesn't represent a valid tuple, and a table that contains at least one such row doesn't represent a valid relation. In other words, *nulls break the relational model!* Let me repeat: If the database contains any nulls, we aren't dealing with the relational model any more.

　　This point is so important, I want to say it a third time, in different words:

---

[11] After all, if it turns out—and in my opinion it does—that UNK and *unk* have implications for scalars that simply can't be tolerated, then there's no point in even considering their implications for rows and tables.

a. A "domain" (type) that contains a null isn't a domain.

b. A "tuple" with an attribute defined on such a "domain" (type) isn't a tuple.

c. A "relation" that contains such a "tuple" isn't a relation.

So the entire relational edifice collapses, and *all bets are off*. I find it very hard to understand why Codd would want to destroy his beautiful relational model by adding nulls and 3VL to it, but that, in effect, is exactly what he did.

■ In order to proceed with our discussion, however, we have to suspend disbelief, as it were (at least for the time being). So I'm going to have to assume until further notice that it's possible after all for a row to have an UNK component, or in fact any number of such components. Note, however, that such a row isn't itself an "UNK row" or "null row." In fact, an UNK row is a whole different concept.[12]

■ Likewise, I'm going to have to assume that it's possible for a table to contain a row with UNK components, or in fact any number of such rows. Note, however, that such a table isn't itself an "UNK table" or "null table." In fact, an UNK table is a whole different concept.[13]

■ Recall now that UNKs are considered as duplicates of one another for purposes of duplicate elimination, even though the expression UNK = UNK doesn't evaluate to *true*. We can extend this idea to rows as follows. Let x and y be rows of the same type,[14] and let corresponding components of x and y be $(x1,y1)$, $(x2,y2)$, ..., (xn,yn). Then x and y are duplicates of one another if and only if, for all i ($i = 1, 2, ..., n$), xi and yi are duplicates of one another—i.e., either $xi = yi$, or xi and yi are both UNK.

---

[12] It's also one that SQL gets itself into a terrible muddle over. See Chapter 1 ("Equality") of my book *Stating the Obvious, and Other Database Writings* (Technics Publications, 2020).

[13] SQL gets itself into a muddle over this one too.

[14] Reference [1] says the rows have to be "union compatible," but I prefer to replace this very ad hoc notion by a much more carefully thought out notion of *type*. See my book *E. F. Codd and Relational Theory, Revised Edition* (Technics Publications, 2021).

We can also extend the operator DUP_OF to deal with rows. To be specific, the expression *x* DUP_OF *y* (where *x* and *y* are rows of the same type) is defined to evaluate to *true* if *x* and *y* are duplicates of one another, *false* otherwise.

IN

What exactly does it mean for a given row to be "in" a given table? The following definition is deliberately framed in such a manner as to simplify certain subsequent definitions (in particular, the definition of relational projection). It's not a direct counterpart to the set membership operator "belongs to" ("ε"), because it returns *true* in certain cases where "ε" would more correctly return *unk*. (My reason for not wanting to define "ε" properly is that it turns out to be extremely tricky—perhaps impossible?—to define projection precisely in terms of "ε." You might like to try it as an exercise, if you're interested.)

Let *T* be a table containing rows *r1*, *r2*, ..., *rm* (only). By definition, *r1*, *r2*, ..., *rm* must all be of the same (row) type. Let *r* be a row of that same row type. Then the expression

```
r IN T
```

is defined to be equivalent to the expression

```
( r DUP_OF r1 ) OR ( r DUP_OF r2 ) OR ... OR ( r DUP_OF rm )
```

Note, therefore, that expressions of the form *r* IN *T* always return *true* or *false*, never *unk*.

Examples: Let *a*, *b*, *c*, *d*, *e* be rows all of the same type, with components as follows:[15]

```
a : (    1 ,   2 ,   3   )
b : (    1 ,   2 ,   4   )
c : (    1 ,   2 , UNK   )
d : (    1 ,   5 , UNK   )
e : (  UNK , UNK , UNK   )
```

---

[15] Here—for display purposes only, let me stress—it's necessary to assume that rows have a left to right ordering to their components. (Of course, rows in SQL do have such an ordering, but their relational counterparts, tuples, don't.)

Also, let T be a table containing just the following rows (all of the same type as the ones shown above):

```
(    1 ,    2 ,    3   )
(    1 ,    2 , UNK  )
(  UNK , UNK , UNK  )
```

Then the expressions a IN T, c IN T, and e IN T evaluate to *true*, and the expressions b IN T and d IN T evaluate to *false*. (By contrast, if we were to replace each "IN" by "$\in$", then the expressions for b, c, d, and e would each evaluate to *unk*.)

Quantifiers

I now define the quantifiers EXISTS and FORALL as iterated OR and AND, respectively. More precisely, let T be a table with rows $r1$, $r2$, ..., rm (only), and let r be a range variable that ranges over the rows of that table. Also, let $p(r)$ be a boolean expression (typically but not necessarily one that references r). Then the expression

```
EXISTS r ( p ( r ) )
```

is defined to be equivalent to the expression

```
FALSE OR
    ( p ( r1 ) ) OR ( p ( r2 ) ) OR ... OR ( p ( rm ) )
```

And the expression

```
FORALL r ( p ( r ) )
```

is defined to be equivalent to the expression

```
TRUE AND
    ( p ( r1 ) ) AND ( p ( r2 ) ) AND ... AND ( p ( rm ) )
```

Note, therefore, that if T is empty (i.e., $m = 0$), then EXISTS and FORALL return *false* and *true*, respectively.

Examples: As in the examples in the previous subsection, let T be a table containing just the following rows:

```
(    1  ,    2  ,    3   )
(    1  ,    2  ,  UNK   )
(  UNK  ,  UNK  ,  UNK   )
```

Also, let's assume for the sake of the example that the three columns of table *T*, in left to right order as shown, are named *C1*, *C2*, *C3*, respectively. Then the following expressions have the indicated values:

```
EXISTS  r ( r.C3 > 1 )               :    true
EXISTS  r ( r.C2 > 2 )               :    unk
EXISTS  r ( MAYBE ( r.C1 > 3 ) )     :    true
EXISTS  r ( IS_UNK ( r.C3 ) )        :    true

FORALL  r ( r.C1 > 1 )               :    false
FORALL  r ( r.C2 > 1 )               :    unk
FORALL  r ( MAYBE ( r.C3 > 1 ) )     :    false
```

Relational Algebra

I consider here only the operators restrict, project, product, union, intersection, and difference, since the other usual algebraic operators can all be defined in terms of them.[16]

■ Restrict

Restriction is unaffected. Remember, however, that it returns only those rows for which the pertinent boolean (or conditional) expression evaluates to *true*, not to *false* and not to *unk*.

■ Project

The projection of table *T* on column *C*, written *T{C}*, is obtained by eliminating all other columns and then eliminating redundant duplicates from what remains:

$$T\{C\} \overset{\text{def}}{=} \{ \ r.C \ : \ r \ \text{IN} \ T \ \}$$

---

[16] At least in 2VL! It might not be true in the 3VL treatment we're considering here. In fact, the distinction we're drawing between equality and duplication—i.e., between "=" and DUP_OF—has a number of surprising consequences. For one thing, intersection turns out to be no longer a special case of natural join. For another, the natural join of a table with itself over all of its columns is no longer guaranteed to return the original table. Exploring the consequences of such anomalies is left as an exercise.

The symbol "$\overset{\text{def}}{=}$" means "is defined as." *Note:* I limit the definition to projection on just a single column here for simplicity. Extending it to cater for an arbitrary number of columns is tedious but essentially straightforward.

■ Product

Product is unaffected.

■ Union

The union of two tables *T1* and *T2* of the same type[17] is the set of rows *r* such that *r* is a duplicate of some row of *T1* or some row of *T2* or both:

$$T1 \text{ UNION } T2 \overset{\text{def}}{=} \{ r : (r \text{ IN } T1) \text{ OR } (r \text{ IN } T2) \}$$

■ Intersection

The intersection of two tables *T1* and *T2* of the same type is the set of rows *r* such that *r* is a duplicate of some row of *T1* and some row of *T2*:

$$T1 \text{ INTERSECT } T2 \overset{\text{def}}{=} \{ r : (r \text{ IN } T1) \text{ AND } (r \text{ IN } T2) \}$$

■ Difference

The intersection between two tables *T1* and *T2* (in that order) of the same type is the set of rows *r* such that *r* is a duplicate of some row of *T1* and not of any row of *T2*:

$$T1 \text{ MINUS } T2 \overset{\text{def}}{=} \{ r : (r \text{ IN } T1) \text{ AND NOT } (r \text{ IN } T2)) \}$$

MAYBE Operators

Codd also defines what he calls "maybe" versions of restrict, join, and divide.[18] Since I omitted consideration of join and divide in the previous subsection, however, I'll do the same for their "maybe" counterparts here. As for "maybe

---

[17] Footnote 14 applies here also, mutatis mutandis.

[18] Why do you think he omitted "maybe" versions of the other operators?

restrict," it differs from the normal—i.e., "true"—restrict operator in that it returns those rows for which the boolean or conditional expression evaluates to *unk* instead of *true*. In other words, the expression

```
MAYBE_RESTRICT tx WHERE bx
```

(where *tx* is a table expression and *bx* is a boolean expression) is logically equivalent to the expression

```
RESTRICT tx WHERE MAYBE ( bx )
```

In fact, Codd would have had no need for his "maybe" algebraic operators, nor for his MAYBE qualifier on expressions, if only he'd defined the MAYBE boolean operator (and allowed it to be used fully orthogonally, of course)—but he didn't. (Of course, I'm assuming here that we actually want 3VL support, which I don't in fact believe. But if it's to be done at all, then I do think it should be done right—and doing it right includes supporting the MAYBE operator.)

To be continued.

Chapter 13

NOT Is Not "Not"!

Part 2

For a description of the background to this chapter, please see the preamble to Chapter 12. This version copyright © 2022 C. J. Date.

TAUTOLOGIES AND CONTRADICTIONS

In logic, (a) a tautology is an expression that always evaluates to *true* and (b) a contradiction is an expression that always evaluates to *false*, regardless in both cases of the values of any variables involved. Tautologies and contradictions are important in the transformation of expressions (either by the user or by the system) into simpler forms. In this section, I briefly discuss a few important examples (I've numbered them for purposes of future reference):

Let *bx* be a boolean expression. Then the following is an obvious tautology in 2VL:

```
1. bx OR NOT ( bx )
```

And the following is an obvious contradiction (again, in 2VL):

```
2. bx AND NOT ( bx )
```

Note carefully, however, that a tautology in 2VL isn't necessarily a tautology in 3VL, and the same goes for contradictions. To be specific, if *bx* evaluates to *unk*, then the two expressions just shown both evaluate to *unk* as well—so No. 1 isn't a tautology in 3VL, and No. 2 isn't a contradiction in 3VL.

The failure of No. 1 in particular (I mean, its failure to continue to be a tautology) accounts for a well known counterintuitive property of 3VL, which can be illustrated thus: If we ask the system to "Get all suppliers in London," and then to "Get all suppliers not in London," and then we take the union of the two results, we don't necessarily get all suppliers. Instead, we have to include "all suppliers who *might* be in London."

As this example suggests, an expression that *is* a tautology in 3VL—the 3VL counterpart to No. 1 above—is:

3. *bx* OR NOT (*bx*) OR MAYBE (*bx*)

(Informally: Any 3VL boolean expression *bx* must be *true* or *false* or *unk*.)

As for the 3VL counterpart to No. 2, it's slightly tricky. Note first that the following expression, which might be proposed as the "obvious" counterpart to No. 2, is neither a tautology nor a contradiction in 3VL (why not, exactly?):

4. *bx* AND NOT (*bx*) AND MAYBE (*bx*)

The correct 3VL counterpart to No. 2 is:

5. *bx* AND NOT (*bx*) AND NOT (MAYBE (*bx*))

By contrast, the following tautologies (usually known as De Morgan's Laws) hold in both 2VL and 3VL (the equivalence symbol "≡" as used in these tautologies means "has the same truth value as"):

6. NOT (*bx* AND *by*) ≡ (NOT (*bx*)) OR (NOT (*by*))
7. NOT (*bx* OR *by*) ≡ (NOT (*bx*)) AND (NOT (*by*))

Here's a truth table proof of the validity of No. 6 (the proof of No. 7 is left as an exercise):

bx	by	bx AND by	lhs	NOT bx	NOT by	rhs
t	t	t	f	f	f	f
t	u	u	u	f	u	u
t	f	f	t	f	t	t
u	t	u	u	u	f	u
u	u	u	u	u	u	u
u	f	f	t	u	t	t
f	t	f	t	t	f	t
f	u	f	t	t	u	t
f	f	f	t	t	t	t

The columns headed *lhs* and *rhs* denote the values of the expressions on the left and right hand side, respectively, of the equivalence symbol. Since these two columns are identical, the tautology is proved.

The following expressions are also tautologies in both 2VL and 3VL (again the proofs are left as an exercise). *Note:* The expression *p(x)* denotes an arbitrary boolean or truth valued expression involving *x* as a parameter (*aka* a "free variable").

```
8. FORALL x ( p ( x ) ) ≡ NOT ( EXISTS x ( NOT ( p ( x ) ) ) )

9. EXISTS x ( p ( x ) ) ≡ NOT ( FORALL x ( NOT ( p ( x ) ) ) )
```

EXAMPLES

Intuition is often misleading in dealing with problems involving three-valued logic. The present section discusses some examples that demonstrate the truth of this claim. As a basis for those examples, I'll use a slight variation on the usual suppliers-and-parts database. Here's the database definition in outline:

```
S    { SNO , SNAME , STATUS , CITY }
     KEY { SNO }

P    { PNO , PNAME , COLOR , WEIGHT , CITY }
     KEY { PNO }

SP   { SHIPNO , SNO , PNO , QTY }
     KEY { SHIPNO }
     KEY { SNO , PNO }
     FOREIGN KEY { SNO } REFERENCES S
     FOREIGN KEY ( PNO ) REFERENCES P
```

The only structural difference between this version of the database and the more familiar version is that table SP includes an additional column, SHIPNO ("shipment number"), which serves as another key for that table. Also, the definition doesn't show it, but I assume that certain columns—columns S.CITY, SP.SNO, and SP.PNO in particular—allow nulls (UNKs).

Suppose now that these tables look like this at the present time: [1]

---

[1] Actually, nowhere in the remainder of this chapter is any use made of the parts table P. I include it here only to avoid questions from readers who might wonder where it was if I didn't.

S

SNO	SNAME	STATUS	CITY
S1	Smith	20	London
S2	Jones	10	Paris
S3	Blake	30	Paris
S4	Clark	20	UNK

SP

SHIPNO	SNO	PNO	QTY
SHIP1	S1	P1	300
SHIP2	S2	P2	200
SHIP3	S3	UNK	400

P

PNO	PNAME	COLOR	WEIGHT	CITY
P1	Nut	Red	12.0	London
P2	Bolt	Green	17.0	Paris

The first difficulty is illustrated by the following state of affairs (repeated from the previous chapter): Given the sample data values shown, the query "Get all suppliers in London" together with the query "Get all suppliers not in London" will *not* between them yield all suppliers. To be specific, the first will return supplier S1 and the second will return suppliers S2 and S3, and supplier S4 won't appear in either result.

The point, of course, is that while the two conditions "location is London" and "location isn't London" are mutually exclusive and exhaust the full range of possibilities in the real world, the database doesn't contain the real world—rather, it contains *the system's knowledge about* the real world. And in the case at hand there are three possibilities, not two, regarding knowledge of the real world—"location is known to be London," "location is known not to be London," and "location is unknown." And we obviously can't ask the system questions about the real world, we can only ask it about its knowledge of the real world, as represented by the data in the database. Thus, the counterintuitive nature—or what advocates of 3VL might call the *alleged* counterintuitive nature—of this first example derives from a simple confusion over levels: The user is thinking at the real world level, but the system is thinking at the level of its knowledge about that real world.

Now, if the foregoing were the only kind of difficulty arising in connection with 3VL and intuition, I don't think there'd be much of a problem—it would just be a matter of absorbing and understanding, and taking to heart, the substance of the previous paragraph. Unfortunately, however, matters don't stop there, as I'll now show.

Consider the following expression ("Query 1"):[2]

```
S.SNAME WHERE EXISTS SP ( SP.SNO = S.SNO AND SP.PNO = 'P2' )
```

What's the real world interpretation of this expression?—i.e., what does the expression "mean"? The obvious answer is: It means "Get names of suppliers who supply part P2." But, of course, this interpretation is incorrect. What the expression really means is "Get names of suppliers who are *known to the system* to supply part P2." (To say it again, we can only ask questions about the system's knowledge of the real world, not about the real world per se.)

Let's consider how the foregoing expression is evaluated. (The following explanation will probably be familiar to you, but I want to go through it in detail in order to set the scene for subsequent discussion.)

1.   The variable S (which is actually a range variable that ranges over the table with the same name, i.e., the suppliers table S) takes on one of its permitted values. Let's assume, just to be definite, that the variable S iterates over the rows of table S in the top to bottom order as shown on the previous page, so that the first value it takes on is the row for supplier S1. The expression in the WHERE clause thus effectively becomes

```
EXISTS SP ( SP.SNO = 'S1' AND SP.PNO = 'P2' )
```

This expression evaluates to *false* (there's no row in table SP for S1 and P2), and so the SNAME for supplier S1 doesn't appear in the final result.

2.   For the next supplier row (which is for supplier S2), the expression in the WHERE clause becomes

```
EXISTS SP ( SP.SNO = 'S2' AND SP.PNO = 'P2' )
```

This expression evaluates to *true* (a row does exist in table SP for S2 and P2), and so the SNAME for supplier S2 ("Jones") does appear in the final result.

---

[2] The queries in this section are formulated in relational calculus, not SQL, because (as explained in the next chapter) EXISTS in SQL suffers from problems of its own.

3. For the next supplier row (for supplier S3), the expression in the WHERE clause becomes

```
EXISTS SP ( SP.SNO = 'S3' AND SP.PNO = 'P2' )
```

This expression evaluates to *unk* (there's no row in SP for S3 and P2, but there does exist a row in SP for S3 in which the PNO value is UNK). So for S3 the overall expression effectively becomes

```
S.SNAME WHERE unk
```

Recall now that restriction returns only those rows for which the expression in the WHERE clause evaluates to *true*, not to *false* and not to *unk*. So the SNAME for supplier S3 doesn't appear in the final result.

4. For the last supplier row (for supplier S4), the expression in the WHERE clause becomes

```
EXISTS SP ( SP.SNO = 'S4' AND SP.PNO = 'P2' )
```

This expression evaluates to *false* (there's no row at all in SP for S4), so the SNAME for supplier S4 doesn't appear in the final result.

So the final result is a set containing just the single supplier name "Jones."

Given the foregoing analysis and explanation, then, what can we say about the following expression ("Query 2")? In other words, again, what does the following expression really mean?[3]

```
S.SNAME WHERE NOT
       ( EXISTS SP ( SP.SNO = S.SNO AND SP.PNO = 'P2' ) )
```

Possible interpretations include at least all of the following:

a. Get names of suppliers who don't supply part P2.

---

[3] It's relevant (in fact, highly relevant) to my thesis here to mention that when I first discussed this question with Ted Codd and a colleague (Nat Goodman), we all got it wrong. Even Ted got it wrong!—and Ted *believed* in 3VL and nulls and thought they were a good thing, which Nat and I most certainly did not. PS: Despite this latter state of affairs, I do think it's fair to claim that at least all three of us understood the concepts involved pretty thoroughly—and yet, to repeat, we all got it wrong. So what chance do you think there is that "the naïve end user" will answer such questions correctly?

b. Get names of suppliers who aren't known to supply part P2 (i.e., they might supply part P2, but the system doesn't know whether they do or not).

c. Get names of suppliers who are known not to supply part P2 (i.e., they're definitely known not to supply part P2).

d. Get names of suppliers who are either known not or not known to supply part P2 (the union of b. and c.).

I suggest you try to decide which of these interpretations (if any) you think is correct before continuing. *Note:* If you're having difficulties over the difference between b. and c. here (i.e., over the "not known" vs. "known not" distinction), thinking about the exactly parallel difference between these two statements might help:

b'. I don't know if you have measles.

c'. I know you don't have measles.

Discussion: Interpretation a. is clearly not correct—even though it's the one most people would given, because it's "obviously" and "intuitively" right! It's incorrect because (once again) it talks in terms of the real world instead of what the system knows about the real world. By contrast, the other three interpretations do talk in terms of what the system knows. How do they differ? In order to answer this question, let's consider what knowledge the system does have regarding which suppliers supply part P2. I'll assume the same sample values as before, but I'll repeat them here for convenience:

S

SNO	SNAME	STATUS	CITY
S1	Smith	20	London
S2	Jones	10	Paris
S3	Blake	30	Paris
S4	Clark	20	UNK

SP

SHIPNO	SNO	PNO	QTY
SHIP1	S1	P1	300
SHIP2	S2	P2	200
SHIP3	S3	UNK	400

With respect to the subject query, then ("Who supplies part P2?"), here's what's known to the system:

- Supplier S1 (Smith) is definitely known not to supply part P2.[4]

- Supplier S2 (Jones) is definitely known to supply part P2.

- Supplier S3 (Blake) is not known to supply part P2 (but not known not to, either).

- Supplier S4 (Clark) is definitely known not to supply part P2—nor any other part, as a matter of fact.

For Query 2, therefore, if interpretation b. is the correct one, the result should be "Blake"; if interpretation c. is correct, it should be "Smith" and "Clark"; and if interpretation d. is correct, it should be "Smith," "Blake," and "Clark." So let's now consider exactly how the query is evaluated:

1. For supplier S1, the expression in the WHERE clause becomes

```
NOT ( EXISTS SP ( SP.SNO = 'S1' AND SP.PNO = 'P2' ) )
```

which evaluates to NOT *false* (i.e., *true*), since there's no SP row for S1 and P2, and so the SNAME for supplier S1 ("Smith") does appear in the result.

2. For supplier S2, the expression in the WHERE clause becomes

```
NOT ( EXISTS SP ( SP.SNO = 'S2' AND SP.PNO = 'P2' ) )
```

---

[4] Here I'm appealing to *The Closed World Assumption*, a crucially important principle that states, in effect, that if a row appears in a table, then it represents something that's known to be a "true fact"; conversely, if it could appear but doesn't, then it represents something that's known not to be a "true fact." Thus, since there's no row for S1 and P2 (and also no row for S1 and an unknown part number) in table SP, we're entitled to interpret that state of affairs as meaning that "S1 supplies P2" is known not to be true. See Chapter 5 ("*The Closed World Assumption*") of my book *Logic and Relational Theory, and Other Database Writings* (Technics Publications, 2020) for further explanation.

    Note: Actually, there are those who might argue that in a world that embraces 3VL, even *The Closed World Assumption* might need revision. Sorry, but I don't want to go there (and nor should you). Let me add, however, that the referenced Chapter 5 shows among other things how we can get "don't know" answers out of a database—when "don't know" is the right answer, of course!—*even in a system that abides entirely by 2VL.* No need for nulls at all, in other words.

which evaluates to NOT *true* (i.e., *false*), since there does exist an SP row for S2 and P2, and so the SNAME for supplier S2 doesn't appear in the result.

3. For supplier S3, the expression in the WHERE clause becomes

    ```
    NOT ( EXISTS SP ( SP.SNO = 'S3' AND SP.PNO = 'P2' ) )
    ```

    which evaluates to NOT *unk* (i.e., *unk*), since there's no SP row for S3 and P2, but there does exist an SP row for S3 in which PNO is UNK. So for S3 the overall expression effectively becomes

    ```
    S.SNAME WHERE unk
    ```

    So the SNAME for supplier S3 doesn't appear in the final result.

4. For supplier S4, the expression in the WHERE clause becomes

    ```
    NOT ( EXISTS SP ( SP.SNO = 'S4' AND SP.PNO = 'P2' ) )
    ```

    which evaluates to NOT *false* (i.e., *true*), since there's no SP row for S4 and P2 (actually, of course, there are no SP rows for S4 at all), and so the SNAME for supplier S4 ("Clark") does appear in the result.

So the final result is the set {"Smith", "Clark"}. *Conclusion:* Interpretations b. and d. are definitely incorrect; the correct one is c. (Are you sure?)

I'm not finished with this example. The obvious next question is: Given that interpretation c. was the right one, how can we formulate a query for interpretation b.? (Of course, we must be able to. If we can't, then there'd be something wrong with our query language; I mean, there'd be some sense in which it wouldn't be complete. See the next section for further discussion.)

Just to remind you, interpretation b. was:

b. Get names of suppliers who aren't known to supply part P2 (i.e., they might supply part P2, but the system doesn't know whether they do or not).

Observe now that (as the parenthetical remark indicates) the natural language statement of the problem can perhaps be reduced to the following simpler form:

b. Get names of suppliers who might supply part P2.

"Might" here means "might, according to the system's knowledge," of course. In other words, we want to exclude any suppliers who (according to the system) either definitely do supply part P2 or definitely don't. Here then is a first attempt ("Query 3"):

```
S.SNAME WHERE EXISTS SP
            ( MAYBE ( SP.SNO = S.SNO AND SP.PNO = 'P2' ) )
```

("supplier names where there exists a shipment saying the supplier might supply part P2"). However, this formulation is incorrect (though it does happen to produce the right answer, given our usual sample data). In order to see how it's incorrect, suppose we add another row to table SP, viz., a row for S3 and P2, thus:

SP

SHIPNO	SNO	PNO	QTY
SHIP1	S1	P1	300
SHIP2	S2	P2	200
SHIP3	S3	UNK	400
SHIP4	S3	P2	500

Now consider what happens when the range variable S takes as its value the row from table S for supplier S3:

■ The expression in the WHERE clause becomes

```
EXISTS SP
      ( MAYBE ( SP.SNO = 'S3' AND SP.PNO = 'P2' ) ) )
```

which evaluates to *true*, since there does exist an SP row—namely, the row (SHIP3,S3,UNK,400)—for which the subexpression

```
      ( SP.SNO = 'S3' AND SP.PNO = 'P2' )
```

evaluates to *unk*. Thus the SNAME for supplier S3 ("Blake") appears in the final result. But it shouldn't, because there's also an SP row—namely, the row (SHIP4,S3,P2,500)—that says that supplier S3 definitely does supply part P2. Error!

It follows that the correct interpretation of Query 3 is this: "Get names of suppliers who, regardless of whether they're definitely known to supply part P2, are definitely known to be *possible* suppliers of part P2" (!).

Here then is another attempt at formulating an expression ("Query 4") for interpretation b.:

```
S.SNAME WHERE MAYBE
      ( EXISTS SP ( SP.SNO = S.SNO AND SP.PNO = 'P2' ) )
```

("supplier names where there might exist a shipment saying the supplier supplies part P2"). This formulation is correct. *Exercise:* Convince yourself that this is so.

Note: It follows from all of the above that a correct formulation for interpretation d. is:

```
S.SNAME WHERE
      NOT   ( EXISTS SP ( SP.SNO = S.SNO AND SP.PNO = 'P2' ) )
      OR
      MAYBE ( EXISTS SP ( SP.SNO = S.SNO AND SP.PNO = 'P2' ) )
```

("supplier names where either there does not exist a shipment, or there might exist a shipment, saying the supplier supplies part P2").

One final point regarding the foregoing example: If table SP includes a row in which the supplier number is UNK and the part number is P2, then Query 3 will produce a result containing the SNAME of every supplier! This makes sense (?), because if table SP includes such a row, it means that every supplier *might* supply part P2, regardless of whether there exists another SP row saying the supplier in question actually does.

QUESTIONS

This section raises some questions that I feel ought to have been asked (and satisfactorily answered, of course) before the IT world committed itself to becoming so heavily reliant on something as suspect as 3VL and nulls.

Aside: The foregoing sentence was worded a little differently in the original paper:

> I raise a couple of questions that I believe need to be answered before we commit ourselves wholeheartedly to the [3VL] approach.

Well, that was then and this is now; my plea clearly fell on deaf ears, and now we're stuck with that approach. But the questions are still germane! In other words, even though we are indeed "stuck with" it, I still hope the discussion in these two chapters (and other discussions like it) can serve to persuade you not to use it. Personally, I wouldn't touch nulls and 3VL with a ten foot pole. *End of aside.*

Anyway, the first of those questions (a very fundamental one) is this:

Is 3VL as described in these two chapters a sound and complete logic for dealing with databases that contain UNKs?

In other words:

a. *Soundness:* Is it possible to derive a logical inconsistency using 3VL as here defined?[5] If so, that 3VL is unsound.

b. *Completeness:* Does there exist an expression that is in fact *true* but can't be shown to be *true* using 3VL as here defined? If so, that 3VL is incomplete.

Now, perhaps these questions can be answered satisfactorily. Until they have been, however, I feel the logical defensibility of the approach hasn't been shown, and we should therefore tread very warily in trying to incorporate it into our formal database theories and systems.

Second, assuming the foregoing questions can indeed be answered satisfactorily, is there anything that can be done about the mismatch between 3VL and ordinary intuition? If the answer has to be "It's an education problem,"

---

[5] I'm using the word "defined" here somewhat loosely. The fact is, I've *described* a certain 3VL (one of many possible such) fairly carefully, but I certainly haven't *defined* it—there are many, many aspects of any such logic that I haven't even mentioned. For one thing, any such logic necessarily involves over 19,000 monadic and dyadic logical operators (actually 19,710 of them), and I've defined only three (NOT, AND, and OR). PS: I note in passing that SQL doesn't define its particular brand of 3VL either.

then I have to say it doesn't seem to be a particularly *easy* education problem. The big advantage of the traditional approach to missing information—viz., the approach described in the appendix, which incidentally is the approach adopted outside the world of databases—is precisely that it's intuitively understandable and isn't a big education problem. It's also easier to implement (which suggests the pragmatic point that the implementation is likely to contain fewer errors).

CONCLUDING REMARKS

What I've tried to do in these two chapters is present a careful and yet not too formal treatment of the 3VL approach to missing information, on the assumption that users are probably going to have to grapple with these ideas at some time in the near future.[6]   However, as I've repeatedly said, I do have serious reservations regarding the merits of that approach. Here are some of the items seem to me to deserve further study:

- The soundness and completeness questions from the previous section

- The psychological questions (i.e., the problems of intuition) sketched in the "Examples" section

- The suitability of the approach for extension to deal with other kinds of nulls (see the section "Kinds of Missing Information" in Part 1)

- The question of how many different kinds of nulls exist, or at least how many are needed in practice (again, see the section "Kinds of Missing Information")

- What it means to deal with boolean variables that happen to be UNK rather than *unk* (see the section "UNK and 3VL," also in Part 1)

- The justification for the distinction between duplicate elimination and testing for equality (again, see the section "UNK and 3VL")

---

[6] That assumption turned out to be truer than I first realized—*much* truer, in fact, and true in far too many ways. I stand by my contention that, despite the fact that (a) SQL "supports" nulls and 3VL, and despite the fact that (b) SQL DBMSs are built on the assumption that users will make use of that support, a sensible response to these facts on the part of users is (c) to do everything in their power not to use that "support" at all, if they can possibly manage without it.

- The justification for the fact that "$x - x$" fails to give zero, and "$x = x$" fails to give *true*, if x happens to be UNK (see the section "UNK and 3VL" yet again)

- The assertion in reference [4] that "a fundamental theorem of normalization" breaks down.[7] *Note:* It's true that Codd states in reference [2] that he doesn't agree with this assertion, but his counterarguments are unconvincing.

   In addition, there's one question I deliberately haven't addressed prior to this point. viz.: Can a set can contain a null? Codd apparently assumes the answer is *yes*, because in reference [1] he considers the truth value of the boolean expression $\{\omega\} \subseteq X$, where ω (omega) denotes a null, "$\subseteq$" denotes set inclusion, and X denotes a nonempty set. *Note:* An equivalent expression is $\omega \in X$, where "$\in$" denotes set membership.

   If a set can contain a null, however, then numerous further questions arise:

- The expression UNK $\in X$ will return *unk* for any nonempty set X, regardless of whether X does actually contain an UNK, so we'll need a new operator to test whether a given set does in fact contain an UNK.

- The expression $v \in X$ will return *unk* or *true* (never *false*) for any v if set X does in fact contain an UNK, so we'll need a new operator to test whether a given set that does contain an UNK does *not* contain some specified nonUNK value.

- As a consequence of the previous point, if a domain (type) contains an UNK, checking the pertinent type constraint will never fail. I conclude from this fact that domains (types) shouldn't include UNKs!

- As a consequence of the previous point, a relation that contains an UNK— more precisely, a relation that contains a tuple that contains an UNK— won't be a subset of the cartesian product of its underlying domains, counter to Codd's original definition of relation.

---

[7] The theorem in question states that if relation $R\{A,B,C\}$ satisfies the functional dependency $R.A \rightarrow R.B$, then R is equal to the join of its projections on $\{A,B\}$ and $\{A,C\}$. It's easy to see that this theorem is no longer valid if $R.A$ has "nulls allowed."

Note: An advocate of UNKs might claim this assertion is false and is due to a "value oriented misinterpretation" [2]: If the EMP relation includes a row saying "Joe's salary is UNK," then that UNK is merely a placeholder, not a value; in other words, presumably there does exist some value *v* that actually is Joe's salary, and when we replace the UNK by that value *v* (and replace all other UNKs in the EMP relation in a similar fashion), then what results is indeed a subset of the cartesian product of the domains. But this counterargument, even if we accept it in the case of UNKs, doesn't seem to be valid for other kinds of nulls (consider, e.g., the "value is the empty set" null).

■ If a set can contain an UNK, the expression $X \subseteq X$ will return *unk*, not *true*, if X does in fact contain an UNK. (This anomaly is reminiscent of, and of course a consequence of, the anomaly that the comparison $x = x$ also returns *unk*, not *true*, if x is UNK.) So we'll need, first, an appropriately extended interpretation of what it means for one set to be included in another; second, a new operator to test whether one set is indeed included in another according to that extended definition.

■ What's the cardinality of a set that contains an UNK? Is it UNK also? (Note, however, that the cardinality of such a set isn't *completely* unknown; e.g., consider the set {1,2,UNK}—if such a set is legitimate, that is—for which the cardinality is unknown but must be either two or three. Such considerations lead us into another problem, however—viz., the "distinguished nulls" problem. See reference [4] for further discussion.)

■ If a set does contain an UNK, is that set itself in fact UNK also (given that a set is known if and only if its members are known)? And if so, does it mean that the set contains itself as a member? If so, then ... ?

And doubtless other questions also. Do we really want to go down this path?

ACKNOWLEDGMENTS

I'm grateful, first of all, to Nat Goodman, who, through his comments on my original note to Codd regarding these matters [5], made me understand the precise nature of some of the difficulties discussed in this chapter. I'm also grateful to Charley Bontempo and Hugh Darwen for numerous discussions and for their helpful reviews of earlier drafts.

REFERENCES

1. E. F. Codd: "Extending the Database Relational Model to Capture More Meaning," *ACM Transactions on Database Systems 4*, No. 4 (December 1979).

2. E. F. Codd: "Missing Information (Applicable and Inapplicable) in Relational Databases," *ACM SIGMOD Record 15*, No. 4 (December 1986).

3. E. F. Codd: "More Commentary on Missing Information in Relational Databases (Applicable and Inapplicable Information)," *ACM SIGMOD Record 16*, No. 1 (March 1987).

4. C. J. Date: "Null Values in Database Management," in C. J. Date, *Relational Database: Selected Writings* (Addison-Wesley, 1986).

5. C. J. Date: "Three-Valued Logic" (private communication to E. F. Codd, March 31st, 1988).

APPENDIX

In reference [4], I proposed an approach to missing information based on the *systematic*—I stress that word—use of default values. The following summary of that proposal is based on the one given in reference [4], though numerous details are omitted here.

Note: The original proposal in reference [4] treated just one kind of missing information (viz., "value unknown"), but it could obviously be extended to deal with other kinds as well. If so, however, it would be desirable to replace keywords such as DEFAULT (see below) by some more explicit term such as UNKNOWN. Additional keywords such as INAPPLICABLE, UNDEFINED, etc., could then be introduced to deal with other kinds of missing information. The present discussion stays with the single DEFAULT of the original proposal, however.

1. Associated with the declaration of each column of each named table is either a DEFAULT specification (designating the default value for that column), or else the specification NODEFAULT (meaning the column in question doesn't have a default value). Here's an outline example, using an SQL-based syntax:

```
CREATE TABLE S /* suppliers */
     ( SNO    ... NODEFAULT ,
       SNAME  ... DEFAULT ( '    ' ) ,
       STATUS ... DEFAULT ( -1 ) ,
       CITY   ... DEFAULT ( '???' ) )
       KEY ( SNO ) ;
```

If no default is specified explicitly for a given column (and NODEFAULT isn't specified), then it might be possible for the system to assume a "default default" (e.g., blanks for character string columns, zero for numeric columns).

2. When a new row is inserted into a base table:

   a. A value must be provided for every column that has no default value.

   b. For other columns, the system will supply the applicable default value if the user doesn't provide a value.

3. When a column is added to a base table:

   a. The new column must have an (explicit or implicit) DEFAULT specification (i.e., NODEFAULT can't be specified).

   b. The value of the new column is automatically set to the applicable default value in all existing rows in the table.

4. The operator DEFAULT $(R.C)$, where R is a range variable ranging over some named table and C is a column of that table, returns the default value applicable to that column. It's an error if no such default value exists.

5. In applying an aggregate operator such as AVG to a particular column, the user must explicitly exclude default values, if that's what's desired. For example:

```
SELECT  AVG ( SP.QTY )
FROM    SP
WHERE   SP.QTY ≠ DEFAULT ( SP.QTY )
```

6. The operator IS_DEFAULT (*R.C*) returns *true* if its argument *R.C* evaluates to the applicable default value, *false* otherwise. Thus, the foregoing SELECT could alternatively have been formulated as follows:

```
SELECT  AVG ( SP.QTY )
FROM    SP
WHERE   NOT ( IS_DEFAULT ( SP.QTY ) )
```

7. Aggregate operators such as AVG are extended to include an optional second argument, defining the value to be returned if the first argument is empty. It's an error if the first argument is empty and the second argument is omitted.

8. For some columns it might be the case that every value of the pertinent type (domain) is a legitimate nondefault value. Such cases must be handled by explicit, separate, user controlled indicator columns (as with the host side of the interface in embedded SQL today)—though it would be desirable to be able to tell the system that those separate columns are indeed indicator columns, and to specify the indicator values declaratively so that the system understands them.

Discussion

Advantages of the foregoing scheme, compared to the 3VL approach described in the body of these two chapters, include the following:

- No nulls! No 3VL! In other words, it's intuitively easier to understand.

- It's also easier to implement.

- It directly reflects the way we handle missing information in the real world.

- There are fewer traps for the unwary.

- As already mentioned, it's extendable to other kinds of missing information without the need to resort to *n*-valued logic for any $n > 2$.

In reference [2], however, Codd argues strongly against such a scheme on the grounds that (a) it's unsystematic, (b) it misrepresents the semantics, and (c) it's a significant burden on DBAs and users, inasmuch as they have to choose and understand and manipulate the default values (possibly many different default values). My response to these arguments is as follows:

a. *"Unsystematic"*: It seems to me that DBAs and users (and DBMSs, I might add) are always going to be able to use system facilities in an unsystematic manner, no matter how carefully defined those facilities might be. The default values approach isn't totally unsystematic. At least the default values are explicitly made known to the system, and appropriate operators are provided to avoid the need for hardcoding those values into programs (in fact, users shouldn't normally even have to know what the specific default values are). A systematic treatment of empty sets is also part of the proposal.

b. *"Misrepresenting semantics"*: If it's true that default values "misrepresent the semantics," then the 3VL scheme does so too!—at least, it does so as soon as it becomes necessary to deal with more than one kind of missing information. To repeat an argument from the body of this chapter: To my way of thinking, it's at least as dangerous to represent, say, "not applicable" as "value unknown" as it is to represent, say, "value unknown" as "-1"— possibly even more dangerous, in fact, because in the first case the user might be lulled into a false sense of security. Indeed, we can see exactly this kind of mistake in the design of the SQL language itself (in other words, system designers and implementers can make just the same kinds of mistakes as users). For example, the fact that SQL regards the MAX of an empty set to be null (meaning "value unknown") is just plain wrong, in my opinion.

c. *"Burden"*: I agree that default values represent a significant burden on DBAs and users—but so too does three-valued logic, in my opinion (not to mention four- and five- ... and *n*-valued logic), as I think the discussions of these two chapters have clearly demonstrated. So which burden do you think is the greater?

To conclude, therefore, I freely admit that the default values scheme isn't a particularly elegant approach to the problem, but I'm far from convinced that

3VL is any better, and indeed I believe there are reasons to think it's much worse. In other words, I believe the whole area of missing information stands in need of considerable further research.

Chapter 14

EXISTS Is Not "Exists"!

This chapter can be seen as a companion to Chapters 12 and 13. In those chapters, I criticized the use of nulls and three-valued logic (3VL) as a basis for dealing with the problem of missing information. Of course, SQL in particular does base its approach to that problem on nulls and 3VL, so the criticisms of those chapters certainly apply to SQL specifically—but SQL manages to introduce additional flaws of its own in this area, or in other words flaws that are over and above the ones that I claim are intrinsic to the very idea of nulls and 3VL. The present chapter focuses on just one aspect of those additional flaws, viz., SQL's support for quantification.

Background: It was in late 1987 or so that I first realized there was a problem with SQL's EXISTS operator, inasmuch as invocations of that operator always returned true or false, never unknown. Moreover, one particular consequence of this state of affairs was that SQL's "quantified comparisons" (i.e., comparisons involving a scalar and a table), which generally might be expected to be—and ought to be—equivalent to some expression involving EXISTS, sometimes weren't. A telephone call on such matters from an old acquaintance, Don Slutz of the SQL group at Tandem, in November 1988 set me thinking about the problem more deeply. I came to the conclusion that the matter was quite serious, and decided to try and pull the various points together and try to present them in a coherent manner. What follows is the result.

Incidentally, an interesting sidelight on the issue is the following: When I demonstrated the problem to various SQL apologists, the typical reaction wasn't one of distress at the gravity of the situation; rather, the parties concerned would simply try to show me how to reformulate the examples so that SQL would get the right answer!

> *Publishing history: This is a major revision of, and supersedes, a paper that first appeared under the same title (but with the addition of the subtitle "Some Logical Flaws in SQL") as Chapter 13 of my book Relational Database Writings 1985-1989 (Addison-Wesley, 1990). This version copyright © 2022 C. J. Date.*

SQL's support for three-valued logic (3VL) is defective. The fundamental problem can be stated quite simply as follows:

> In 3VL in general, boolean expressions—also known as truth valued or logical expressions—evaluate to one of three possible values, *true*, *false*, and *unknown* (abbreviated in what follows to just *unk*). In SQL, by contrast, there's one such expression, viz., an invocation of SQL's EXISTS operator, that always returns *true* or *false*, never *unk*, even when *unk* is the logically correct response.

As a consequence, SQL's EXISTS operator isn't a faithful representation of the existential quantifier ("there exists") of 3VL—a fact that accounts for the somewhat tongue in cheek title of this chapter, of course.

Let's look at an example. Let the set *Z* contain just the values 1 and 2, together with a null,[1] and let *v* be a variable that ranges over *Z*. In 3VL, then, the existentially quantified expression

```
EXISTS v ( v > 5 )        /* or ∃v ( v > 5 ) */
```

evaluates to *unk*, because it's unknown whether there's any element *v* of *Z* for which *v* > 5 evaluates to *true*. More precisely, the expression is defined to be equivalent to the following "iterated OR" expression [4]:

```
FALSE OR ( 1 > 5 ) OR ( 2 > 5 ) OR ( null > 5 )
```

This expression in turn is equivalent to *false* OR *false* OR *false* OR *unk*, which reduces to just *unk*. *Note:* The truth tables for 3VL can be found in many places (see, e.g., reference [4]).

---

[1] Of course, null isn't a value, but I have to assume for the purposes of this chapter that it makes sense for a set to contain one (or possibly more than one?). See reference [4] for further discussion of such matters.

However, an SQL analog of the foregoing example looks something like this:

```
EXISTS ( SELECT DISTINCT V.*
         FROM    Z V
         WHERE   V.N > 5 )
```

(Z is now a table of one column, called N, and V is a range variable that ranges over Z.)[2] So what happens? Well, the SELECT expression evaluates to an empty result, because SELECT in SQL is defined to select only the values for which the expression in the WHERE clause evaluates to *true*, not to *false* and not to *unk*. So the expression overall returns *false*, not *unk*, because EXISTS in SQL is defined to return *false* if its argument is empty and *true* otherwise.

It follows from this rather trivial example that the existential quantifier of 3VL and the EXISTS operator in SQL are indeed not the same thing. In principle, therefore, the chapter could stop right here—once it has been established that the EXISTS in SQL is logically flawed, it's obvious that (as a colleague of mine, Nat Goodman, once put it) "SQL will break." In other words, problems will occur. Thus, identifying specific places where it does break—i.e., describing the specific problems in detail—might be regarded as just beating a dead horse. But some of those problems are so significant, and at the same time so subtle, that it does seem worthwhile, at least from a pedagogic standpoint, to examine them in some depth, and so I will.

A CONTRADICTION

Consider the following table (essentially a very much reduced version of the shipments table SP from the familiar suppliers-and-parts database):

SP

SNO	PNO	QTY
S1	P1	null
S2	P1	200

---

[2] I'll use explicit range variables in examples throughout this chapter, for clarity. I'll also specify DISTINCT in all SELECT expressions, even when it's logically unnecessary, simply to be sure without having to think about the matter that such expressions do always evaluate to sets as such, without any duplicates.

Note that the null in the row for S1 and P1 in this example would normally be (and indeed is meant to be) interpreted as "value unknown"—i.e., supplier S1 does supply part P1, we just don't know in what quantity.

Consider now the query "Get supplier numbers for suppliers who supply part P1, but not in a quantity of 1000"—meaning, more precisely, suppliers who are *known* to supply part P1, and the corresponding quantity is *known* not to be 1000. (As explained in reference [4], we can't ask questions about the real world per se, only about the system's knowledge of the real world as represented by the values in the database.) Given the sample data shown above, then, the right answer to this query is clearly just the single supplier number S2; the system doesn't know whether supplier S1 supplies part P1 in a quantity of 1000, because of that null.

Now, the "obvious" formulation of the query in SQL is:[3]

```
SELECT  DISTINCT SPX.SNO
FROM    SP SPX
WHERE   SPX.PNO = 'P1'
AND     SPX.QTY <> 1000
```

In fact this formulation is correct—it does indeed return just S2 (S1 doesn't qualify, because for S1 the boolean expression in the WHERE clause becomes *true* AND *unk*, which reduces to just *unk*).

Observe now, however, that the foregoing formulation can be regarded as shorthand for a kind of "UNION" or "iterated OR" formulation: In effect, what it does is examine the rows of table SP one by one, extracting the supplier number from a given row if and only if the expression in the WHERE clause evaluates to *true* for that row, and returning the UNION of all supplier numbers so extracted.[4] In other words, it's effectively equivalent to an expanded formulation that might look something like this:

---

[3] I'm tempted to add one of my favorite quotes here: "Obvious is the most dangerous word in mathematics" (from reference [1]). PS: In case you're not familiar with it, the symbol "<>" in the last line of the example is SQL's syntax for the "not equals" operator ("≠").

[4] More precisely, it returns the union of a collection of *tables*, each such table containing just one column and one row, with a supplier number as the sole value at that row and column position.

```
SELECT  DISTINCT SPX.SNO
FROM    SP SPX
WHERE   SPX.SNO = 'S1'            /* "first" supplier number */
AND     SPX.PNO = 'P1'
AND     SPX.QTY <> 1000

UNION

SELECT  DISTINCT SPX.SNO
FROM    SP SPX
WHERE   SPX.SNO = 'S2'            /* "second" supplier number */
AND     SPX.PNO = 'P1'
AND     SPX.QTY <> 1000

UNION

. . . . .

UNION

SELECT  DISTINCT SPX.SNO
FROM    SP SPX
WHERE   SPX.SNO = 'Sn'            /* "last" supplier number   */
AND     SPX.PNO = 'P1'
AND     SPX.QTY <> 1000
```

Here now is another formulation, one that logically should be equivalent to the foregoing "UNION" formulation:

```
SELECT  DISTINCT SPX.SNO
FROM    SP SPX
WHERE   SPX.PNO = 'P1'
AND     NOT EXISTS
      ( SELECT DISTINCT SPY.*
        FROM    SP SPY
        WHERE   SPY.SNO = SPX.SNO
        AND     SPY.PNO = 'P1'
        AND     SPY.QTY = 1000 )
```

In stilted natural language: "Select supplier numbers from shipments SPX such that the supplier in question does supply part P1, but there doesn't exist a shipment SPY saying the same supplier supplies part P1 in a quantity of 1000." Note that this latter formulation would in fact be the "obvious" one if there could be two or more rows having the same supplier number and same part number—i.e., if the combination (SNO,PNO) wasn't a key.

So let's see how this expression is evaluated. For definiteness, let's suppose the rows of table SP are processed in top to bottom order as shown. For the "first" row, then:

■ The expression denoting the argument to the EXISTS invocation effectively becomes:

```
SELECT  DISTINCT SPY.*
FROM    SP SPY
WHERE   SPY.SNO = 'S1'
AND     SPY.PNO = 'P1'
AND     SPY.QTY = 1000
```

And this expression evaluates to an empty table, since there's no row (S1,P1,1000) in table SP.

■ The EXISTS invocation therefore evaluates to *false*. The NOT invocation therefore evaluates to *true*, and the outer SELECT expression thus effectively becomes:

```
SELECT  DISTINCT SPX.SNO
FROM    SP SPX
WHERE   SPX.PNO = 'P1'
AND     TRUE
```

So supplier number S1 appears in the final result. Error!

■ Supplier number S2 also appears in the final result, as you might like to confirm, but of course it's correct that it should.

The message from the foregoing example is this: (a) There are two different ways to formulate the query, one (conceptually) using "UNION" or "iterated OR" and the other using EXISTS; (b) the two formulations ought to be logically equivalent; but (c) they aren't—they return different results. As a consequence, *it's possible to derive contradictions from an SQL DBMS.*[5]

I'd like to take a moment to stress the momentous nature of this state of affairs. What I've shown, in effect, is that an SQL DBMS can answer the very same question either *yes* or *no*, depending purely on how we choose to frame that question in the first place. Would you really want to put your business in the

---

[5] As noted in the previous chapter, the term *contradiction* has a rather specific meaning in logic—it refers to a boolean expression such *p* AND NOT *p* that evaluates to *false* regardless of the values of any variables involved. Here, however, I'm using it in its more usual natural language sense, meaning something that's apparently both true and false at the same time and is thus an impossibility.

hands of such a DBMS? Seriously? What about your life savings? What about your life?

A PROBLEM OF INTERPRETATION

Suppose we have two tables, S (suppliers) and SP (shipments), with values as follows:

S

SNO	SNAME	STATUS	CITY
S1	Smith	20	London
S2	Jones	10	Paris

SP

SNO	PNO
S1	P1

Here's a sample query on this database: "Get names of cities for suppliers who supply at least one part." A correct formulation of this query in SQL is as follows:

```
SELECT DISTINCT X.CITY
FROM    S X
WHERE   EXISTS
     ( SELECT DISTINCT Y.PNO
       FROM    SP Y
       WHERE   Y.SNO = X.SNO )
```

In stilted natural language: "Select cities for suppliers, X say, such that there exists at least one part that supplier X supplies." This formulation does return the correct answer, which is a table of one column and one row containing just one city name, viz., London.

However, suppose we now form the *left outer natural join* of tables S and SP on supplier numbers (call the result SSP):

SSP

SNO	SNAME	STATUS	CITY	PNO
S1	Smith	20	London	P1
S2	Jones	10	Paris	null

What exactly does this table mean? Most people would probably say it means something like the following:

Supplier SNO has name SNAME, status STATUS, and city CITY, and supplies part PNO.

Given this interpretation, a simple formulation of the original query "Get names of cities for suppliers who supply at least one part" would appear to be straightforward:

```
SELECT DISTINCT X.CITY
FROM    SSP X
```

But this formulation is obviously incorrect; to be specific, it produces a result that includes the city for supplier S2 (Paris), even though that supplier doesn't supply any parts. And of course the root of the problem is that null in table SSP (were you surprised?). More specifically, the problem is that the null in question is *not* the usual "value unknown" null. More specifically still, that null doesn't mean (a) that supplier S2 does supply some part, but we don't know which; rather, it means (b) that what we do know is that supplier S2 doesn't supply any parts at all.

The foregoing explanation notwithstanding, I venture to suggest that not too many people will realize that the interpretation of table SSP I gave previously—*Supplier SNO has name SNAME, status STATUS, and city CITY, and supplies part PNO*—is incorrect. So I'd like to explore some of the consequences of this state of affairs.

First of all, if that interpretation were indeed correct after all, the following alternative formulation of the original query would be correct as well :

```
SELECT DISTINCT X.CITY
FROM    SSP X
WHERE   EXISTS
      ( SELECT DISTINCT Y.PNO
        FROM    SSP Y
        WHERE   Y.SNO = X.SNO )
```

(The only difference between this formulation and the earlier correct one is that the references to tables S and SP in the previous version have been replaced by references to table SSP.) Now consider what happens when the range variable X takes as its value the SSP row for supplier S2, in which "the part number is null":

■ The expression denoting the argument to the EXISTS invocation effectively becomes:

```
SELECT  DISTINCT Y.PNO
FROM    SSP Y
WHERE   Y.SNO = 'S2'
```

And this expression yields a nonempty table (actually a table containing nothing but a null).

■ The EXISTS invocation therefore evaluates to *true*, because, to repeat, the argument is nonempty. So the city for supplier number S2 appears in the final result. Error!

Now, the rationale for defining EXISTS to return *true* in such a case (i.e., the case where the argument set contains just one element and that element is null) is presumably that the null in question means "value unknown"—i.e., a value does exist to make the existence test *true*, we just don't happen to know what that value is. But as explained above, the particular null in the case at hand doesn't mean "value unknown," it means "value doesn't exist." That's why (as indicated in the title to this section) I regard this particular flaw as a problem of interpretation.

There's one more point I want to make in connection with this example. In principle, it ought to be possible to recast any SQL expression involving EXISTS into another involving COUNT instead, because:

a. Loosely speaking, if *tx* ("table expression") is a SELECT expression, then the expression EXISTS (*tx*) evaluates to *false* if and only if the expression COUNT (*tx*) evaluates to 0.

   Note: I say "loosely speaking" here because SQL's COUNT operator has problems of its own (see reference [3]). In particular, SQL's syntax rules don't allow a SELECT expression to be used to denote the table argument, though logically they should.[6]

---

[6] Which incidentally is why a comparand in an SQL WHERE clause can't be specified by means of a simple COUNT invocation. The pseudoSQL examples later in this section show how (in my opinion) matters would be considerably improved if the syntax for COUNT did follow the same general style as that of EXISTS after all.

b. Likewise—ignoring nulls for the moment—the expression EXISTS (*tx*) evaluates to *true* if and only if the expression COUNT (*tx*) evaluates to some *n* such that *n* > 0.

In SQL, however, these equivalences break down when nulls are taken into account, because COUNT simply ignores any nulls in its argument and EXISTS doesn't. But the fact that they do break down when nulls are involved is precisely the point I'm trying to make! If we assume the existence of an improved "pseudoSQL" version of SQL in which COUNT (*tx*) is syntactically legal, then analogs of the two expressions shown earlier in this section (the ones that used EXISTS) would look like this:

```
SELECT DISTINCT X.CITY          SELECT DISTINCT X.CITY
FROM    S X                     FROM    SSP X
WHERE   COUNT                   WHERE   COUNT
  ( SELECT DISTINCT Y.PNO         ( SELECT DISTINCT Y.PNO
    FROM    SP Y                     FROM    SSP Y
    WHERE   Y.SNO = X.SNO ) > 0      WHERE   Y.SNO = X.SNO ) > 0
```

I show these two pseudoSQL versions side by side for ease of comparison; the query, to repeat, is "Get names of cities for suppliers who supply at least one part."

The interesting thing about these pseudoSQL formulations is that (unlike their EXISTS counterparts) they *both* return the right answer! (With the EXISTS versions, you'll recall, one returned the right answer but the other one didn't.) Consider what happens in each of these pseudoSQL formulations when the range variable X takes as its value the row for supplier S2:

a. In the formulation on the left, the COUNT argument is empty (there are no part numbers in table SP for supplier S2); the COUNT invocation therefore returns zero, and hence Paris doesn't appear in the final result (correct).

b. In the formulation on the right, by contrast, the COUNT argument contains just one element, a null. However, COUNT in SQL ignores nulls in its argument;[7] the COUNT invocation therefore again returns zero, and again Paris doesn't appear in the final result (again correct).

---

[7] Unless the COUNT reference takes the special form COUNT(*), which it doen't here. PS: I'm not arguing here that ignoring nulls in the argument is itself correct behavior!—I'm just explaining one of the consequences of how the SQL COUNT operator works.

Here for interest is a valid, legitimate SQL expression that's equivalent to the pseudoSQL formulation shown above on the right:

```
SELECT  DISTINCT X.CITY
FROM    SSP X
GROUP   BY X.SNO , X.CITY
HAVING  COUNT ( DISTINCT X.PNO ) > 0
```

Exercise: Convince yourself that this expression does indeed deliver the correct result. Then ask yourself these questions:

- Do you think this is an obvious way to formulate the query? Note that GROUP BY and HAVING haven't even been mentioned in our discussions prior to this point. Why are they suddenly needed here? (*Are* they needed here?)

- What would happen if replaced the COUNT invocation in the HAVING clause here by just COUNT (*)—which would surely seem on the face of it to be a perfectly reasonable simplification? (*Answer:* The result would be yet another logically incorrect formulation. Why, exactly?)

- Given that for every value of X.SNO there's just one corresponding value of X.CITY, why is it necessary to mention X.CITY in the GROUP BY clause at all? *Is* it necessary? What difference would it make to the grouping if it were omitted?

QUANTIFIED COMPARISONS

There are two features of SQL that are quantifier-like, or at least have something to with quantification as usually understood. One is the EXISTS operator, which I've now extensively discussed. The other, the subject of the present section, is quantified comparisons.

Now, if what we had here were just an example of syntactic substitution at work [2], I'd have nothing to complain about—in fact I'd probably be all in favor. That is, if quantified comparisons were nothing but a syntactic shorthand for something that could alternatively be expressed, possibly more longwindedly, using the EXISTS operator, then everything would be fine. Sadly, however, such is not the case. (It's *nearly* the case, but in my opinion "nearly" here is much worse than if there were no overlap in functionality at all.) Let me elaborate.

First, I should explain that "quantified comparisons" is just another name for what elsewhere I've referred to as "ANY or ALL comparisons" (i.e., they're comparisons that involve the operators <ANY, >ALL, and so on).

Second, contrary to what I said in the last paragraph but one, I'm on record as claiming that such comparisons *can* be recast as existence tests. For example, here's an extract from reference [3]:

> [The] comparison operators =ANY (etc.) need never be used. If we assume for simplicity that no nulls are involved anywhere (as I would strongly recommend), then (a) the WHERE clause
>
> ```
>     WHERE x $ANY ( SELECT y FROM T WHERE bx )
> ```
>
> (where $ is any one of "=", ">", etc.) is logically equivalent to
>
> ```
>     WHERE EXISTS ( SELECT * FROM T
>                      WHERE ( bx ) AND x $ T.y )
> ```
>
> And (b) the WHERE clause
>
> ```
>     WHERE x $ALL ( SELECT y FROM T WHERE bx )
> ```
>
> is logically equivalent to
>
> ```
>     WHERE NOT EXISTS ( SELECT * FROM T
>                          WHERE ( bx ) AND NOT ( x $ T.y ) )
> ```

OK ... but now let me draw your attention to that important qualification, or disclaimer: "[We] assume for simplicity that no nulls are involved." Right! The foregoing transformations certainly *ought* to be valid (and if they were, then we would indeed be talking about an example of syntactic substitution in action). What's more, they *are* valid, so long as there aren't any nulls involved. But (sadly) if nulls are involved, then of course they aren't valid any longer ... Here's an accurate statement of the situation that, in effect, does take nulls into account:

■ The boolean expression

```
x $ANY ( SELECT y FROM T WHERE bx )
```

evaluates to *true* if the expression

```
x $ ( y )
```

evaluates to *true* for at least one value *y* in the result of evaluating the parenthesized SELECT expression; it evaluates to *false* if the expression

```
x $ ( y )
```

evaluates to *false* for every value *y* in the result of evaluating that SELECT expression, or if that result is empty; and it evaluates to *unk* otherwise.

■ The boolean expression

```
x $ALL ( SELECT y FROM T WHERE bx )
```

evaluates to *true* if the expression

```
x $ ( y )
```

evaluates to *true* for every value *y* in the result of evaluating the parenthesized SELECT expression, or if that result is empty; it evaluates to *false* if the expression

```
x $ ( y )
```

evaluates to *false* for at least one value *y* in the result of evaluating that SELECT expression; and it evaluates to *unk* otherwise.

Again consider the query (I deliberately repeat it in detail) "Get supplier numbers for suppliers who are known to supply part P1, where the corresponding quantity is known not to be 1000." Here's another plausible SQL formulation:[8]

---

[8] The operator <>ALL used in this formulation is logically equivalent to, and really just another spelling for, the more familiar SQL operator NOT IN.

```
SELECT  DISTINCT SPX.SNO
FROM    SP SPX
WHERE   SPX.PNO = 'P1'
AND     1000 <>ALL
      ( SELECT DISTINCT SPY.QTY
        FROM    SP SPY
        WHERE   SPY.SNO = SPX.SNO
        AND     SPY.PNO = 'P1' )
```

In fact this formulation is correct, but try to convince yourself that it is so before going on to read the explanation that follows.

Explanation: Assume once again that table SP looks like this—

```
SP
```

SNO	PNO	QTY
S1	P1	null
S2	P1	200

—and assume too as before that the rows of the table are processed in top to bottom order as shown. Then:

■ For the "first" row, viz., (S1,P1,null), the expression denoting the right comparand to the <>ALL operator effectively becomes:

```
SELECT  DISTINCT SPY.QTY
FROM    SP SPY
WHERE   SPY.SNO = 'S1'
AND     SPY.PNO = 'P1'
```

This expression returns a table of one column and one row, containing a null. The overall query expression thus effectively becomes

```
SELECT  DISTINCT SPX.SNO
FROM    SP SPX
WHERE   SPX.PNO = 'P1'
AND     1000 <>ALL ( null )
```

Now (a) the comparison SPX.PNO = 'P1' returns *true*; (b) the comparison 1000 <> null returns *unk*, and so (c) the comparison 1000 <> ALL (null) returns *unk* as well; thus (d) the boolean expression in the WHERE clause reduces to *true* AND *unk*, which is *unk*, and so supplier S1 doesn't appear in the final result (which is of course correct).

■ For the "second" row, viz., (S2,P1,200), the expression denoting the right comparand to the <>ALL operator effectively becomes:

```
SELECT  DISTINCT SPY.QTY
FROM    SP SPY
WHERE   SPY.SNO = 'S2'
AND     SPY.PNO = 'P1'
```

This expression returns a table of one column and one row, containing the value 200. The overall query expression thus effectively becomes

```
SELECT  DISTINCT SPX.SNO
FROM    SP SPX
WHERE   SPX.PNO = 'P2'
AND     1000 <>ALL ( 200 )
```

Now (a) the comparison SPX.PNO = 'P2' returns *true*; (b) the comparison 1000 <> 200 also returns *true*, and so (c) the comparison 1000 <> ALL (200) returns *true* as well; thus (d) the boolean expression in the WHERE clause reduces to *true* AND *true*, which is *true*, and so supplier S2 does appear in the final result, which is correct.

So the formulation involving <>ALL is indeed correct. But suppose we now try transforming that formulation into another "equivalent" version, using the transformation rule for ALL comparisons given near the beginning of this section. We obtain the following expression:

```
SELECT  DISTINCT SPX.SNO
FROM    SP SPX
WHERE   SPX.PNO = 'P1'
AND     NOT EXISTS
      ( SELECT DISTINCT SPY.*
        FROM    SP SPY
        WHERE   SPY.SNO = SPX.SNO
        AND     SPY.PNO = 'P1'
        AND     NOT ( 1000 <> SPY.QTY ) )
```

And now, if we simplify the comparison in the last line here to just SPY.QTY = 1000, we wind up with a formulation that's identical to one that we've already seen (on pages 253-254) isn't valid. So the message is: By all means use the transformation rules from near the beginning of this section if you want to—but not if there are any nulls around, because SQL's EXISTS operator doesn't deal with them correctly.

ANOTHER ANOMALY

The discussions of the preceding section pave the way for an explanation of another anomaly concerning quantification in SQL. This one has to do with the fact that, if the parenthesized SELECT expression following an ANY or ALL comparison operator returns a table of one column and one row (so containing just one item), then the ANY or ALL keyword can be omitted, thereby reducing the operator in question to a simple scalar comparison operator. Here are the rules. Let *tx* be the expression SELECT *y* FROM *T* WHERE *bx*, and let *tx* evaluate to a table of exactly one row and one column (containing just one item, *y*). Then the expressions

```
x $ANY ( tx )
```

and

```
x $ALL ( tx )
```

are both equivalent to just

```
x $ y
```

Here's a simple example ("Get supplier numbers for suppliers who are located in the same city as supplier S1"):[9]

```
SELECT  DISTINCT SX.SNO
FROM    S SX
WHERE   SX.CITY =ANY
      ( SELECT DISTINCT SY.CITY
        FROM    S SY
        WHERE   SY.SNO = 'S1' )
```

Given table S as shown on page 255, the expression in parentheses returns a table of one column and one row (containing the name of supplier S1's city, viz.,

---

[9] The operator =ANY used in this formulation is logically equivalent to, and really just another spelling for, the more familiar SQL operator IN.

London), and so the =ANY comparison effectively reduces to a simple equality test. As a consequence, SQL will actually allow the comparison to be written using a simple equals sign instead of =ANY, like this:

```
SELECT  DISTINCT SX.SNO
FROM    S SX
WHERE   SX.CITY =               /* the change is in this line */
      ( SELECT DISTINCT SY.CITY
        FROM    S SY
        WHERE   SY.SNO = 'S1' )
```

So consider now the (admittedly somewhat contrived) query "Get supplier numbers for suppliers who (a) do supply at least one part, and (b) if they supply part P1, also supply some other part in a quantity greater than the quantity in which they supply part P1." Here's one possible SQL formulation:

```
SELECT  DISTINCT SPX.SNO
FROM    SP SPX
WHERE   NOT ( SPX.QTY <=ANY
      ( SELECT DISTINCT SPY.QTY
        FROM    SP SPY
        WHERE   SPY.SNO = SPX.SNO
        AND     SPY.PNO = 'P1' ) )
```

In stilted natural language: "Select supplier numbers from shipments SPX such that it's not the case that the corresponding shipment quantity is less than or equal to some quantity in which the supplier in question supplies part P1").

However, there's at most one shipment for a given supplier and given part. For a given value of the range variable SPX, therefore, the SELECT expression in parentheses will return a table of one column and at most one row, containing therefore at most a single item. We can therefore drop the ANY, yielding:

```
SELECT  DISTINCT SPX.SNO
FROM    SP SPX
WHERE   NOT ( SPX.QTY <=      /* the change is in this line */
      ( SELECT DISTINCT SPY.QTY
        FROM    SP SPY
        WHERE   SPY.SNO = SPX.SNO
        AND     SPY.PNO = 'P1' ) )
```

So there's a trivial syntactic difference between the two formulations. But is there a semantic difference? As a basis for considering this question, suppose table SP looks like this:

SP

SNO	PNO	QTY
S2	P2	400

Consider now how the first formulation (the one using =ANY) is evaluated, given this sample value for table SP:

- The range variable SPX takes on the value (S2,P2,400). The SELECT expression in parentheses thus logically becomes:

```
SELECT  DISTINCT SPY.QTY
FROM    SP SPY
WHERE   SPY.SNO = 'S2'
AND     SPY.PNO = 'P1'
```

This expression returns an empty table, and the formulation overall thus reduces to the following:

```
SELECT  DISTINCT SPX.SNO
FROM    SP SPX
WHERE   NOT ( SPX.QTY <=ANY ( ) )
```

(using "( )" to represent that empty table). The expression in the WHERE clause here thus becomes NOT *false*—see the definition of the ANY or ALL operators in terms of EXISTS as given in that extract from reference [3] near the beginning of the previous section—which reduces to *true*, and so the final result does contain the supplier number S2, and nothing else. (By the way, this result is logically correct!—perhaps a little surprisingly.)

What about the second formulation? Well:

- Once again the range variable SPX takes on the value (S2,P2,400) and the SELECT expression in parentheses returns an empty table, as before. The formulation overall thus reduces to the following:

```
SELECT  DISTINCT SPX.SNO
FROM    SP SPX
WHERE   NOT ( SPX.QTY <= ( ) )
```

This time, however, the expression in the WHERE clause becomes NOT *unk*, because SQL defines a "simple comparison" (of which the parenthesized expression following the NOT is an example) to return *unk* if the pertinent comparand is empty. As a consequence, the final result doesn't include the supplier number S2. Contradiction!

Well, I was tempted to leave it as another exercise to spot the sleight of hand in the foregoing discussion, but I decided that would be a little unfriendly— so let me spell it out.

- The expressions *x* $ANY (*tx*) and *x* $ALL (*tx*) can both be abbreviated to just *x* $ (*tx*) if *tx* returns a table of *exactly* one row.

- But in the case at hand the pertinent table expression *tx* is:

```
SELECT  DISTINCT SPY.QTY
FROM    SP SPY
WHERE   SPY.SNO = SPX.SNO
AND     SPY.PNO = 'P1'
```

And as we know, for a given value of SPX.SNO this expression returns a table of *at most* one row.

So the transformation I carried out in the example, from the first to the second formulation of the query, wasn't valid! But the point is a subtle one, and I venture to suggest that the trap is one that's all too easy to fall into.[10]

AND ANOTHER

There's at least one more surprise that can occur in connection with quantification in SQL. Consider, e.g., the operator <ANY. Intuitively speaking, if some value *x* is "less than any" value in some set, then it's obvious that it must

---

[10] In fact I believe it was a serious mistake in the original design of SQL to allow comparisons of the form *<scalar value> <scalar comparison operator> <table value>* in the first place. At the very least, such comparisons require some kind of implicit conversion, or *coercion*, of a table value to some scalar type, and coercions in general are widely recognized to be A Very Bad Idea. Quite apart from anything else—and this is certainly the case in the example we've been discussing—they increase the number of possible programming errors that can't be caught until run time. If then.

must be less than the *maximum* value in that set. [11] (Analogous remarks can be made regarding most if not all of the ANY or ALL operators, of course.) And comparing a value with the maximum in some set is often intuitively easier to understand than comparing it with "any" (i.e., every) value in that set. The following "obvious" transformation rule thus suggests itself (be aware, however, that this rule is not entirely valid):

- The boolean expression

      x <ANY (SELECT y FROM T WHERE bx)

  is equivalent to the expression

      x < (SELECT MAX (y) FROM T WHERE bx)

To see what's wrong with this putative "rule," consider the following rather complicated query: "Get supplier numbers for suppliers such that (a) they supply at least one part, and (b) it's not the case that they supply some part in a quantity less than that in which they supply some other part." Here's an SQL formulation of this query:

```
SELECT  DISTINCT SPX.SNO
FROM    SP SPX
WHERE   NOT( SPX.QTY <ANY
                ( SELECT DISTINCT SPY.QTY
                  FROM   SP SPY
                  WHERE  SPY.PNO <> SPX.PNO ) )
```

Now if we suppose again that table SP contains just the single row (S2,P2,400)—

SP

SNO	PNO	QTY
S2	P2	400

---

[11] By the way, "less than any" value in the set must be understood here to mean "less than *some*" value in that set, not less than all of them, which is how "less than any" would normally be understood in colloquial English. Another trap for the unwary! PS: SQL does actually allow SOME as an alternative spelling for ANY, but of course that doesn't solve the problem (e.g., what do you think <>SOME means?).

—then the foregoing formulation of the query reurns a result containing just the supplier number S2, which is correct.

Now here's another formulation of the query that's at least plausible, one that's derived from the previous (correct) one by applying the "obvious" transformation rule given above:

```
SELECT DISTINCT SPX.SNO
FROM    SP SPX
WHERE   NOT( SPX.QTY <
                  ( SELECT DISTINCT MAX ( SPY.QTY )
                    FROM    SP SPY
                    WHERE   SPY.PNO <> SPX.PNO ) )
```

But (surprise, surprise) this second formulation is incorrect. Suppose again that table SP contains just the single row (S2,P2,400). When the range variable SPX takes on this row as its value, the expression

```
SELECT DISTINCT SPY.QTY
FROM    SP SPY
WHERE   SPY.PNO <> SPX.PNO
```

evaluates to an empty table; the expression

```
SELECT DISTINCT MAX ( SPY.QTY )
FROM    SP SPY
WHERE   SPY.PNO <> SPX.PNO
```

therefore evaluates to a table containing nothing but a null (the MAX of an empty set is—incorrectly, in my very strong opinion!—defined to be null in SQL); the conditional expression in the outer WHERE clause thus evaluates to *unk*, and supplier number S2 therefore doesn't appear in the final result. Error!

CONCLUDING REMARKS

This is all pretty tricky stuff, and I'm tempted to say that if you're not confused by it, then you haven't been paying attention ... Be that as it may, the original paper on which this chapter is based concluded by saying simply "SQL is not sound." On reflection, I'm not sure that conclusion was fair. A formal system is unsound if it's possible, within that system, to derive an inconsistency—i.e., to find some boolean expression that evaluates to different truth values. The present chapter hasn't demonstrated any such failure on SQL's part. What it has

demonstrated, though (several times over, in fact), is that there can exist
expressions in SQL that can reasonably be believed to be equivalent but in fact
aren't—they have different truth values. Thus, users are likely to perceive the
language as unsound even if strictly speaking it isn't. In other words, they're
likely to encounter what they see as contradictions, even if the "contradictions"
in question aren't really contradictions (or inconsistencies) as such but merely
look as if they are. But this is certainly not a happy state of affairs! The fact that
expressions that look equivalent, and logically ought to be equivalent, can
produce different results isn't just an academic concern—there are serious
implications for real world applications. What's more, it's not easy to place
bounds on the scope of the damage that might be caused. In fact, of course, there
are no bounds: Medical diagnoses and treatments could be incorrect; bridges
could collapse spacecraft could fall out of the sky; and worse.

The point, of course, is not just that users are likely to make mistakes—
though they certainly are, even if they thoroughly understand 3VL (which in any
case most users probably don't), because SQL's version of 3VL is defective (not
to say incorrect). At least as significant is the fact that implementations are likely
to be incorrect also, because they perform expression transformations internally
that should be valid but in fact aren't. Indeed, I know for a fact that there are
implementations on the market today that were certainly incorrect in this sense at
some point in their history, and I daresay still are. And even if an
implementation is "correct" (whatever "correct" might mean when the language
itself is arguably incorrect), there's still the point that the errors act as
optimization inhibitors—i.e., the optimizer is prevented from making certain
transformations that have the potential to improve performance, and should have
been legal, but in fact aren't.

Note too that users can't avoid the problems by simply avoiding nulls in the
database (i.e., by explicitly defining all columns in all base tables to be NOT
NULL), because empty sets and nulls can be generated dynamically at run time.
However, it's probably true that avoiding nulls in the database (which I would
definitely recommend anyway) will have the effect of reducing the error
potential—but unfortunately not to zero.[12] The only way to avoid the problem
entirely, at least as far as SQL is concerned, would be to eliminate every aspect

---

[12] And even if you do make the (in my view, very sensible) decision to avoid nulls entirely, they'll still act
as an optimization inhibitor, *because there's no way to tell the system what you've done.* Thus, the system
still has to avoid making certain transformations to improve performance, because it has to operate on the
conservative assumption that there might always be some nulls lurking around somewhere.

of the language that has anything to do with nulls and 3VL. But that's not going to happen. So, sadly, my closing piece of advice has to be:

> If you possibly can, avoid all aspects of SQL's 3VL support entirely. If you can't do that, then exercise *extreme caution* when dealing with these aspects of the language.

ACKNOWLEDGMENTS

I'm grateful to Nagraj Alur, Hugh Darwen, Nat Goodman, and Colin White for their numerous helpful comments on the original version of this paper. I'm also grateful to Colin in particular for checking out my SQL examples on Oracle.

REFERENCES

1. Eric Temple Bell: *Mathematics: Queen and Servant of Science* (McGraw-Hill, 1951).

2. C. J. Date: "Some Principles of Good Language Design," Chapter 7 of the present book.

3. C. J. Date: "A Critique of SQL/86" (in three parts), Chapters 8-10 of the present book.

4. C. J. Date: "NOT Is Not 'Not'!" (in two parts), Chapters 12-13 of the present book.

Chapter 15

A Normalization Problem

The normalization problem referred to in this chapter's title was originally posed in an article by Joe Celko [1]. I wrote the original paper on which this chapter is based as a response to that article, and more specifically as an attempt to clarify in my own mind exactly what was wrong with the five "solutions" to that problem—in other words, the five proposed designs—presented by Celko in that article.

The statement of the problem in reference [1] concluded with the words "This problem will give you respect for a database normalizer tool you probably never had." (I assume the phrase "you probably never had" here is to be understood as qualifying "respect," not "a database normalizer tool.") On the contrary!—if I'm to take it that the five designs discussed in reference [1] are what some "database normalizer tool" would actually propose, then the problem serves rather to increase my suspicion of such tools. So I agree there's a valuable lesson to be learned here, but I'm not sure it's the lesson the author of reference [1] had in mind.

Publishing history: This is a heavily revised version of, and supersedes, a paper that first appeared in The Relational Journal 4, No. 2 (April/May 1992) and was later republished in my book Relational Database Writings 1991-1994 (Addison-Wesley, 1995). This version copyright © C. J. Date 2022.

The normalization problem referred to in the title of this chapter is taken from reference [1]. It concerns a simple airline application, for which we're told the following self-explanatory functional dependencies—"FDs" for short—hold:

```
 1. { FLIGHT }                → { DESTINATION}
 2. { FLIGHT }                → { HOUR}
 3. { DAY , FLIGHT }          → { GATE }
 4. { DAY , FLIGHT }          → { PILOT }
 5. { DAY , HOUR , GATE }     → { DESTINATION }
 6. { DAY , HOUR , GATE }     → { FLIGHT }
 7. { DAY , HOUR , GATE }     → { PILOT }
 8. { DAY , HOUR , PILOT }    → { DESTINATION }
 9. { DAY , HOUR , PILOT }    → { FLIGHT }
10. { DAY , HOUR , PILOT }    → { GATE }
```

Note: Here and throughout this chapter I depart slightly from the notation and terminology used in reference [1]. First, in FDs I use braces "{" and "}" where reference [1] uses parentheses. Second, I talk in terms of just keys, unqualified, rather than primary keys as such, which is what reference [1] does. Also, I occasionally use the terms *determinant* and *dependant* to refer to what appears on the left side and right side (i.e., before and after the arrow), respectively, of any given FD.

Before you read any further, I suggest you take the time to convince yourself that it's reasonable to claim that the foregoing FDs hold—or at the very least to make sure you know what they're saying. No. 10, for example, says in effect that if a given pilot is taking some flight out on a given day at a given hour, then there must be exactly one departure gate for the flight in question.

Reference [1] then goes on to say: "Try to find all five 3NF database schemas in these relationships." Well, there are several things I want to say right away (several criticisms I want to make, rather) regarding this initial instruction:

■ First of all, the wording is sloppy. To be specific:

    a. The instruction talks about "schemas." But there's no consensus on exactly what the term *schema* means (certainly it's used with a variety of different meanings in the literature). Thus, I think it would have been be better to talk in terms of [database] *designs* rather than [database]schemas, like this: "Give five designs for this database." (As for that "3NF" qualification, please read on.)

    b. The wording suggests there are *exactly* five such designs (or "3NF schemas"), which manifestly isn't the case.

    c. "3NF" should preferably be BCNF, if not 5NF or even 6NF [4]. Of course, people often do say "3NF" when what they really mean is

BCNF, but such sloppiness should be resisted. *Note:* I'll spell out the difference between 3NF and BCNF in the next section.

d. It's not the "schemas" as such that are in 3NF, but rather the tables defined by those schemas.

e. The schemas aren't "in" the "relationships"; rather, they *represent*, or *capture*, or *reflect* them.

f. The use of the term "relationships" to refer to FDs is unusual. It's not exactly incorrect, but there's an obvious possibility of confusion with tables (or relations), and it would have been better to use some other term—perhaps "FDs"?

To all of the above I have to add that it's particularly galling to encounter such sloppiness in (of all things) a relational context, given that—as I've had occasion to remark elsewhere (see, e.g., reference [6])—it was always one of the objectives of the relational model to inject some precision and clarity into the database field.

■ Second, note the form in which the problem is stated: "Here are some FDs; now go figure out an appropriate set of tables." In other words, we're given a set of FDs as *input* and asked to come up with an appropriate design as *output*. Note, however, that:

a. The FDs in question are, of course, supposed to be ones that *hold*. But the notion of some FD $X \rightarrow Y$ holding has meaning only in the context of some table that actually has columns X and Y.[1] In other words, it would be more accurate to regard the input as a set of tables for which the given FDs hold, and the output as a certain restructuring of those given tables.

b. I don't think starting with a set of FDs—especially one in which the FDs are so obviously not even independent of one another—is a good way to do database design. I believe some top down methodology, such as that described in reference [2], is to be preferred in practice.

---

[1] More correctly, *sets* of columns X and Y.

3NF AND BCNF

I assume the objectives and advantages of third normal form (3NF), and more particularly Boyce/Codd normal form (BCNF), are too well known to need rehearsing here. Tutorial presentations on such matters can be found in many places (see, e.g., reference [4]). For the record, however, I'll at least give a couple of reasonably precise definitions of those terms. *Note:* Several different definitions, equivalent to the ones shown, can be given, but the ones below are the most satisfactory for my purposes in this chapter. [2]

> **Definition (third normal form):** Let T be a table, let X be any subset of the set of columns of T, and let A be any column of T. Then T is in third normal form, 3NF, if and only if, for every FD $X \rightarrow \{A\}$ that holds in T, at least one of the following is true:
>
> a. X contains A (so the FD is trivial).
>
> b. X includes a key of T.
>
> c. A is contained in some key of T.

> **Definition (Boyce/Codd normal form):** Let T be a table, let X be any subset of the set of columns of T, and let A be any column of T. Then T is in Boyce/Codd normal form, BCNF, if and only if, for every FD $X \rightarrow \{A\}$ that holds in T, at least one of the following is true:
>
> a. X contains A (so the FD is trivial).
>
> b. X includes a key of T.

To put matters more informally (albeit much less precisely): BCNF means that every nontrivial FD that holds is "an FD out of a key"; 3NF means that every nontrivial FD that holds is *either* an FD out of a key *or* an FD in which the

---

[2] I'd really much prefer to state the definitions in terms of *relation variables* ("relvars") and *attributes* instead of tables and columns (see, e.g., references [3], [4], and [6]). However, talking in terms of tables and columns is good enough for present purposes.

dependent column is a component of some key. Note, therefore, that BCNF implies 3NF, meaning that if a table is in BCNF then it's certainly in 3NF. But the converse is false—a table can be in 3NF and not in BCNF. Developing an example to illustrate this point is left as an exercise.

THE RIGHT DESIGN

What I'm here choosing to call "the right design" for the problem at hand can be obtained as follows. First, we rewrite the given set of FDs in an obvious way, combining FDs that have the same determinant. (In other words, we combine Nos. 1 and 2; Nos. 3 and 4; Nos. 5-7; and Nos. 8-10.) We obtain the following revised set (note the renumbering):

```
1. { FLIGHT }              → { DESTINATION , HOUR }
2. { DAY , FLIGHT }        → { GATE , PILOT }
3. { DAY , HOUR , GATE }   → { DESTINATION , FLIGHT , PILOT }
4. { DAY , HOUR , PILOT }  → { DESTINATION , FLIGHT , GATE }
```

However, it follows from FD No. 1 here that the following FD holds:

```
{ FLIGHT } → { DESTINATION }
```

(In fact, of course, this was FD No. 1 in the original set.) So we can drop DESTINATION from the dependant in each of Nos. 3 and 4, yielding as our final simplified set of FDs the following:

```
1. { FLIGHT }              → { DESTINATION , HOUR }
2. { DAY , FLIGHT }        → { GATE , PILOT }
3. { DAY , HOUR , GATE }   → { FLIGHT , PILOT }
4. { DAY , HOUR , PILOT }  → { FLIGHT , GATE }
```

The most immediately obvious attempt at a design would thus involve four tables, one for each of the four FDs, with the determinant of the pertinent FD forming a key for the corresponding table. Of those four tables, however, the ones corresponding to FDs Nos. 3 and 4 are clearly not in BCNF, because they both satisfy the additional FD {FLIGHT} → {HOUR}[3]—see the definition of BCNF in the previous section—and hence both involve some internal data

---

[3] This was FD No. 2 in the original set.

redundancy. The "obvious" design—and, I claim, the right one—therefore consists of just two tables, corresponding to FDs Nos. 1 and 2:

```
FDH { FLIGHT , DESTINATION , HOUR }
    KEY { FLIGHT }

DFGP { DAY , FLIGHT , GATE , PILOT }
    KEY { DAY , FLIGHT }
```

These tables are both in BCNF.

But what about FDs Nos. 3 and 4? These two correspond to certain additional integrity constraints that apply to the foregoing tables and need to be separately stated. Informally, the constraints in question might look something like this:

```
IF ( f1 , t1 , h ) , ( f2 , t2 , h ) ∈ FDH AND
    ( d , f1 , g , p1 ) , ( d , f2 , g, p2 ) ∈ DFGP
THEN f1 = f2 AND p1 = p2

IF ( f1 , t1 , h ) , ( f2 , t2 , h ) ∈ FDH AND
    ( d , f1 , g1 , p ), ( d , f2 , g2 , p ) ∈ DFGP
THEN f1 = f2 AND g1 = g2
```

Explanation: The notation I'm using here is loosely based on relational calculus; in particular, the symbol "∈" denotes the set membership operator (it can be read as *is an element of*, or *appears in*, or simply as *[is] in*). Thus, the first constraint says that:

a. If two rows of FDH have the same HOUR h, and

b. Two rows of DFGP, one each for the two FLIGHTs *f1* and *f2* in the two FDH rows, have the same DAY d and GATE g, then

c. The two FDH rows must be the same, and

d. The two DFGP rows must be the same.

In other words, if we know the HOUR, DAY, and GATE, then the FLIGHT and PILOT are determined. The other constraint (corresponding to FD No. 4) is interpreted analogously. *Note:* I'll have more to say on the question of integrity constraints—specifically, on how to declare them formally—in the section "Declaring Constraints" later in the chapter.

By the way, {FLIGHT} in table DFGP is a foreign key, of course, referencing the key {FLIGHT} of table FDH. Reference [1] doesn't mention foreign keys at all, and so I'll ignore them too (mostly); I remark, however, that the process of identifying foreign keys is a very important part of database design in practice. (In other words, database design isn't just a matter of getting the tables right—integrity constraints are a crucial aspect too.) I remark further that if reference [1] had in fact taken foreign keys into account, some of the problems with its proposed designs (see the section immediately following) would have become apparent very quickly.

THE FIVE PROPOSED DESIGNS

I now turn to the five designs proposed in reference [1]. Before discussing them in detail, though, let me stress the point that, in my opinion, the designs in question are all extremely bad!—and in fact probably unacceptable, as I hope you'll quickly agree.

Note: The discussion that follows is somewhat repetitious, as you'll soon see. But I don't think you need to read the whole thing, exhaustively (unless you want to, of course); rather, I offer it principally as a source for future reference. You might prefer to go directly to the end of the section, where the flaws in the five designs are summarized in tabular form.

Design No. 1

The first design proposed in reference [1] ("Design No. 1") looks like this:

```
DEPARTURES { FLIGHT , DESTINATION , HOUR }
        KEY { FLIGHT }

WEEKLY_ROSTER { DAY , HOUR , GATE , FLIGHT , PILOT }
          KEY ( DAY , HOUR , GATE )
```

DEPARTURES here is the same as our FDH, so that one's OK. As for WEEKLY_ROSTER, it corresponds to FD No. 3, and thus (as we saw in the previous section) isn't in BCNF—but that's not the only problem with this design. To spell out the problems in detail:

■ WEEKLY_ROSTER has an additional (but undeclared) key, viz., {DAY,HOUR,PILOT}. Because it's not declared, the corresponding key constraint can't be enforced by the DBMS.

■ WEEKLY_ROSTER has another undeclared key, viz., {DAY,FLIGHT}. Because it's not declared, the corresponding key constraint can't be enforced by the DBMS.

■ WEEKLY_ROSTER is subject to an additional (but undeclared) FD, viz.. {FLIGHT} → {HOUR}. Because it's not declared, the FD constraint can't be enforced by the DBMS.

■ Because of that FD {FLIGHT} → {HOUR}, WEEKLY_ROSTER isn't in BCNF. As a result, WEEKLY_ROSTER includes some internal redundancy (the fact that a given FLIGHT operates at a given HOUR appears seven times in the table, in general—once for each possible value of DAY).

■ Because of that FD {FLIGHT} → {HOUR} again, the design involves some redundancy across the two tables. Specifically, the fact that a given FLIGHT operates at a given HOUR appears not only seven times in the WEEKLY_ROSTER table but once in the DEPARTURES table as well.

Design No. 2

The second design proposed in reference [1] looks like this:

```
DEPARTURES { FLIGHT , DESTINATION , HOUR }
        KEY { FLIGHT }

WEEKLY_ROSTER { DAY , HOUR , PILOT , FLIGHT , GATE }
            KEY ( DAY , HOUR , PILOT )
```

This design is very similar to Design No. 1; the main difference is that WEEKLY_ROSTER now corresponds to FD No. 4 instead of No. 3. The problems with this design are essentially identical to those discussed under Design No. 1 the above, mutatis mutandis.

Design No. 3

```
DEPARTURES { FLIGHT , DESTINATION , HOUR }
          KEY { FLIGHT }

GATE_PILOT_SCHEDULE { DAY , FLIGHT , GATE , PILOT }
                  KEY { DAY , FLIGHT }

GATE_FLIGHT_SCHEDULE { DAY , HOUR , GATE , FLIGHT }
                   KEY { DAY , HOUR , GATE }

PILOT_FLIGHT_SCHEDULE { DAY , HOUR , PILOT , FLIGHT }
                    KEY { DAY , HOUR , PILOT }
```

DEPARTURES and GATE_PILOT_SCHEDULE here are the same as our FDH and DFGP, respectively. The other two tables correspond to FDs Nos. 6 and 9, respectively, in the original (unsimplified) set of FDs. Problems:

- GATE_FLIGHT_SCHEDULE has an additional (undeclared) key, viz., {DAY,FLIGHT}. Because it's not declared, the corresponding key constraint can't be enforced by the DBMS.

- GATE_FLIGHT_SCHEDULE is subject to an additional (but undeclared) FD, viz.. {FLIGHT} → {HOUR}. Because it's not declared, the FD constraint can't be enforced by the DBMS.

- Because of the FD {FLIGHT} → {HOUR}, GATE_FLIGHT_SCHEDULE isn't in BCNF.

- PILOT_FLIGHT_SCHEDULE has an additional (undeclared) key, viz., {DAY,FLIGHT}. Because it's not declared, the corresponding key constraint can't be enforced by the DBMS.

- PILOT_FLIGHT_SCHEDULE is subject to an additional (but undeclared) FD, viz.. {FLIGHT} → {HOUR}. Because it's not declared, the FD constraint can't be enforced by the DBMS.

- Because of the FD {FLIGHT} → {HOUR}, PILOT_FLIGHT_SCHEDULE isn't in BCNF.

■ The design involves a grossly excessive amount of cross-table redundancy. The details are left as an exercise.

Design No. 4

```
DEPARTURES { DESTINATION , HOUR }
        KEY { FLIGHT }

GATE_FLIGHT_SCHEDULE { DAY , FLIGHT , GATE }
                KEY { DAY , FLIGHT }

GATE_PILOT_SCHEDULE { DAY , HOUR , GATE , PILOT }
                KEY { DAY , HOUR , GATE }

PILOT_FLIGHT_SCHEDULE { DAY , HOUR , PILOT , FLIGHT }
                 KEY { DAY , HOUR , PILOT }
```

DEPARTURES here is the same as our FDH, except that column FLIGHT is missing (but this is presumably just a typo, since {FLIGHT} is given as a key). GATE_FLIGHT_SCHEDULE is the same as our DFGP, except that column PILOT is missing (this is probably *not* just a typo). The other two tables correspond to FDs Nos. 7 and 9, respectively, in the original unsimplified set. Problems:

■ GATE_PILOT_SCHEDULE has an additional (undeclared) key, viz., {DAY,HOUR,PILOT}. Because it's not declared, the corresponding key constraint can't be enforced by the DBMS.

■ PILOT_FLIGHT_SCHEDULE has an additional (undeclared) key, viz., {DAY,FLIGHT}. Because it's not declared, the corresponding key constraint can't be enforced by the DBMS.

■ PILOT_FLIGHT_SCHEDULE is subject to an additional (but undeclared) FD, viz.. {FLIGHT} → {HOUR}. Because it's not declared, the FD constraint can't be enforced by the DBMS.

■ Because of that FD {FLIGHT} → {HOUR}, PILOT_FLIGHT_ SCHEDULE isn't in BCNF.

■ The symmetry between GATEs and PILOTs has been destroyed.

■ Again the design involves a great deal of cross-table redundancy, and again the details are left as an exercise.

Design No. 5

```
DEPARTURES { DESTINATION , HOUR }
        KEY { FLIGHT }

DUTY_ROSTER { DAY , FLIGHT , PILOT }
        KEY { DAY , FLIGHT }

GATE_FLIGHT_SCHEDULE { DAY , HOUR , GATE , FLIGHT }
                KEY { DAY , HOUR , GATE }

GATE_PILOT_SCHEDULE { DAY , HOUR , PILOT , GATE }
                KEY { DAY , HOUR , PILOT }
```

DEPARTURES here is the same as our FDH, except that column FLIGHT is missing (again this is presumably just a typo, though, since {FLIGHT} is given as a key). DUTY_ROSTER is the same as our DFGP, except that column GATE is missing (this is probably not just a typo). The other two tables correspond to FDs Nos. 6 and 10, respectively, in the original unsimplified set. Problems:

■ GATE_FLIGHT_SCHEDULE has an additional (undeclared) key, viz., {DAY,FLIGHT}. Because it's not declared, the corresponding key constraint can't be enforced by the DBMS.

■ GATE_FLIGHT_SCHEDULE is subject to an additional (but undeclared) FD, viz.. {FLIGHT} → {HOUR}. Because it's not declared, the FD constraint can't be enforced by the DBMS.

■ Because of the FD {FLIGHT} → {HOUR}, GATE_FLIGHT_SCHEDULE isn't in BCNF.

■ GATE_PILOT_SCHEDULE has an additional (undeclared) key, viz., {DAY,HOUR,GATE}. Because it's not declared, the corresponding key constraint can't be enforced by the DBMS.

■ The symmetry between GATEs and PILOTs has been destroyed.

- Once again the design involves a great deal of cross-table redundancy.
  Once again the details are left as an exercise.

Summary

Well, I hope it's clear that:

- None of the foregoing five designs is the same as the one I claimed was the
  "obviously" right one.

- None of them is complete—each omits two key declarations and at least
  one additional integrity constraint.

- Each includes at least one nonBCNF table.

- Each involves some cross-table redundancy, as well as the internal
  redundancy that results from having tables that aren't in BCNF.

These criticisms are summarized in the following table. A couple of points
of clarification regarding that table:

- For space reasons I've abbreviated DAY, FLIGHT, GATE, HOUR, and
  PILOT to D, F, G, H, and P, respectively.

- Note that the various table names are "design local." For example, table
  GATE_PILOT_SCHEDULE in Design No. 4 isn't the same as table
  GATE_PILOT_SCHEDULE in Design No. 5 (in particular they have
  different declared keys).

Design	Undeclared keys	Undeclared FDs	Not BCNF
1	{D,H,P} & {D,F} in WEEKLY_ROSTER	{F} → {H} in WEEKLY_ROSTER	WEEKLY_ ROSTER
2	{D,H,G} & {D,F} in WEEKLY_ROSTER	{F} → {H} in WEEKLY_ROSTER	WEEKLY_ ROSTER

Design	Undeclared keys	Undeclared FDs	Not BCNF
3	{D,F} in GATE_FLIGHT_SCHEDULE	{F} → {H} in GATE_FLIGHT_SCHEDULE	GATE_FLIGHT_SCHEDULE
	{D,F} in PILOT_FLIGHT_SCHEDULE	{F} → {H} in PILOT_FLIGHT_SCHEDULE	PILOT_FLIGHT_SCHEDULE
4	{D,F} in PILOT_FLIGHT_SCHEDULE	{F} → {H} in PILOT_FLIGHT_SCHEDULE	PILOT_FLIGHT_SCHEDULE
	{D,H,P} in GATE_PILOT_SCHEDULE		
5	{D,F} in GATE_FLIGHT_SCHEDULE	{F} → {H} in GATE_FLIGHT_SCHEDULE	GATE_FLIGHT_SCHEDULE
	{D,H,G} in GATE_PILOT_SCHEDULE		

DECLARING CONSTRAINTS

Note: The material of this section first appeared in somewhat different form in Chapter 9 ("SQL and Views") of reference [3].

Despite my numerous criticisms of its proposed designs, reference [1] does serve one useful purpose, as follows: It shows very clearly why, although normalization is helpful, in that (among other things) it lets us represent certain integrity constraints—specifically, certain FDs[4]—very simply, it doesn't let us represent *all* constraints (not even all FDs) in that simple manner: at least, not in general. In practice, therefore, it'll sometimes be necessary—actually I'd say it'll *always* be necessary—to declare certain constraints explicitly. In the case at hand, even given what I called "the right design," explicit declarations for the following additional constraints were needed:

---

[4] Which FDs, exactly?

```
IF ( f1 , t1 , h ) , ( f2 , t2 , h ) ∈ FDH AND
    ( d , f1 , g , p1 ) , ( d , f2 , g, p2 ) ∈ DFGP
THEN f1 = f2 AND p1 = p2

IF ( f1 , t1 , h ) , ( f2 , t2 , h ) ∈ FDH AND
    ( d , f1 , g1 , p ), ( d , f2 , g2 , p ) ∈ DFGP
THEN f1 = f2 AND g1 = g2
```

These constraints correspond to FDs Nos. 3 and 4 in the simplified set (despite the fact that they don't look very much like FDs as such, a point I'll return to in just a moment). As noted earlier, they're expressed in relational calculus. Here by contrast is what they might look like in SQL:

```
CREATE ASSERTION DHGFP CHECK
  ( NOT ( EXISTS ( SELECT * FROM FDH FDH1 WHERE
          EXISTS ( SELECT * FROM FDH FDH2 WHERE
          EXISTS ( SELECT * FROM DFGP DFGP1 WHERE
          EXISTS ( SELECT * FROM DFGP DFGP2 WHERE
                   FDH2.HOUR = FDH1.HOUR AND
                   DFGP1.FLIGHT = FDH1.FLIGHT AND
                   DFGP2.FLIGHT = FDH2.FLIGHT AND
                   DFGP2.DAY = DFGP1.DAY AND
                   DFGP2.GATE = DFGP1.GATE AND
                   ( FDH1.FLIGHT <> FDH2.FLIGHT OR
                     DFGP1.PILOT <> DFGP2.PILOT ) ) ) ) ) ) ) ;

CREATE ASSERTION DHPFG CHECK
  ( NOT ( EXISTS ( SELECT * FROM FDH FDH1 WHERE
          EXISTS ( SELECT * FROM FDH FDH2 WHERE
          EXISTS ( SELECT * FROM DFGP DFGP1 WHERE
          EXISTS ( SELECT * FROM DFGP DFGP2 WHERE
                   FDH2.HOUR = FDH1.HOUR AND
                   DFGP1.FLIGHT = FDH1.FLIGHT AND
                   DFGP2.FLIGHT = FDH2.FLIGHT AND
                   DFGP2.DAY = DFGP1.DAY AND
                   DFGP2.PILOT = DFGP1.PILOT AND
                   ( FDH1.FLIGHT <> FDH2.FLIGHT AND
                     DFGP1.GATE <> DFGP2.GATE ) ) ) ) ) ) ) ;
```

The relational calculus formulations seem preferable!

As an aside, I note that this part of SQL is actually based on relational calculus; but the trouble is, certain useful calculus features are missing, including in particular the universal quantifier FORALL and the logical implication operator IF ... THEN ... . Now, it's true that these missing features are logically unnecessary, thanks to the following identities:[5]

---

[5] But are these identities valid in SQL's three-valued logic?

```
FORALL x ( p )   ≡   NOT EXISTS x ( NOT p )

IF p THEN q      ≡   ( NOT p ) OR q
```

But it's the fact (in large part) that the features in question are missing that makes the SQL declarations so verbose—not to mention hard to understand.

Now, I've already said that the calculus versions of the constraints don't look much like FDs, even though they do in fact correspond to FDs Nos. 3 and 4 in the simplified set. But what if we had the ability to declare keys for *views*? Consider the following example. First let me repeat what I called the "right design" earlier:

```
FDH { FLIGHT , DESTINATION , HOUR }
    KEY { FLIGHT }

DFGP { DAY , FLIGHT , GATE , PILOT }
    KEY { DAY , FLIGHT }
```

Now let V be a view, defined as the natural join of these two tables (i.e., the join on FLIGHT, which is, please note, a join based on a foreign key in DFGP and the matching target or referenced key in FDH):

```
CREATE VIEW V AS ( FDH JOIN DFGP ) ;
```

(using a kind of hybrid of SQL and the syntax of reference [7]). If we could additionally declare keys for this view, thus—

```
CREATE VIEW V AS ( FDH JOIN DFGP )
       KEY { DAY , HOUR , GATE }
       KEY { DAY , HOUR , PILOT } ;
```

—then these two key declarations would serve very nicely to define the integrity constraints in question. Thus, the discussions of this chapter provide an additional argument in support of a position I've argued in favor of, for other reasons, elsewhere [3]: namely, that it should be possible to declare keys for views as well as for base tables.[6]

---

[6] It's worth noting in passing that the keys in question (i.e., the ones for view V in the example) certainly can't be inferred from the FDs that hold within the underlying base tables (i.e., base tables FDH and DFGP in the example).

By the way, did you spot the omission? Given that (a) FDH JOIN DFGP is a key to foreign key join and (b) {DAY, FLIGHT} is a key for the table on the foreign key side of that join, it follows that (c) {DAY, FLIGHT} is a key for the view also:

```
CREATE VIEW V AS ( FDH JOIN DFGP )
       KEY { DAY , FLIGHT }
       KEY { DAY , HOUR , GATE }
       KEY { DAY , HOUR , PILOT } ;
```

Now let me take the argument one step further. Why not allow keys to be declared, more generally, for relational *expressions* of any kind? I mean, it seems kind of silly, or at least awkward, to have to define some view if the only purpose of doing so is to simplify the formulation of some constraint. Surely it would be better to allow that constraint be specified directly (i.e., without involving a view a all), perhaps as follows:

```
CONSTRAINT DHGFP ( FDH JOIN DFGP )
               KEY { DAY , FLIGHT }
               KEY { DAY , HOUR , GATE }
               KEY { DAY , HOUR , PILOT } ;
```

As a matter of fact, SQL almost does let us do what I've just suggested, thanks to its UNIQUE operator. Loosely speaking, the boolean expression UNIQUE (*tx*), where *tx* is an arbitrary SQL table expression, returns *true* if and only if the result of evaluating *tx* doesn't contain any duplicate rows. So, e.g., we can write:

```
CREATE ASSERTION DHGFP CHECK
       UNIQUE ( SELECT DAY , FLIGHT
                FROM   FDH NATURAL JOIN DFGP ) AND
       UNIQUE ( SELECT DAY , HOUR , GATE
                FROM   FDH NATURAL JOIN DFGP ) AND
       UNIQUE ( SELECT DAY , HOUR , PILOT
                FROM   FDH NATURAL JOIN DFGP ) ;
```

(Of course, I'm assuming here that the product we happen to be working with does support both UNIQUE and CREATE ASSERTION, which I don't believe they all do—at least, not at the time of writing.)

There's one final issue I'd like to raise in connection with constraint declarations (more specifically, *key* declarations, which are of course an important special case of constraint declarations in general). As we saw, every one of the designs proposed in reference [1] involved some undeclared keys; in

Design No. 1, for example, table WEEKLY_ROSTER had one explicitly declared key, viz., {DAY,HOUR,GATE}, and two undeclared keys, viz., {DAY,HOUR,PILOT} and {DAY,FLIGHT}. So the table has three keys altogether. Well, whatever happened to the old and familiar notion of *primary* keys? In this example, I guess it *might* be argued that {DAY,FLIGHT} is the "natural" choice for primary key (though reference [1] didn't in fact make that choice), because it involves the fewest columns. But that argument is hardly a very strong one. As for the other two keys, there seems to be no good reason at all to prefer either one over its rival. Indeed, *any* choice that makes one of the keys somehow "more equal than the other two" introduces an unpleasant degree of awkwardness and arbitrariness and asymmetry into the situation. I've examined such matters in more detail elsewhere [5]; here let me just say that I no longer feel as strongly as I once did regarding the need to choose one key and make it primary.

ACKNOWLEDGMENTS

I'd like to thank Joe Celko for posing the original problem, and my reviewers Hugh Darwen, David McGoveran, and (especially) Paul Winsberg for their helpful comments on an earlier draft of this chapter.

REFERENCES

1. Joe Celko: "Back to the Future," *Database Programming & Design 4*, No. 12 (December 1991).

2. C. J. Date: "A Practical Approach to Database Design," in *Relational Database: Selected Writings* (Addison-Wesley, 1986).

3. C. J. Date: *SQL and Relational Theory: How to Write Accurate SQL Code*, 3rd edition (O'Reilly, 2015).

4. C. J. Date: *Database Design and Relational Theory: Normal Forms and All That Jazz*, 2nd edition (Apress, 2019).

5. C. J. Date: "Primary Keys Are Nice but Not Essential," Appendix C of reference [4].

6. C. J. Date: *E. F. Codd and Relational Theory, Revised Edition: A Detailed Review and Analysis of Codd's Major Database Writings* (Technics Publications, 2021).

7. C. J. Date and Hugh Darwen: "**Tutorial D**," Chapter 11 of *Database Explorations: Essays on The Third Manifesto and Related Topics* (Trafford Publishing, 2010; see also *www.thethirdmanifesto.com*).

Appendix

Love Me,

Love My Doggerel

This appendix contains a series of—well, I hesitate to dignify them by calling them "poems"; perhaps "verses" will do—on the general subject of database management, composed by myself in various idle moments as a little light relief from my day job. I offer them here in the hope that they might provide you with a little light relief too: relief, that is, from the comparatively heavy nature of some of the foregoing chapters. Note: My title ("Love Me, Love My Doggerel") is actually the working title for another work in progress, a book that includes the poems in this appendix and much else of a similar nature—but since that work is, I strongly suspect, never going to be finished, I thought I might at least borrow the title and use it here.

For over 50 years now my professional life has been inextricably tangled up with SQL and relational database theory. SQL (variously pronounced "sequel" or "ess cue ell," the latter pronunciation being rendered in what follows as "S-Q-L") is—as of course you know—a commercially available computer language that attempts to realize the ideas of relational theory in concrete syntactic form but, sadly, fails in all too many ways to do so. Two of its worst failures have to do with duplicates and nulls. The first stanza of what follows came to me suddenly over breakfast one morning, and by the time I'd finished breakfast I'd finished the verses too.

Heed Relation Rules

a squib

The tables in the database
Though fully normalized
Were still somewhat anomalous—
It couldn't be disguised.

The trouble was the schema
Had, sad enough to tell,
Been designed by someone who
Believed in S-Q-L.

As a result, the tables
Were filled with nulls—a state
Of affairs that SQL
Allows, though one I hate.

(As an aside, I note that
To say a table might
"Contain a null" is nonsense!—
In fact the very height

Of auto-contradiction—
Since nulls "do not exist";
But suchlike solecisms
Always arise in this

Absurd and self-negating
Approach to this whole mess.
I could go on much longer—
However, I digress.)

What's more, the tables also
Had duplicates! I mean,
In table *T*, rows *A* and *B*—
No diff'rence to be seen—

Could be identical in all
Respects (it's really true!)
And yet the users had to know
They were not one but two.

The set containing *A* and *B*
Has cardinality
Not two but one!—and here I speak
Completely logically.

It follows that in S-Q-L
A table's not a set;
In fact a table is a *bag*
Aka multiset.

How *can* a crazy concept
Like this one possibly
Make sense to poor old users
Plain folks like you and me?

I haven't even mentioned yet
The way the silly notions
Discussed so far interreact
And lead us into oceans

Of complication and despond
And general distress.
Are two nulls equal (duplicates)?
I fear, both *no* and *yes.*

The moral of my poem is
(In case it isn't plain)
We should eschew those concepts
That don't seem very sane.

The duplicity of duplicates,
The senselessness of nulls:
Both lead to awful problems;
The combination dulls

(Unless we're very careful)
The analytic sense,
The intellectual faculty,
And causes much intense

Frustration, pain, and frenzied
Attempts to extricate
Data from the database
And make the crooked straight.

And so I say it one more time:
Do what you know is cool;
Take my advice, as One Who Knows,
And **heed relation rules**.

—from Installment No. 46 of my regular column *According to Date*
("The Art of the Possible"),
Database Programming & Design 9, No. 6 (June 1996),
republished in my book *Relational Database Writings 1994-1997*
(Addison-Wesley, 1998)

In an attempt to get away from the ills of SQL (among other things), my friend
and colleague Hugh Darwen and I have been working for many years on what we
call *The Third Manifesto*. One of our objectives has been to see if we could
marry relational theory and what we regarded as the sensible parts of object
orientation (abbreviated OO, appropriately pronounced "oh oh").

The Third Manifesto

a call for common sense

Objects and relations:
Can they work together?
An interesting question!
It all depends on whether

We first agree on what
Objects as such might be
There's surely no consensus—
In fact, it's hard to see

Why so much current int'rest
Is focused on the notion
Of object databases.
The famous magic potion

Of Astérix the Gaul
Makes just about as much sense
(At least it seems to me)
As "object data" does!—whence

What we really need to do
Is figure out precisely
Just what the real problem is
And then attack it nicely

By thinking very clearly
Not being swayed by fashion
Though truth to tell it's tough:
Thought oft gives way to passion.

(*Sigh*) Contemplating clearly
Is very hard to do—
My thoughts are often muddled
My guess is yours are, too.

By dint of application, though,
My good friend Hugh and I
Have tackled this great question
And grappled with the *Why*

Of objects and relations
And (more germane) the *How*
And so we're pleased to offer you
Our *Manifesto* now.

The *Manifesto* (sadly)
Is several pages long
And so I've tried to précis it
In this, my little song.

Careful and exhaustive search
Through all the object hype
Reveals a single good idea—
The *Abstract Data Type*.

Of course, we want to follow
The principles of Codd:
Be relationally pure!
It would be very odd

Not to support relations
At this stage in our history
And so the issue facing us
(Some might say, the mystery)

Is this: What do we need to do
To "tables" (if you please)
That they might thus be able
To deal with ADTs?

The answer is: *Do nothing!*
This answer I explain
By claiming that an ADT
Is simply a domain!

That is, the single good idea
Of objects—ADTs—
Can be combined with tables
As leaves combine with trees

Codd's model of relations
Already had support
For object functionality;
The trouble is, none thought

To *implement* that model,
And so we never got
A product that delivered
More than a part of what

Codd's vision should have led to.
Now twenty-five years later[1]
The pundits are proclaiming
Relations cannot cater

For "complex" applications
And "high performance" needs.
And yet it's all so silly!—
As anyone who reads

The *Manifesto* clearly
Will surely realize.
No: What we really need to do
To cut them down to size

---

[1] This was originally written in the 1990s. For "twenty-five" here, read "fifty plus."

Is get back to our future,
To our *relation* roots;
Build a true RDMS
And hence enjoy the fruits

Of true relational support
Including ADTs.
So: Read the *Manifesto*
And do the right thing—***please***.

—from Installment No. 72 of my regular column *According to Date*
("Back to the Relational Future"),
Database Programming & Design 11, No. 8 (August 1999)

———— ♦♦♦♦ ————

As part of our *Third Manifesto* work, Hugh and I had to come to grips with the issue of type inheritance. After much struggle, we constructed an inheritance model of our own, one that (unlike other schemes we studied) seemed to us to make good logical sense. I wrote the following celebratory piece in 1998.

The Modern Data Modeler

to be sung to a well known tune

I am the very model of a modern data modeler,
You couldn't say my knowledge was just that of a mere toddler.
With entities, relationships, and attributes and suchlike stuff,
I'm totally at home, in fact I challenge you to call my bluff.

Designing databases is a trivial little game for me—
It doesn't matter what you want, a network or a hi'rarchee;
Of objects and relations I know ever such a great big lot,
And I can tell you whether SQL's "NOT" is really NOT or not.

For some time now I've focused on the problems of inheritance,
A complicated topic that can lead you on a merry dance
As you try to comprehend all of its byzantine[2] complexities,
Affronts to intuition, and its horrible perplexities.

To make some sense of all of this
                I've struggled and I've worked and worked,
I've read the papers, read the books,
                I've thought and thought and never shirked;
And all of this great effort has, I'm glad to say, not been in vain,
Despite the times I've had to stop and hold my poor old head in pain

Be ... cause ... now ... **(deep breath)** ...

I **understand** inheritance, its subtypes and its supertypes!—
I understand it all as clear as water flows through waterpipes—
Sophisticated notions like type *alpha* and type *o-me-ga*
(Though as for objects, well, I feel, nice try perhaps but no cigar).

Yes, I understand inheritance, behavioral and structural,
And type constraints declarative and methods though procedural,
And substitutability and co- and contra-variance,
The logical connectives of those context-free grammarians,

And polymorphic operators, code reuse, and dummy types,
And specializing by constraint and SQL3 and other hypes,
And multiple inheritance as well as just the single kind,
Type lattices, TREAT UP and DOWN, and static and dynamic bind.

What's more, it's not just scalar types that I can explicate to you,
But tuple and relation types, and sub- and super-tables too
(Albeit I must tell you that I don't think much of *that* idea
To talk of tables being types is pretty silly, dear oh dear!)

---

[2] To be pronounced *bizz'-an-teen'*, of course.

And though I don't know anything of DB2 or Oracle—
You might as well try asking me to navigate by coracle—
Still, as regards inheritance I am no tiny toddler,
I am the very model of a modern data modeler!

——— ♦ ♦ ♦ ♦ ———

The following is a kind of postscript to those two *Manifesto* poems ... One specific construct we found we needed was something we called a multiple assignment statement. The details don't matter here, but the crux of the idea was that we could assign values to any number of targets and defer the necessary integrity constraint checking until all of the individual assignments had been done. As this short verse puts it:

> To targets properly defined
> Separate values are assigned;
> Disbelief we can suspend—
> Constraints are checked at statement end.

——— ♦ ♦ ♦ ♦ ———

I wrote this next before we'd fully taken on board the message of the previous one:

> The structure of the database
>   Is easily defined
> But keeping it consistent
>   Is much more of a bind.

——— ♦ ♦ ♦ ♦ ———

A plea for more precision in speaking and writing and (above all) thinking:

> What's formal is normal
>   What's not so is not
> And if normal is formal,
>   Informal is what?

——— ♦ ♦ ♦ ♦ ♦ ———

I used this one as an epigraph to my book *Fifty Years of Relational, and Other Database Writings* (Technics Publications, 2020):

> Database management isn't so tough
>> Set theory, logic—that's all there is to it
> So why are the products so terribly rough?
>> Why make such a mess?—why don't they just *do* it?
>
> Part of the answer and part of the blame
>> Lies with the language that industry chose—
> A travesty, crime, a sin, and a shame
>> For something so simple as columns and rows!

—Anon:
Where Bugs Go

——— ♦ ♦ ♦ ♦ ♦ ———

A *triolet* is a verse of eight lines with this structure:

A B a A a b A B

To be more specific, lines 1, 4, and 7 are identical (though preferably with the words differently stressed), and rhyme with lines 3 and 5; similarly, lines 2 and 8 are identical (though, again, preferably with different stress), and rhyme with line 6. Here's one that I composed on the fly (almost) and used to conclude my keynote speech at the Very Large Data Base Conference ("VLDB") in Hong Kong in 2002. My point was that the major focus of that conference seemed to me to be on what I saw as very much a secondary issue (the so called "DBA problem"), and I wanted people to think about more fundamental matters (the title of my keynote was "Foundation Matters").

> At VLDB in Hong Kong
> > The DBA problem is *it*
> No matter if all else is wrong!—
> > At VLDB in Hong Kong.
> But *foundations* are what make us strong
> > Even here they can help quite a bit
> At VLDB in Hong Kong
> > Where the DBA problem is *it*.

——— ♦ ♦ ♦ ♦ ———

As a kind of coda to this appendix, I'd like to include the following splendid piece. It's not my own—it originally appeared in (I think) the British Computer Society *Bulletin*, at least 45 or so years ago (!), and was attributed at the time to someone calling himself simply Howard. My profound apologies if I'm inadvertently violating someone's copyright.

The Computer Programere

> When traidres can not cope with their afaires
> som see the answere to destracted preyers
> in a computre's trompeted precisioun,
> and greet celeritie of composicioun.
> In trouthe, when prikklie problems press arond them,
> computres may serve onlie to confond them,
> but wher computres governe everich thing,
> amonges the staf the programere is king.
> And oon swich king I hadde upon my Ryde
> that used to be my solitarie gyde
> thru all the trakkes of his owne straunge contree
> of alpha and numerik binarie.
>
> His Companye sente forth bukes of alle sortes
> throughout the lande, and eek to foregn portes,
> but journel or sales daye buke they hadde non,
> instead, computre prynt-outs by the tonne.

And he wolde helpe me oer these papre dunes,
sith, like a dragoman, he wist the runes:
Fortran and Cobol he graspt at a luke,
and papre tape he coude rede like a buke;
octal he knew, prime data coude define—
he was in alle respectes a man on lyne.

He smokt a pype, and quietlie puffed at it
the whyles he spake of caractre and bit,
magnetik diskes, and all the trials he suffred
that his computre was nat fully buffred.
Natheless he was of his machene most proude,
and sceptic gibes he sternlie disalowed;
If I implyd som detayle porelie rekkoned
he wolde disclame it in a microsecond,
and, thumming his punched cards, he wolde assure
the data was alle in the backing stor,
and som test program wolde anon devize
to prove it, with prodigious entreprize.
Computres coude in ne wyse err, quod he,
mistakes deryved but fro humanitie.

In his professioun nedes must shote this lyne,
but ay he kept a twinkel in his eyen,
and spak nat like som stoffed sherte fro greet height,
but was alwey a merie-humored wight.
Long houres aloon I spent on visites ther,
but export rebate was my onlie care,
so now I see the programere ne more,
ne stryve to folow his computre lore.

Index

For alphabetization purposes, (a) differences in fonts and case are ignored; (b) quotation marks are ignored; (c) other punctuation symbols—hyphens, underscores, parentheses, etc.—are treated as blanks; (d) numerals precede letters; (e) blanks precede everything else.

www.ingramcontent.com/pod-product-compliance
Lightning Source LLC
Chambersburg PA
CBHW080624060326
40690CB00021B/4802